Brain Quest®

Dear Parent,

"It's Fun to Be Smart!" That's not just our slogan, it's our philosophy. For fifteen years we've been adding a big dose of "fun" into learning—first with our bestselling Q&A Brain Quest card decks; then with all the licensed games and products bearing the Brain Quest brand; and now with BRAIN QUEST WORKBOOKS.

At Brain Quest we believe:

- All kids are smart—though they learn at their own speed.
- All kids learn best when they're having fun.
- All kids deserve the chance to reach their potential—given the tools they need, there's no limit to how far they can go!

BRAIN QUEST WORKBOOKS are the perfect tools to help children get a leg up in all areas of curriculum; they can hone their reading skills or dig in with math drills, review the basics or get a preview of lessons to come. These are not textbooks, but rather true workbooks—best used as supplements to what kids are learning in school, reinforcing curricular concepts while encouraging creative problem solving and higher-level thinking. You and your child can tackle a page or two a day—or an entire chapter over the course of a long holiday break. Your child will be getting great help with basic schoolwork, and you will be better able to gauge how well he or she is understanding course material.

Each BRAIN QUEST WORKBOOK has been written in consultation with an award-winning teacher specializing in that grade, and is compliant with most school curricula across the country. We cover the core competencies of reading, writing, and math in depth—with chapters on science, social studies, and other popular units rounding out the curriculum. Easy-to-navigate pages with color-coded tabs help identify chapters, while Brain Boxes offer parent-friendly explanations of key concepts and study units. That means parents can use the workbooks in conjunction with what their children are learning in school, or to explain material in ways that are consistent with current teaching strategies. In either case, the workbooks create an important bridge to the classroom, an effective tool for parents, homeschoolers, tutors, and teachers alike.

BRAIN QUEST WORKBOOKS all come with a variety of fun extras: a pull-out poster; Brain Quest "mini-cards" based on the bestselling Brain Quest game; two pages of stickers; and a Brainiac Award Certificate to celebrate successful completion of the workbook.

Learning is an adventure—a quest for knowledge. At Brain Quest we strive to guide children on that quest, to keep them motivated and curious, and to give them the confidence they need to do well in school . . . and beyond. We're confident that BRAIN QUEST WORKBOOKS will play an integral role in your child's adventure. So let the learning—and the fun—begin!

—The editors of Brain Quest

Library of Congress Cataloging-in-Publication Data is available.

ISBN 978-0-7611-4916-3

Workbook series design by Raquel Jaramillo
Illustrations by Kimble Mead

Workman books are available at special discounts when purchased in bulk for premiums and sales promotions as well as for fund-raising or educational use. Special editions or book excerpts also can be created to specification. For details, contact the Special Sales Director at the address below or send an email to specialmarkets@workman.com.

Workman Publishing Co., Inc.
225 Varick Street
New York, NY 10014-4381
workman.com

Printed in the United States of America
First printing June 2008

50 49 48 47 46 45 44 43

Brain Quest®
Grade 3 Workbook

Written by Jan Meyer
Consulting Editor: Anna Shults

WORKMAN PUBLISHING
NEW YORK

Contents

5

Spelling and Vocabulary

6

The Long and Short of It

Circle the correct spelling of the **long vowel** word. Then sort the words by spelling pattern on the cards below.

Spelling and Vocabulary

Short and long vowels

Molly gave a bath to the straigh stray straye dog.

Reid wanted extra cheese chease chese on his pizza.

Mackenzie put the blue bloo blu notebook in her toat tote tot bag.

It was a good day to take the bote boat out on the lake laik layk.

Shonda got in lin line lyn to see the rhino rhighno rhyno.

The school should suppli suppligh supply the chalk.

Most of the artists painted paynted on eesels easels.

Gavin used the key kee kea to open oapen his huge hug heug art stuedio studio.

Eight Eaght Ait little ducklings crossed the pathway.

The waitress took a coffee break braik brayk.

long a words

The **long a** sound can be spelled: **a_e, ai, ay, ea,** or **ei**

long e words

The **long e** sound can be spelled: **ee, ea,** or **ey**

long i words

The **long i** sound can be spelled: **i, i_e,** or **y**

long o words

The **long o** sound can be spelled: **o, o_e,** or **oa**

long u words

The **long u** sound can be spelled: **u, u_e,** or **ue**

Spelling and Vocabulary

Short and long vowels

Circle the correct spelling of the **short vowel** word. Then sort the words by spelling pattern on the cards below.

The new girl at school made frends friends quickly.

Ebony called ahead ahed to make a reservation.

Jung left his ombrella umbrella on the bus bos .

Katherine stepped onto the bottom botom bohtom rung of the read red raid ladder.

The audience laffed laughed at all the funny things the actors sed said sead.

He grabbed graibbed his skates and went down to the roller renk rink rynk.

The little pig pyg is bright pynk penk pink.

Dylan put a sauddle saeddle saddle on the horse.

Jenna ordered turkey and ham on rye bred bread .

Raquel needed to wash wosh her bicycle.

short u words

The **short u** sound can be spelled: **u**

short a words

The **short a** sound can be spelled: **au** or **a**

short o words

The **short o** sound is usually spelled: **o** or **a**

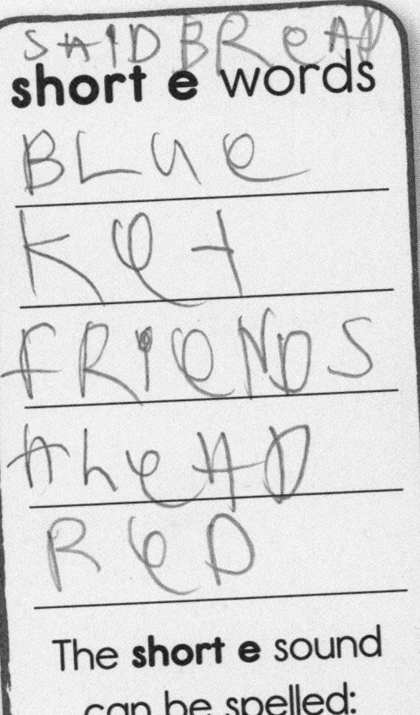

short e words

The **short e** sound can be spelled: **e, ea, ai,** or **ie**

short i words

The **short i** sound can be spelled: **i**

8

Cowabunga!

Label each picture using a word from the Word Box. Then circle the letters that make the **k** sound in each word.

sock	cake	castle
kayak	school	kangaroo
racket	Monarch	chameleon

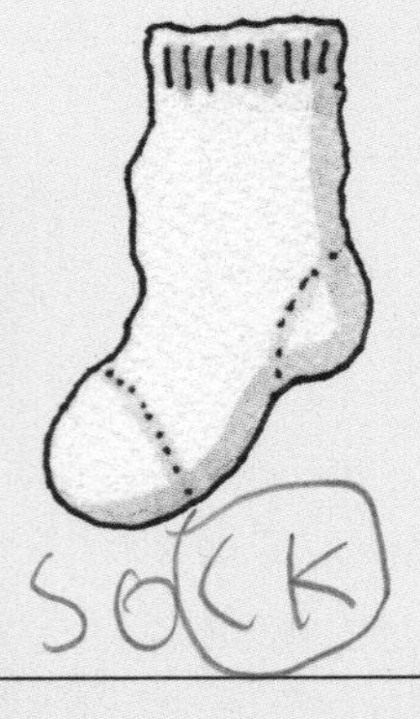

Spelling and Vocabulary

K sounds

Brain Box

The **k** sound can be spelled with a **k, c, ch,** or **ck.** For example: **k**ing, **c**oo**k**, s**ch**ool, bri**ck**

Did You Hear That?

Circle the **silent consonant** in each word. Some words have more than one.

Write a sentence using a **silent b** word.

____

____

Write a sentence using a **silent k** word.

____

____

Write a sentence using a **silent gh** word.

____

____

Write a sentence using a **silent p** word.

____

____

Spelling and Vocabulary

Silent consonants

Brain Box

Silent **consonants** are letters that become silent when combined with other letters. For example:

w as in **w**rist
k as in **k**nock
b as in thum**b**
gh as in ei**gh**t
g as in si**g**n
p as in cu**p**board
h as in w**h**y
n as in colum**n**
d as in le**d**ge

10

Double or Nothing

Rewrite each word using **ing.**

Spelling and Vocabulary

Words ending in **ed** or **ing**

swim	swimming		
dream	DREAMING		
jump	JUMPING	run	RUNNING
ask	ASKING	dig	DIGING
drive	DRIVING	change	CHANGING
write	WRITEING	win	WINING

Now write three sentences that use at least two of the **ing** words above.

____

____

____

____

____

____

Brain Box

Follow these rules when adding **ed** or **ing** to a word:

- If a word ends in a **silent e,** drop the **e:**

hope = hop**ed,** hop**ing**

- If a word ends in a single vowel followed by a single consonant, double the consonant:

hop = hop**ped,** hop**ping**

- If a word ends in a consonant followed by the letter **y,** change the **y** to **i** before adding **ed:**

carry = carr**ied**

Spelling and Vocabulary

Words ending in **ed** or **ing**

Rewrite each word using **ed.**

wish ____________	nod ____________
shop ____________	laugh ____________
live ____________	smile ____________
shine ____________	scrub ____________
hurry ____________	rely ____________

Complete each sentence with a word from the Word Box. Change the spelling by adding **ed** or **ing.**

worry	rob
pop	sneeze
slip	wave

I am ____________ about my social studies test tomorrow.

I started ____________ when I smelled the flowers.

The father ____________ to his daughters as they got on the bus.

Everyone jumped when he ____________ the balloons.

He started ____________ on the icy driveway.

The thief ____________ the bank.

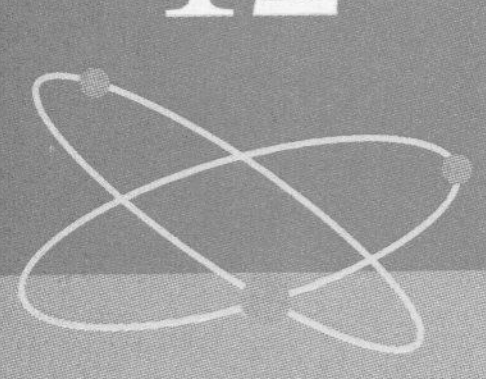

12

Orderly Neighbors

Spelling and Vocabulary

Words with **ie** and **ei**

Complete each word with **ie** or **ei**.

You see your w __ __ ght when you get on a scale.

Another word for "get" is "rec __ __ ve."

A person who steals something is a th __ __ f.

Santa rides a sl __ __ gh on Christmas Eve.

We did an experiment in sc __ __ nce.

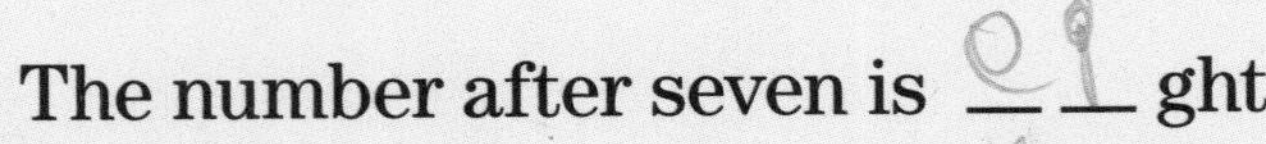

The number after seven is __ __ ght.

The puzzle is missing one p __ __ ce.

If I ever saw a ghost, I would shr __ __ k!

A fr __ __ ght train carries heavy loads.

A ch __ __ f is the leader of a tribe.

Brain Box

When **i** and **e** are side-by-side, the **i** comes before the **e**, except after **c**. For example: gr**ie**f, fr**ie**nd, rec**ei**ve, dec**ei**t

When **i** and **e** make a **long a** sound, **e** comes before the **i**. For example: n**ei**ghbor, v**ei**n

Circle the **ie** and **ei** words in the word search below. Words go across or down.

D	B	K	G	A	S	C	I	E	N	C	E	F	U
M	Y	R	U	O	Z	L	J	D	R	B	H	R	S
S	W	E	I	G	H	T	X	D	C	H	I	E	F
V	B	C	M	V	S	H	R	I	E	K	V	I	F
P	I	E	C	E	N	I	C	A	L	A	J	G	L
O	C	I	G	S	L	E	I	G	H	O	S	H	R
H	D	V	K	Q	U	F	T	B	I	X	H	T	T
X	A	E	I	G	H	T	B	O	F	B	R	C	K

You're Right, They're Wrong

Spelling and Vocabulary

Commonly misspelled words

Circle each misspelled word in the Word Box.

Febuary	enuf	shoping	favrit
busy	because	once	hitting
dinasor	suprise	Wensday	receive
peeple	anser	minit	docter
please	calendar	kwite	giving

Write each misspelled word correctly on the lines below.

February

Write a joke using two or more words you spelled correctly.

Write a sentence using two of the words you spelled correctly.

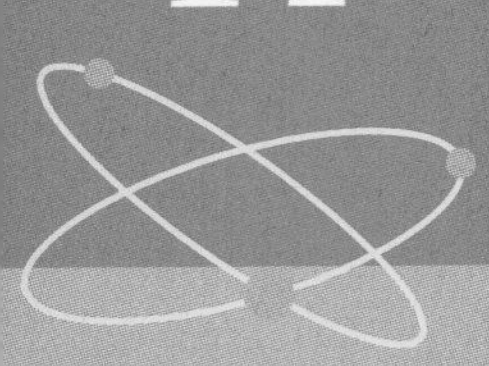

The More the Merrier

Spelling and Vocabulary

Plurals

Write the **plural** for each word.

knife knives

city citts

shelf Shelves

penny pennts

witch witches

turkey turkots

dwarf dworfs

glass Glosses

brush Brushs

tax taxs

candy condys

ray rots

Brain Box

There are special rules for changing some words from singular to **plural:**

- If a noun ends in **sh, ch, ss,** or **x,** add **es.** For example: crush → crush**es**
- If a noun ends in a consonant followed by a **y,** change the **y** to **i** and add **es.** For example: hurry → hurr**ies**
- If a noun ends in a vowel followed by a **y,** add **s.** For example: toy → toy**s**

For many nouns ending in **f** or **fe,** change the **f** or **fe** to **v** and add **es.** For example: loaf → loa**ves**

What other words follow these special plural rules? Write the plural form of as many words as you can think of on the cards.

Nouns ending in **sh, ch, ss, x**	Nouns ending in a consonant followed by **y**	Nouns ending in a vowel followed by **y**	Nouns ending in **f** or **fe**

Two's Company

Write the **plural** for each word.

Then circle the plural forms in the word search. Words go across and down.

baby

babies

house

peach

fox

bunny

boy

puppy

elf

spy

tiger

S	P	I	E	S	Y	E	Q	W	J	L	S
X	V	O	G	U	E	I	T	M	U	N	Y
P	U	B	A	B	I	E	S	H	O	Y	X
U	L	O	Q	W	K	N	E	I	B	G	S
P	J	Y	I	C	P	H	L	T	L	P	L
P	W	S	O	B	U	N	N	I	E	S	M
I	U	K	L	C	P	H	Q	G	A	D	F
E	L	V	E	S	U	Z	I	E	V	Z	F
S	D	I	Q	W	B	M	Y	R	E	R	O
M	R	H	O	U	S	E	S	S	S	B	X
C	I	K	F	M	C	K	W	V	L	I	E
B	V	Q	M	H	P	E	A	C	H	E	S

Spelling and Vocabulary

Plurals

Spelling and Vocabulary

Irregular plurals

Rule Breakers

Fill in the blanks to write the **irregular plural** for each oddball word.

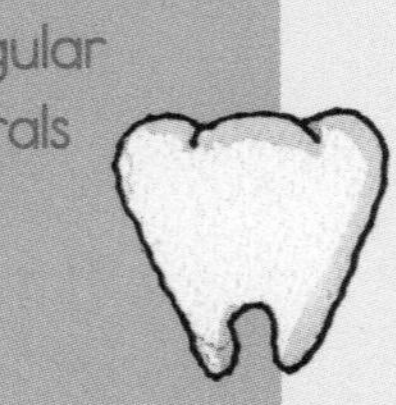

child	child ___ ___ ___	goose	g ___ ___ se
mouse	m ___ ___ e	woman	wom ___ n
man	m ___ n	ox	ox ___ ___
tooth	t ___ ___ th	fish	f ___ sh
sheep	sh ___ ___ p	moose	m ___ ___ se

Finish the story using at least five **irregular plurals.**

The children went to the zoo yesterday. ______________________

____

____

____

____

____

____

Draw a picture to go with your story.

Brain Box

Some words don't follow the rules for making plurals. These are called **irregular plurals.**

Special Beginnings

Complete each word using a **prefix** from the box.

re	pre	mis	sub

Spelling and Vocabulary

Prefixes

I saw that movie before any of my friends.
I went to a ______view of it the day before it opened.

My dog is well trained, but yesterday he ______behaved by jumping up on our best living room chair.

My little sister knocked over her tower of blocks.
Now she has to ______build it.

The bricks were starting to crumble off the side of the building. The construction of the building must be ______standard.

He got only one word wrong on his spelling test.
He ______spelled the word "horrible."

The cookbook said to ______heat the oven for thirty minutes before putting in the cake.

My dad painted the kitchen purple, but the color seemed wrong to him. Now he wants to ______paint the room.

Brain Box

A **prefix** is a group of letters that changes the meaning of a word when added to the beginning of the word.

For example, the prefix **sub** means **below.** A **sub**zero temperature is a temperature below zero.

18

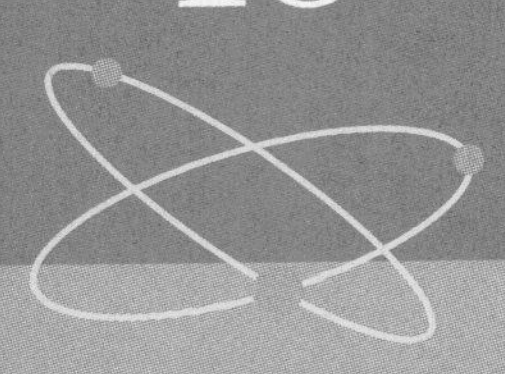

That's a Negative

Spelling and Vocabulary

Prefixes

Complete each word using a **prefix** from the box.

dis	im	in	un

I was so ______happy when we lost the baseball game!

I can hardly wait to ______wrap my birthday presents.

I am ______patient to read my book.

It is ______polite to talk with your mouth full.

The toys are on sale. I can buy two because they are ______expensive.

My brothers and I sometimes ______agree about who should sit by the window.

At first, climbing the hill seemed ______possible, but we stuck with it and got to the top.

Although I ______like brussels sprouts, I love most vegetables.

I form my own opinions. I am an ______dependent thinker.

Write a sentence using at least two words with prefixes.

____

____

Brain Box

The prefixes **dis, in, im,** and **un** mean **not** or **the opposite** of. For example, **dis**interested means **not interested.**

What's Back There?

Spelling and Vocabulary

Suffixes

Read each sentence. Find the missing word in the Word Box and then add **ful** or **less** to make it correct in the sentence.

~~hope~~	care	~~thought~~	~~color~~
fear	power	~~use~~	~~help~~

Dylan loved the feeling of taking off in an airplane. He could feel how __powerful__ the engines were.

Sharise's aunt is __thoughtful__. She sends Sharise a special card every holiday.

Ming is ________ when it comes to gymnastics. He'll try just about anything.

Cole is not the fastest runner in the class, but he is still __hopeful__ that he will win the race.

I love helping my mom cook dinner and set the table. It makes me feel like I'm being __helpful__.

I like trying to spot bright, cheery butterflies. The more __colorful__, the better!

Arguing with my sister is __useful__. She is so stubborn!

He was so __colorful__ with the paint. It splattered all over the canvas.

Brain Box

A **suffix** is a group of letters that changes the meaning of a word when added to the ending of a word.

For example, the suffix **ful** means **full of.** A cheer**ful** person is someone who is **full of cheer.**

What's My Job?

Label each picture using a word from the Word Box. Add **er, or, ist,** or **ian** to complete the word.

Spelling and Vocabulary

Suffixes

violin	sing	write	teach
magic	act	dance	art

teacher

MAGICIAN

SINGER

WRITER

ARTIST

DANCEING

ACTING

VIOLIN

Brain Box

The suffixes **er, or, ist,** and **ian** mean **someone who.** For example:

farm**er** = someone who works on a farm

edit**or** = someone who edits

cell**ist** = someone who plays the cello

comed**ian** = someone who performs comedy

A Cloudy Day

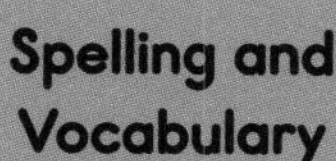

A **prefix** or **suffix** has been added to each of these words. Underline the **root word** (or base word) in each word. Then circle the prefix or suffix.

rainy

forgiveness	attractive	repackage
successful	invention	transportation
childlike	reread	buyer
golden	underground	worthless
	poisonous	

Write a sentence using one of these words. Then draw a picture to match your sentence.

Spelling and Vocabulary

Root words

Brain Box

The word to which a **prefix** or a **suffix** has been added is called a **root word** (or a base word). For example, in the word **cloudy**, the root word is **cloud**.

Antonym Crossword

Finish the clues by writing the **antonym** of the highlighted word.
Then complete the crossword puzzle.

Across

1. She likes candy that is (sour) sweet ________.
3. Luke stepped (under) ____________ the rope.
5. Stephanie wades in the (deep) ____________ end of the pool.
8. He was happy to have a new (enemy) ____________ move in next door.
10. The bag was too (light) ____________ to carry.
12. The cowardly lion had the (most) ____________ courage of everyone in *The Wizard of Oz*.

Down

1. Sean wasn't hungry, so he ordered a (large) ____________ meal.
2. I have to crouch down to get things on the (high) ____________ shelf.
4. Robin Hood stole from the (poor) ____________ to help those in need.
5. Anne's new comforter was cozy and (hard) ____________.
6. The (new) ____________ vase was chipped and cracked.
7. The zoo near my house is home to many (tame) ____________ animals.
9. The bridge is so (wide) ____________ that only one car can go across at a time.
11. Zoe almost fell (awake) ____________ before the end of the movie.

Spelling and Vocabulary

Antonyms

Brain Box

Two words that have the opposite meaning are called **antonyms.** For example: **strong** and **weak** are antonyms.

Cheer Up, Aidan!

Replace each highlighted word with its **antonym.**

Spelling and Vocabulary

Antonyms

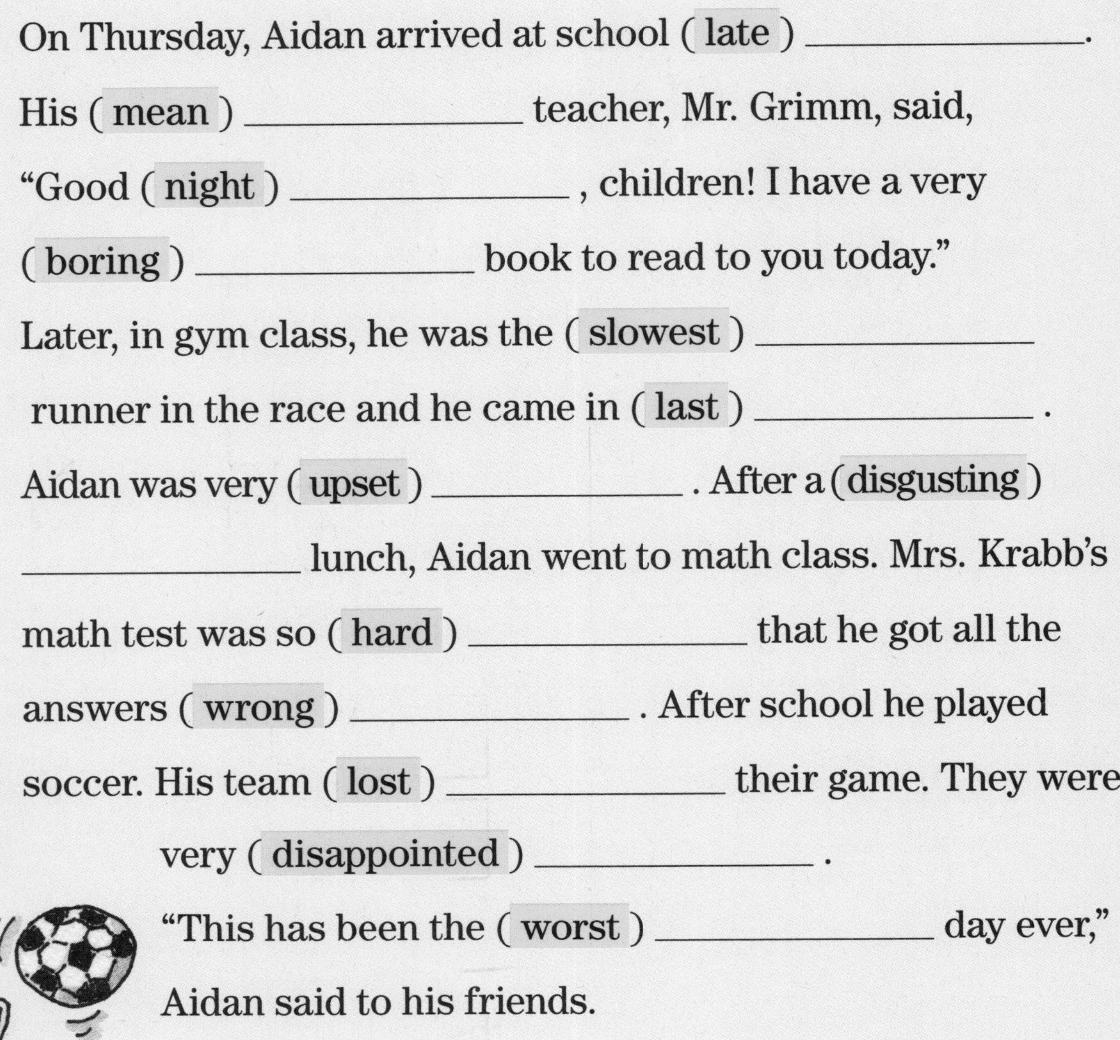

Aidan's (Bad) ____________ Luck Day

On Thursday, Aidan arrived at school (late) ______________.

His (mean) ______________ teacher, Mr. Grimm, said,

"Good (night) ______________ , children! I have a very

(boring) ______________ book to read to you today."

Later, in gym class, he was the (slowest) ______________

runner in the race and he came in (last) ______________ .

Aidan was very (upset) ______________ . After a (disgusting)

______________ lunch, Aidan went to math class. Mrs. Krabb's

math test was so (hard) ______________ that he got all the

answers (wrong) ______________ . After school he played

soccer. His team (lost) ______________ their game. They were

very (disappointed) ______________ .

"This has been the (worst) ______________ day ever,"

Aidan said to his friends.

Write a sentence about your "bad luck" day. Then, rewrite the sentence using an antonym to make it a "good luck" day.

____

____

____

____

Something in Common

Draw a line to match each pair of **synonyms.**

hungry	construct
angry	excited
elevated	cruel
eager	famished
pal	boast
build	rich
wicked	mad
brag	moist
wealthy	high
damp	friend

Write two other synonyms in the boxes below. Then draw a picture to show what they mean.

Brain Box

Words that have the same or nearly the same meaning are called **synonyms.** For example, **dish** and **plate** are synonyms.

Two for One

Spelling and Vocabulary

Antonyms and synonyms

Write a **synonym** and an **antonym** for each word on the chart. Use the words from the Word Box.

ill	break	different	difficult
false	begin	depart	repair
factual	arrive	laugh	energetic
complete	exhausted	alike	cautious
sob	easy	healthy	reckless

	SYNONYM	ANTONYM
careful	cautious	reckless
cry		
hard		
leave		
tired		
fix		
sick		
finish		
similar		
true		

There's an Ant on My Aunt!

Complete each sentence with the correct **homophones.**

Dee ___threw___ the ball ___through___ the hole in the wall.

Logan and Maria saw ____________ friends over ____________ by the hot dog stand.

Jamal wanted ____________ eat ____________ crackers.

I'll ____________ you in the ____________ section of the market.

The Fantastic Fumblers have ____________ only ____________ of their baseball games.

Ms. Ramirez asked us to ____________ the ____________ answers to the math questions.

The brave ____________ spent the ____________ in the haunted castle.

He had enough bus ____________ to get all the way to the county ____________.

Brain Box

Homophones are words that sound the same but have different spellings and meanings. For example, **groan** and **grown** are homophones.

Let's Write Right!

Spelling and Vocabulary

Homophones

Complete each sentence with the correct **homophone.**

The girls waded in the ___creek___.	creak
I heard a scary ___creak___ on the stairs.	creek

allowed	I like to read __________ to my little sister.
aloud	Stop! You're not __________ to go in there.

The rose has a beautiful __________.	scent
Brad __________ his cousin a funny birthday card.	sent

towed	The little __________ hopped onto a stone.
toad	They __________ his car to the garage for repairs.

I tightened the belt around my __________.	waist
It's important not to __________ paper.	waste

principal	Mr. Avila is the __________ of our school.
principle	Martin Luther King Jr. was a man of __________.

Mia wrote her friend a letter on her new __________.	stationary
My dad works out on a __________ bike at the gym.	stationery

pear	I am wearing my favorite __________ of socks.
pair	Kim ate a sandwich and a __________ for lunch.

Be a Word Detective

Use the **context clues** in each sentence to figure out the meaning of the highlighted word. Circle the correct definition.

Mr. Ferris was infuriated when the boys hit a baseball through his living room window.

a. delighted b. very angry c. interested

The tired farmer had toiled in his field all day planting crops.

a. played b. run c. worked hard

The delicious aroma of the cookies baking in the oven made everyone hungry.

a. smell b. color c. heat

Mr. Garcia ascended the ladder to reach the roof of his house.

a. climbed up b. climbed down c. took away

The expert declared, “This is an authentic coin from ancient Rome, so it’s extremely valuable.”

a. dirty b. common c. real

The king’s throne was very elaborate ; it was covered with gold and jewels.

a. soft b. normal c. fancy

The police officer admonished the man not to drive down the flooded street.

a. rewarded b. promised c. warned

Because we had such a hectic weekend, we barely had a moment to rest.

a. slow b. busy c. annoying

When you come across a word you don’t understand, you can often figure out its meaning by looking at the surrounding words. These words are called **context clues.**

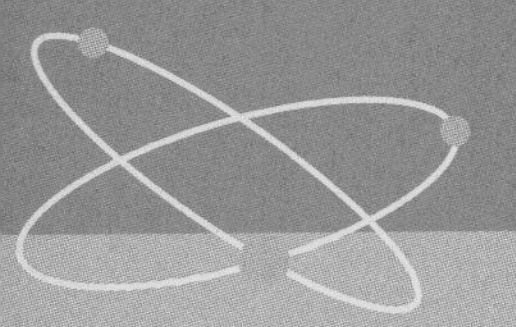

30

What Does That Mean?

Spelling and Vocabulary

Context clues

Use the **context clues** in each sentence to figure out the meaning of the highlighted word.

Then find the correct definition on the cards and write it on the line.

calm | dangerous | easily noticed | amazed | very important | rich | lay back | worn down

It is (crucial) very important to win the game if we want to be in the state championship play-offs.

Only the bravest climbers attempted to climb the (hazardous) ________ mountain.

I was (flabbergasted) ________ when he told me he was really a space alien.

The man was so (prosperous) ________ that he lived in a mansion and had his own private airplane.

The tired boy (reclined) ________ on the sofa and soon fell asleep.

The boat sailed smoothly on the (tranquil) ________ lake.

The building was so (dilapidated) ________ that it was falling apart.

The (conspicuous) ________ man wore a red wig and a bright purple suit.

Put 'Em In Order

Number each group of words to show the correct **alphabetical order.**

2 race
1 rabbit
3 rose

_____ messy
_____ meat
_____ more

_____ map
_____ mouse
_____ mad

_____ has
_____ home
_____ hill

_____ ride
_____ red
_____ read

_____ heavy
_____ happy
_____ hide

_____ hall
_____ hero
_____ hello

_____ rest
_____ road
_____ rug

_____ money
_____ mitten
_____ minus

Spelling and Vocabulary

Alphabetical order

Brain Box

When putting words in **alphabetical order,** sort using the first letter of each word. For example: **a**pple, **b**anana, **c**antaloupe

If the first letter of two or more words is the same, sort using the second letter. For example: with best and bat, **ba**t comes before **be**st.

If the first and second letter is the same, use the third letter to determine alphabetical order. For example: with dance and date, **dan**ce comes before **dat**e.

Look It Up

Read about how to use a **dictionary.**

Spelling and Vocabulary

Dictionary skills

A **dictionary** can tell you how to spell a word, how to pronounce the word, and what it means. The words in a dictionary are listed in **alphabetical order.**

Every word listed in a dictionary is called an **entry word.** For every entry word, you'll usually find:

- the word broken down by syllable
- a pronunciation guide
- an abbreviation for the part of speech
- one or more definitions (if there is more than one meaning, the definitions will be numbered)

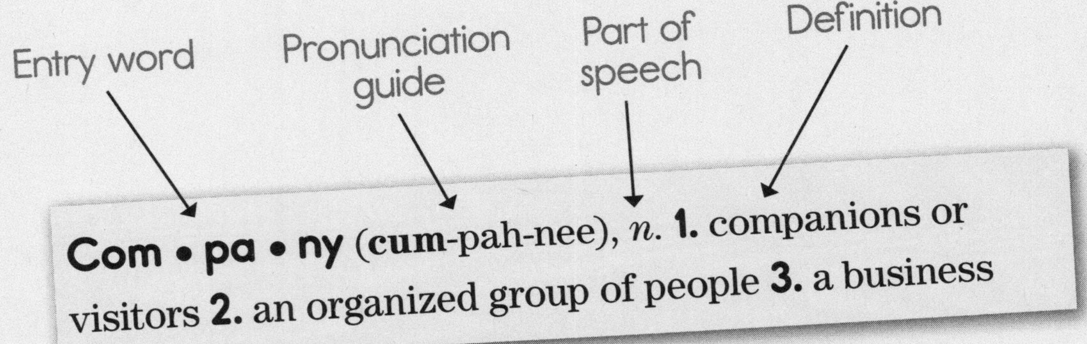

Pronunciation Key		
a short a	i short i	u short u
ā long a	ī long i	ū long u as in mule
e short e	o short o	u̇ long u as in brook
ē long e	ō long o	ü long u as is fool

Abbreviation Key
n = noun
v = verb
adj = adjective
adv = adverb
pron = pronoun

At the top of each dictionary page are two **guide words.** The word on the left is the first entry word on the page. The word on the right is the last entryword on the page.

Use the dictionary pages to answer the questions.

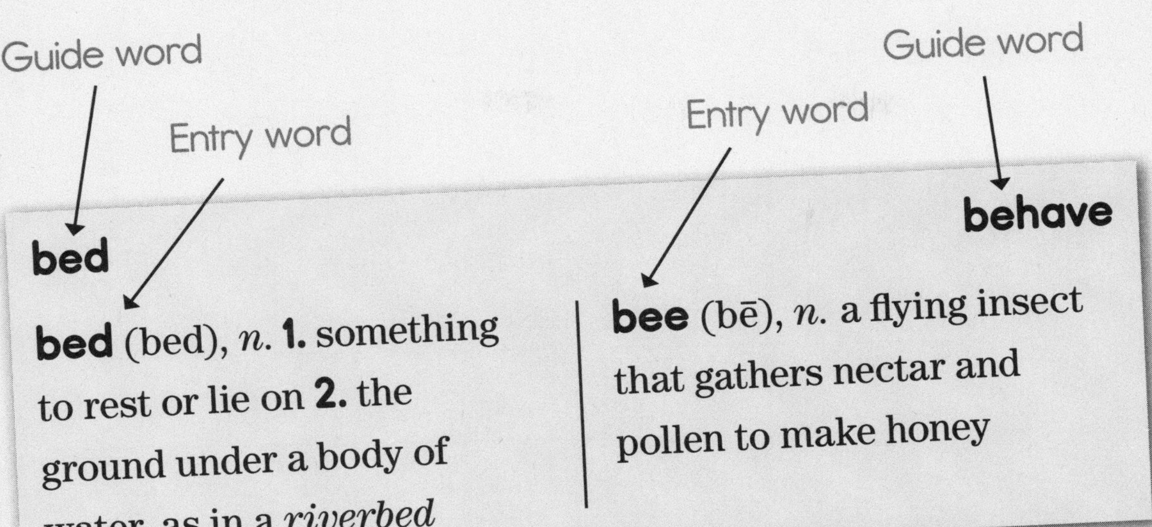

What are the two guide words on the sample dictionary page?

____

What is the last word included on this page? ______________

Would the word **bell** be included on the page? ______________

cap • i • tal (**ka**-pe-tel), *n.* **1.** the city or town where the government of a state is located **2.** a large or uppercase letter such as B, C, or D **3.** the money used in business by a company or a person

What part of speech is the entry word? ______________

How many syllables are in the entry word? ______________

Write a sentence using the word **capital.**

____

____

34

Spelling and Vocabulary

Dictionary skills

Word Search

Look up each word in the dictionary.

Write the definition. Then use the word in a sentence.

chemical

____

____

____

____

electricity

____

____

____

____

wonder

____

____

____

____

Language Arts

Getting Together

Draw a line from each word in column A to a word in column B to make a **common compound** word. Then write the compound words in column C.

Language Arts

Compound words

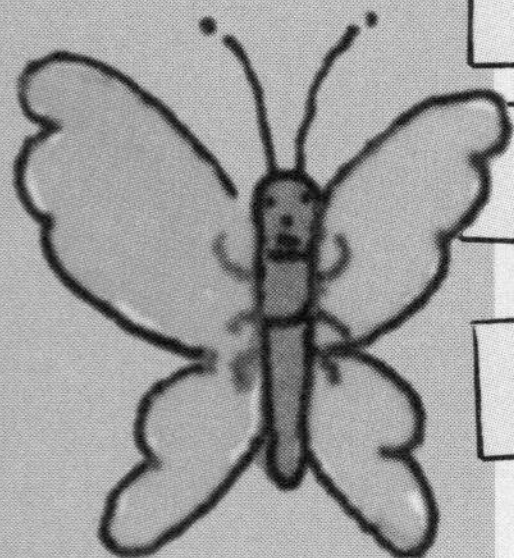

A	B	C
straw	tail	strawberry
eye	walk	
wheel	brow	
side	ground	
pony	fly	
pepper	berry	
butter	mint	
play	barrow	

Now find the compound words in the word search.

H	W	K	J	W	P	O	N	Y	T	A	I	L	F	A
A	H	B	G	B	L	V	I	P	F	C	E	L	B	Q
B	E	S	T	R	A	W	B	E	R	R	Y	P	D	E
U	E	D	L	T	Y	L	M	P	J	M	E	D	I	O
T	L	F	A	H	G	E	H	P	L	C	B	E	R	A
T	B	I	B	F	R	A	C	E	B	G	R	B	G	P
E	A	N	B	U	O	D	K	R	F	E	O	N	J	V
R	R	J	P	D	U	V	J	M	P	O	W	G	U	N
F	R	G	A	K	N	K	S	I	D	E	W	A	L	K
L	O	Q	M	S	D	O	Q	N	H	S	I	V	S	R
Y	W	K	C	H	K	M	D	T	H	T	Y	B	T	F
F	A	D	L	Q	R	K	J	O	B	B	L	A	I	C

Brain Box

A **compound word** is formed when two words are joined together. For example, sun + flower = sunflower.

Circle the compound words in the sentences.

He tiptoed down the hallway to his bedroom.

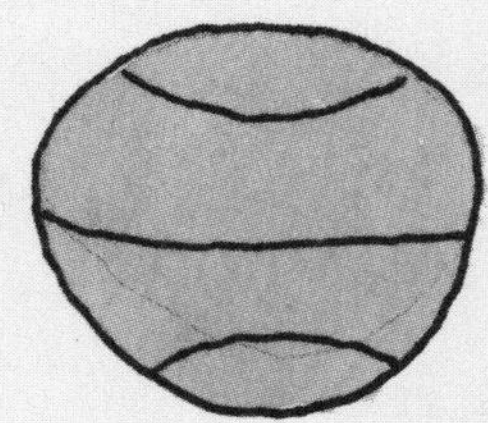

Campbell's dad always wears a necktie to work.

Everyone was going to the big basketball game on Friday night.

She was afraid of being stung by a jellyfish.

There's nothing better than a cozy turtleneck in the wintertime.

Brodie likes to look for starfish on the beach.

They needed to buy a fishbowl for the goldfish.

Ericka and her friends knew the record snowfall meant they could build the biggest snowman ever.

Language Arts

Compound words

Choose three compound words from above. Write each part of the compound word in the spaces below. Then write the whole word.

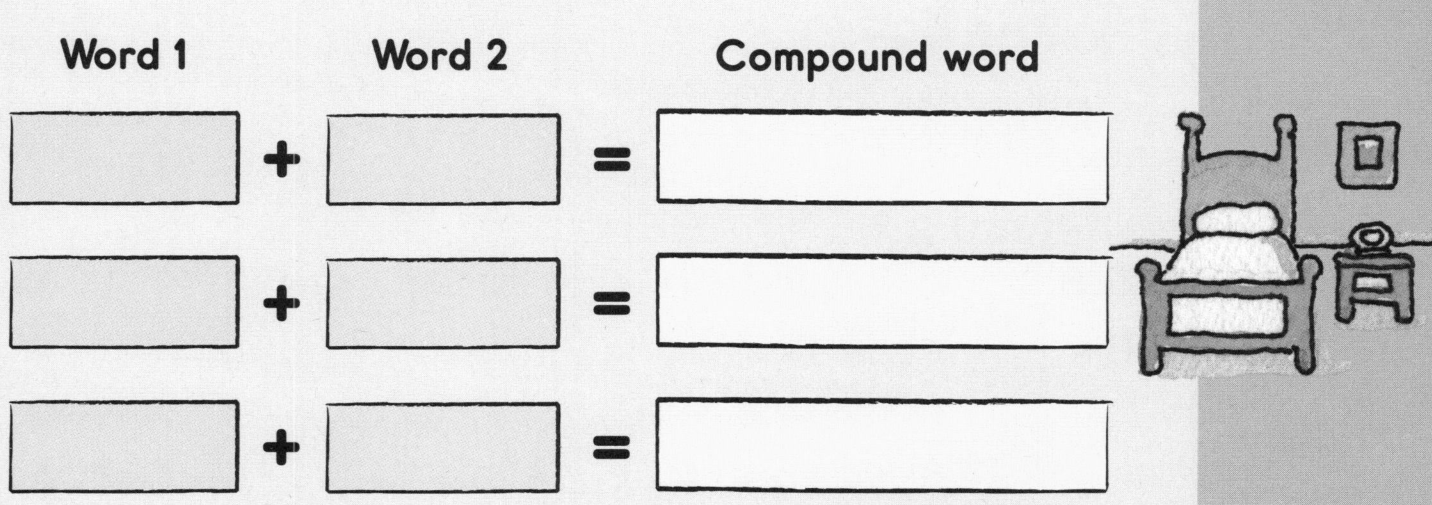

Word Scramble

Language Arts

Scrambled words

Unscramble the following words. Then rearrange the boxed letters to find the fifth word.

Colors

c l a b k

e g n e r

r e p p u l

w e l y o l

Mammals

y e m k o n

r o h i n

d a n a p

g r o a l l i

The Human Body

n i r a b

l n u g s

r a t h e

d o b l o

Rhyme Time

Circle the word that does not **rhyme** with the word in the box.

her	were	where	stir	fur
scratch	catch	hatch	watch	match
ball	fall	stall	small	shall
head	bead	fed	said	dead
purred	word	heard	beard	bird
care	fare	bare	are	dare
stone	phone	moan	gone	bone
wood	could	stood	mood	hood

Circle the word that **rhymes** with the word in the box.

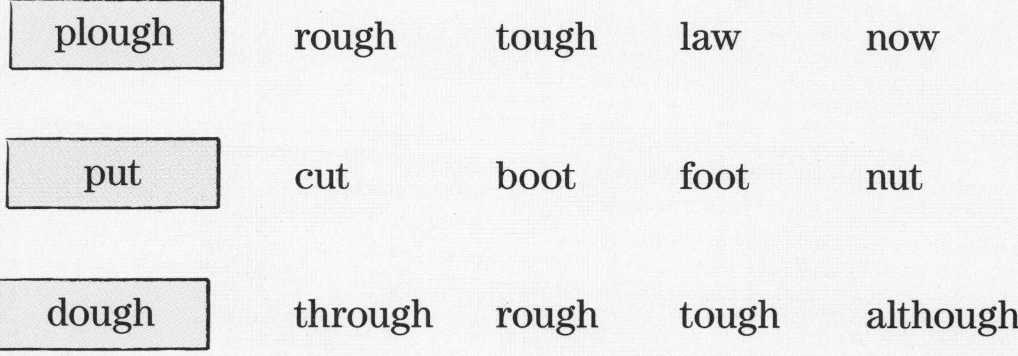

plough	rough	tough	law	now
put	cut	boot	foot	nut
dough	through	rough	tough	although

Clapping and Tapping

Count the **syllables** in each word in the Word Box. Then sort the words on the cards below.

Language Arts

Syllables

spelling	question	operator	ladder
biography	dinosaur	birthday	adorable
bumblebee	caterpillar	accident	grandmother

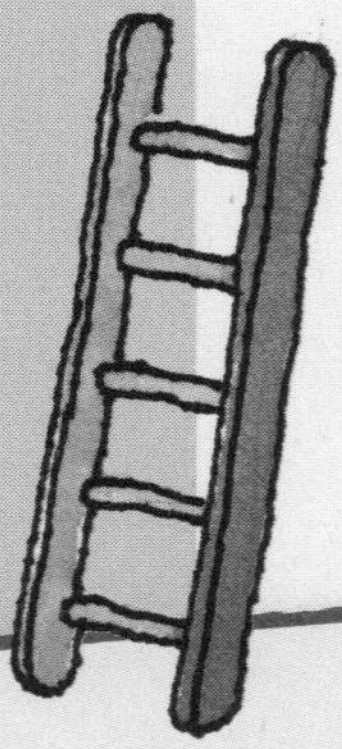

three-syllable words

____

____

____

____

two-syllable words

spelling

____

____

____

four-syllable words

____

____

____

____

Presto Change-o!

Start with the first word in the list. Change just one letter to create a new word that fits the next clue. Continue down the list, changing one letter from the previous word to fit each clue.

it might make you invisible	c l o a k
the sound a frog makes	c r o a k
a dishonest person	___ ___ ___ ___ ___
a small body of water	___ ___ ___ ___ ___
something a witch rides	___ ___ ___ ___ ___

a hair color	b l o n d
it flows through your veins	___ ___ ___ ___ ___
to overflow with water	___ ___ ___ ___ ___
it's opposite the ceiling	___ ___ ___ ___ ___
an ingredient in a cake	___ ___ ___ ___ ___

Language Arts

Word play

Now write your own word play puzzle. Then give it to a friend to solve.

________________	___ ___ ___ ___ ___
________________	___ ___ ___ ___ ___
________________	___ ___ ___ ___ ___
________________	___ ___ ___ ___ ___
________________	___ ___ ___ ___ ___

It's All Relative

Complete each **analogy** using a word from the Word Box.

water	girl	pounds	day
green	food	patient	string

Language Arts

Analogies

Piano is to key as guitar is to string.

Sky is to blue as grass is to ______________.

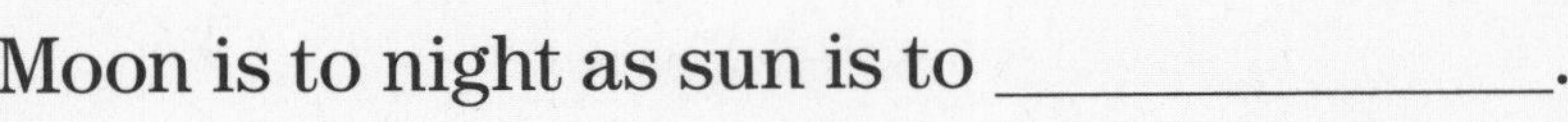

Moon is to night as sun is to ______________.

Teacher is to student as doctor is to ______________.

Brother is to boy as sister is to ______________.

Height is to inches as weight is to ______________.

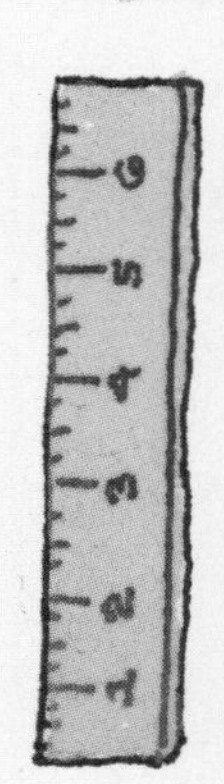

Thirsty is to water as hungry is to ______________.

Car is to road as boat is to ______________.

Brain Box

An **analogy** compares how things are related to each other.

For example: **Hat** is to **head** as **shoe** is to **foot.** A hat **is worn** on a head just like a shoe **is worn** on a foot.

Use your imagination to finish the analogies.
Then draw a picture of your favorite analogy.

Roar is to lion as ______________________________.

Scale is to fish as ______________________________.

January is to winter as ______________________________.

Yesterday is to past as ______________________________.

Hammer is to pound as ______________________________.

Now draw a picture of your favorite analogy.

Construction Zone

Write the two words that make up each **contraction.**

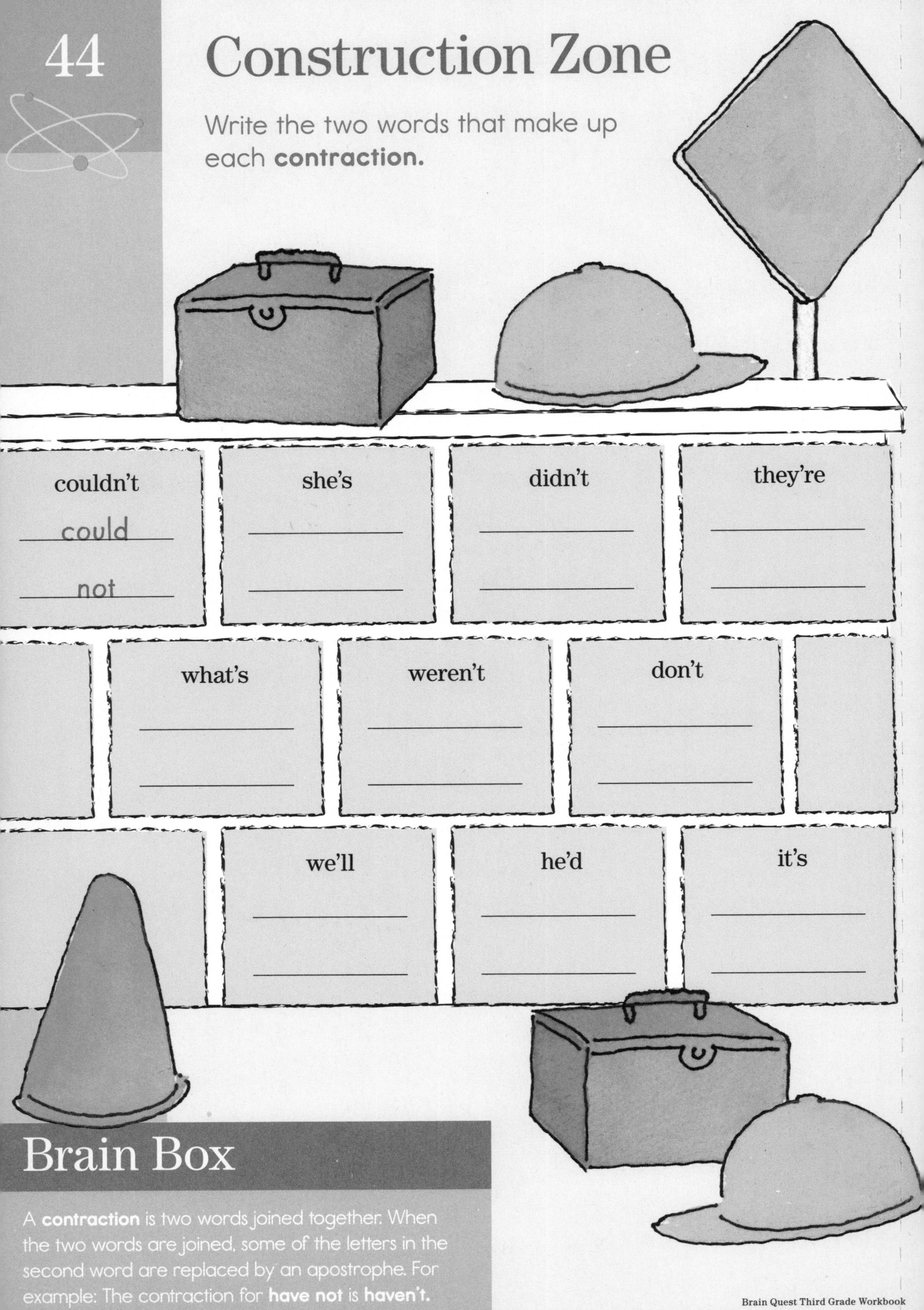

Brain Box

A **contraction** is two words joined together. When the two words are joined, some of the letters in the second word are replaced by an apostrophe. For example: The contraction for **have not** is **haven't.**

It's Me, Connor!

Replace the highlighted words with a **contraction** from the Word Box.

he's	couldn't	we've
I've	I'm	what's
I'll	weren't	they're

Dear Aunt Shelly,

(I am) I'm writing this letter to you from Camp Walnut Creek. I love camp so far! (I have) I've already made a lot of cool friends. My bunkmate is named Ben, and (he is) he's a really good soccer player. (We have) we've been kicking the ball around every day. My two other friends are Thomas and Oliver. (They are) they're identical twins! If it (were not) ________ for the different way they dress, I (could not) ________ tell them apart! I have to go now, so (I will) ________ say goodbye. Please write back and tell me (what is) ________ happening back home!

Love,
Connor

Language Arts

Contractions

Now pretend you're Aunt **Shelly** and write a short **letter back to** Connor. **Use three** contractions.

HI CONNOR. EVERTTHING ISFINE AT HOME. LOVE, AUNT SHELLY

A Figure of Speech

Complete each **simile** with a clue from the next page.

Language Arts

Similes

The baby frog was as light as a feather.

I'm so thirsty, my mouth is as dry as a DeseRT.

Even under pressure, Shanti is as cool as ice.

The boy tiptoed down the hallway, quiet as a mouse.

The center on the basketball team was as tall as a SKYSCRAPER.

He turned as white as a GhOSt when he saw how high the roller coaster was.

If my kitten keeps eating so much she will become as big as an elePhANT.

Now make up your own simile. Then draw your own clue on the blank card.

____

____

____

Brain Box

A **simile** is a phrase or figure of speech that compares two things using the words **as** or **like.** For example: The dancer was as **graceful as a swan.** This phrase compares a **dancer** with a **swan.**

desert

skyscraper

feather

mouse

ice

ghost

elephant

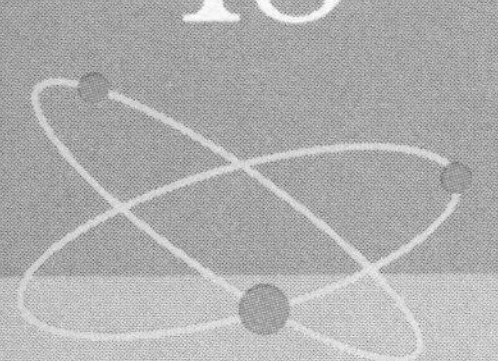

Whatever Do You Mean?

Write what you think each highlighted **idiom** really means.

Lori spilled the beans. Now everyone knows my secret.

____

____

Language Arts

Idioms

Ronald loves to go to the library. He always has his nose in a book.

____

____

Can you give me a hand? I can't lift the box.

____

____

I can't wait to hear about the party. I'm all ears.

____

____

That story about the howling ghost made my hair stand on end.

____

____

Brain Box

Idioms are expressions that mean something different from what the words might seem to actually say. For example: **hold your tongue** is an idiom that means **be quiet.**

I knew every answer on the science test. It was a **piece of cake**.

Is your dad really an astronaut, or are you **pulling my leg**?

Rosita and Jennifer both like to skate and play chess. They're **like two peas in a pod**.

The sound of fingernails on a chalkboard **drives me up a wall**.

Choose an idiom and draw a silly picture of what the words **literally** seem to say.

A Day at the Beach

Circle all the **nouns** in the story. Then sort the nouns on the cards below.

Language Arts

Nouns

Madeline and her family decided to go to the shore in New Jersey. Madeline brought her best friend, Cara, along. Madeline packed extra beach towels and sunscreen. Cara packed a Frisbee and a radio.

Madeline and Cara went to the beach with Madeline's mom, dad, and sister. They also walked along the boardwalk, played games in the arcades, and went to the ice-cream parlor for dessert.

Person

Madeline

______

______

______

______

______

Place

______

______

______

______

______

______

Thing

______

______

______

______

______

______

Brain Box

A **noun** is a word that names a person, place, or thing.

Generally Speaking

Circle the **proper nouns** and underline the **common nouns** in the sentences. Then sort each noun on the cards below.

Ms. Ramos took our class to the zoo.

In January, Penny moved into her new house on Maple Street.

The Grand Canyon is in Arizona.

Dylan tied the shoelaces on his shoes.

Aunt Ethel bought delicious doughnuts at the Sugar Shack.

Dr. Pollock took his family to the beach on Sunday.

The pool is closed on Labor Day.

MAPLE ST.

SUGAR SHACK

CLOSED ON LABOR DAY

Language Arts

Common and proper nouns

Proper Nouns

Ms. Ramos

Common Nouns

Brain Box

A **common noun** names **any** person, place, or thing. Common nouns begin with a lowercase letter. For example: **girl, state, day**

A **proper noun** is the name of a **specific** person, place, or thing. Proper nouns begin with a capital letter. For example: **W**endy, **I**ndiana, **M**onday

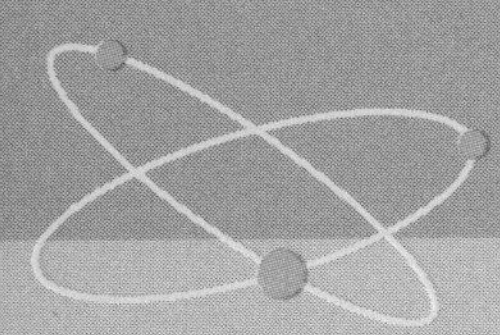

Introducing Nouns

Language Arts

Articles

Circle the correct **article** before each word.

a (an) apple

the a magazines

a an umbrella

the a shoes

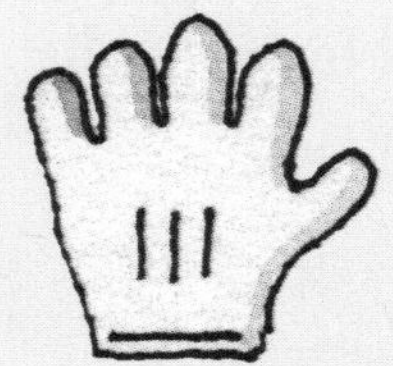

the an glove

a an fish

an the candle

a an pineapple

the an oranges

a an energy bar

the a balloons

the an plant

Brain Box

An **article** is a word that goes before a noun. **A, an,** and **the** are all articles.

When the noun begins with a consonant, use **a** or **the.**

When the noun begins with a vowel, use **an** or **the.**

In most cases, if the noun is plural, use **the.**

Trading Places

Finish each sentence with a **pronoun** that replaces the highlighted word(s).

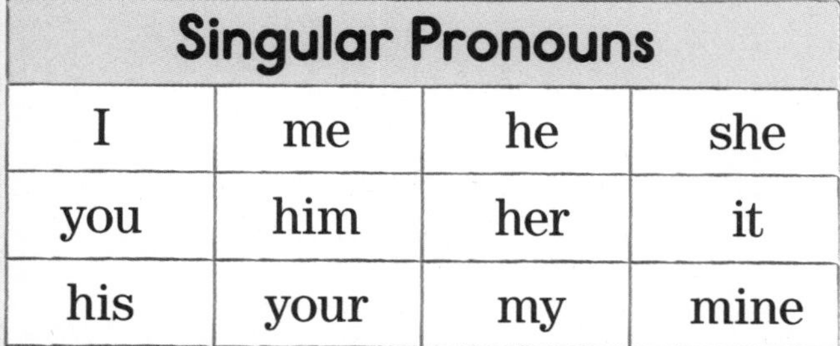

Singular Pronouns			
I	me	he	she
you	him	her	it
his	your	my	mine

Plural Pronouns			
we	us	they	them
their	our	ours	you

Evan hit a double in the first inning.
__He__ hit a triple in the second inning.

The women are going shopping at the mall today.
________ need new shoes.

Can you give that plate to Tamika and me ?
Then can you pass ________ the spinach?

Chitra gave a present to Elijah . ________ couldn't wait for ________ to open it.

Jamal and I put the box on the table.
Then ________ sat and stared at ________ .

The teacher brought a cake for the third graders .
She was excited for ________ to eat it.

I took Amber to the party.
Everyone liked ________ a lot.

Now write your own sentence.
Use the pronouns **I, me,** and **you.**

____

____

____

Brain Box

Pronouns are words that are used in place of nouns. For example:

Ed is wearing a new hat.

He is wearing a new hat. (**He** takes the place of **Ed.**)

A **singular pronoun** takes the place of a singular noun.

A **plural pronoun** takes the place of a plural noun.

54

Whose Is It?

Complete each sentence with the correct **possessive pronoun** from the Word Box.

Possessive Pronouns		
his	her	hers
our	ours	their
theirs	my	mine
your	yours	its

Language Arts

Possessive pronouns

"Whose bike is this?" asked Morgan.

"It belongs to me," said Betsy. "It's ___mine___.

Look, it has ___my___ initials on the seat."

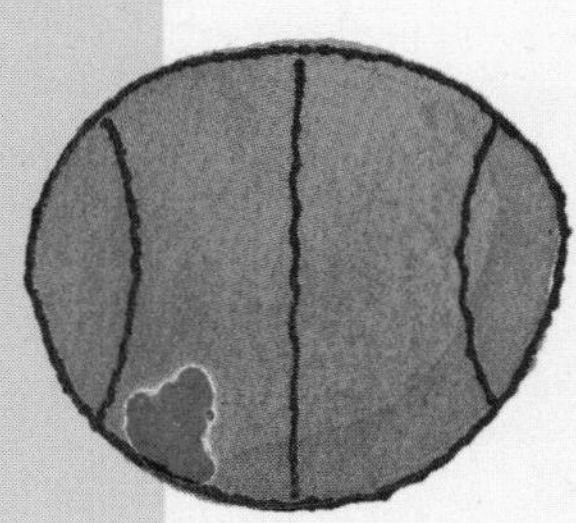

"Whose basketball is this?" asked Elle.

"It belongs to Jon," said Yuri.

"It is ____________.

His dad got it for ____________ birthday."

"Whose dog is this?" asked Tamika.

"It belongs to us," said the twins.

"It is ____________.

____________ dog's name is Buster."

Brain Box

A **possessive pronoun** shows ownership. For example: **Teri** owns a camera. It is **hers. Her** camera is new.

"Whose sweatshirt is this?" Brian asked Claire.
"I saw you wear it yesterday, and it's __________ favorite color. I think it must be __________."

"Whose ice skates are these?" asked Milo.
"They belong to Liz," said Mrs. Randall.
"I know they are __________ because __________ skates have blue laces."

"Whose books are these?" asked Madison.
"They belong to those boys," said Suzie.
"I'm sure they are __________.
They always leave __________ books lying around."

"Whose parrot is this?"
asked Eduardo.
"It belongs to me," said Katie.
"I should put it back in __________ cage."

Noun Ownership

Rewrite these wordy sentences by changing the highlighted words to **possessive nouns.** You may have to switch around some of the other words in the sentence.

Language Arts

Possessives

The reading contest of my teacher is going to start next week.

My teacher's reading contest is going to start next week.

I didn't realize that was the house belonging to Sari.

____

The cupcakes of Samantha were absolutely delicious!

____

That Halloween party of my friend was a little spooky.

____

Did you know that this trumpet belongs to Lalo?

____

I promised I would clean out the car of my dad.

____

The sister of Kody won the spelling bee.

____

Brain Box

When nouns are **possessive,** they tell who or what owns something else. Nouns are made possessive by adding an apostrophe.

For example:

The dog that belongs to Jeff can also be written **Jeff's dog.**

The **possessive nouns** in these sentences are missing their **apostrophes.** Fill in the apostrophes so the sentences make sense.

All of my friends' costumes look great!

I love to hear my English teachers stories.

That trees leaves are starting to turn color.

Mollys birthday is the day after tomorrow.

That girls outfit looks just like mine.

Jamie couldn't believe how high the giraffes necks reached.

Language Arts

Possessives

Choose a noun from the Word Box to complete each sentence. Then change the noun to a plural possessive and write it on the line.

teacher	girl
traveler	bull

The ______________ lounge is on the second floor.

The ______________ horns are white and gray.

The ______________ rest stop has the best doughnuts in town.

The team gathered in the ______________ locker room.

Brain Box

To make a **plural noun** ending in **s** possessive, put the apostrophe after the **s.** For example:

The dogs' dish (two or more dogs have one dish)

The dogs' dishes (two or more dogs have two or more dishes)

It's All in the Details

Language Arts

Adjectives

Underline the **adjectives** in the following descriptions. Then sort them on the cards below.

three enormous and sweet-smelling sunflowers

two delicious, meatless pizzas

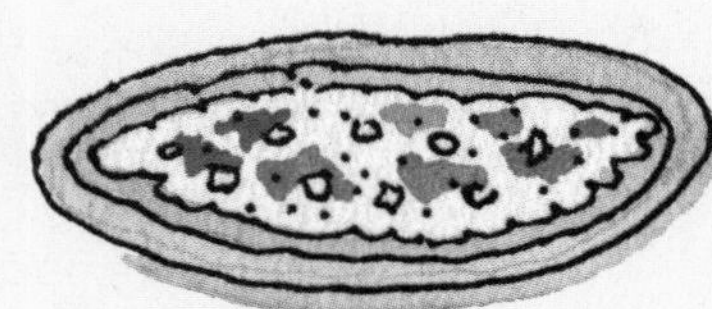

five spicy roasted peppers

a tiny, brown, loud bird

a large, blue pool

the noisy timpani drums

the quiet gray kitten

Number
three

Color

Size
enormous

Taste or Smell
sweet-smelling

Brain Box

Adjectives are words that describe nouns. Adjectives can tell how many, what size, what shape, what color, or what kind. They can tell how something feels, looks, tastes, sounds, or smells. Adjectives can add color and life to sentences and make writing more interesting.

Slimy Snails and Wiggly Worms

Write a creative **adjective** in front of each noun.
For a challenge, try to find an adjective that starts with the same sound as the noun.

dreadful dinosaur

marvelous movie

____________ shirt

____________ dinner

____________ wizard

____________ friend

____________ dog

____________ cat

____________ bug

____________ elf

60

This or That?

Language Arts

Adjectives that compare

Write the correct form of the highlighted **adjective** in each sentence.

This path is (rough) rougher________ than the one behind the barn.

He is always the (hungry) ________________ of all the boys.

She is the (fast) ________________ runner in the school.

A zebra is (short) ________________ than a giraffe.

My turtle was the (slow) ________________ one in the turtle race.

That's the (bright) ________________ color I've ever seen.

Brain Box

When comparing two nouns, add **er** to most one- or two-syllable adjectives. For example: This house is **smaller than** that one.

When comparing more than two nouns, add **est** to most one- or two-syllable adjectives. For example: This house is the **smallest** one on the block.

If the adjective ends in a consonant followed by a **y**, turn the **y** into an **i** before adding **est**. For example: Will was the **happiest** boy on the team.

Some adjectives that compare are irregular. For example:

- good, better, best
- bad, worse, worst
- far, farther, farthest

Circle the incorrect adjective in each sentence. Then write the correct adjective in the box.

I think ham tastes much gooder than chicken.

Seth ran the farest of all the kids in gym class.

Jan's room is cluttered, but Todd's is even badder!

Seize the Day!

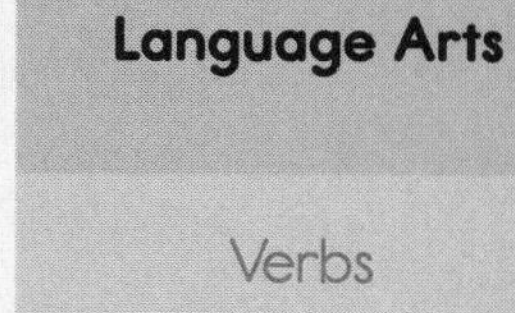

Circle the correct form of the **verb** in each sentence.

Hannah bowl bowls every Saturday with her dad.

Seth and Arturo always figure figures out the answer before anyone else.

The fan work works really well when you put it on full power.

My cats investigate investigates every little spider and ant they see on the ground.

Each Halloween, Sydney dress dresses in a different costume.

Sophie prepare prepares for her game by doing drills in the backyard.

Don't you think we dance dances well together?

Jamal and his sister read reads several books every week.

Brain Box

A **present-tense verb** tells about something that is happening now. For example: Colin **plays** soccer.

If a verb describes the action of one person or thing, it usually ends in **s** or **es.** For example: The swan **floats** on the pond.

If a verb describes the action of more than one person or thing, the verb usually remains as it is, without adding **s** or **es.** For example: The swans **float** on the pond.

Past, Present, Future

Underline the **verb** in each sentence. Then write **past, present,** or **future** to tell when the action is happening.

The twins will go to camp next summer. future

Erik's pet lizard eats crickets.

Our dad cooked steak on the grill last night.

My uncle always sings in the shower.

Olivia hunted everywhere for her missing cat.

I lived in Michigan when I was a baby.

José walks to school with his best friend.

Chloe will ride her bike to the store.

We will plant our garden in the spring.

Language Arts

Verbs

Brain Box

A **past-tense verb** tells about something that has already happened. To change a verb to past tense, add a **d** to most words that end in **e,** and add **ed** to most other words. For example: Colin **exercised** in the gym last night. Colin **pulled** the rope.

A **future-tense verb** tells about something that will happen in the future. The word **will** is usually used with future tense verbs. For example: Colin **will exercise** outside next weekend.

Write three sentences about what you did last weekend. Then circle all the **past-tense** verbs.

Look around the room. Write three sentences about everything that's happening now. Circle all the **present-tense** verbs.

Write three sentences about your plans for next summer's vacation. Circle all the **future-tense** verbs.

Play Ball!

Circle each **action verb** in the story.
Then match each one with a scrambled action verb below and rewrite it correctly on the line.

Language Arts

Action verbs

Today the Queen Bees play the Hornets. In the first inning, Ava hits the ball into left field. Natalie pitches the ball to the next batter.

In the fourth inning, Tonya slams the ball for a home run. Nadia walks to first base when the umpire shouts, "Ball four!"

In the eighth inning, Aiko hurts her ankle when she slides into third base. Coach Monroe examines her ankle and then tapes it.

In the last inning, Carmen catches a fly ball to center field for the third out. The Queen Bees win the game by one run!

malss ______________

issled ______________

klaws ______________

mxienesa ______________

ihst ______________

sshout ______________

iwn ______________

stipche ______________

lyap play

scathec ______________

truhs ______________

steap ______________

Brain Box

An **action verb** tells what the subject of a sentence is doing. For example: Ethan **runs** down the court and **passes** the ball to Jamie. **Runs** and **passes** are both action verbs because they describe what Ethan is doing.

Help Wanted!

Complete each sentence with a **helping verb** from the Word Box.

is	have	has	will	had	are
would	was	were	can	could	am

The girls __________ standing at the bus stop yesterday.

I __________ searching for my pen last night.

We __________ watching the sky for lightning.

My sister __________ wearing her new jeans today.

We __________ skated on this pond before.

I __________ going to the mall in a few minutes.

Your brother __________ like some more popcorn.

Mrs. Takito __________ baked those cookies before.

By the end of the meet, Jabari __________ win three races.

Now write three of your own sentences using the rest of the helping verbs in the Word Box.

____

____

____

____

____

____

Brain Box

Helping verbs can be used to help tell about an action. They are always used before an action verb. For example: The movie star **had** signed autographs. (In this example, **had** is the helping verb for the action verb **signed.**)

Link 'Em Up

Complete each sentence with the correct **linking verb** from the Word Box.

looks	are	is	was
am	feels	seems	smells

Language Arts

Linking verbs

My favorite food __________ hamburgers.

Yesterday I __________ at the pool all day.

I __________ very excited today.

The dogs __________ barking loudly now.

My hamster's fur __________ soft.

This test __________ like it might be hard.

Your hair __________ pretty.

Something __________ bad.

Brain Box

Linking verbs connect a noun to a word or words that tell something about the noun.

For example: Russell **is** happy about the chess tournament.

The linking verb **is** connects Russell to his feelings about the chess tournament.

The Time Machine

Complete each clue by changing the highlighted present tense verb to an **irregular past-tense** verb. Then complete the crossword puzzle.

Language Arts

Irregular verbs

ACROSS

3. Tony (read) ______ his book after dinner.

4. I (give) ______ Adam a computer game for his birthday.

5. Donald (throw) ______ the ball.

7. Janie (ring) ______ the bell after school.

9. He (bring) ______ his violin to school.

DOWN

1. We (drink) ______ strawberry milkshakes at the diner.

2. Alicia (catch) ______ the ball.

6. Ellie (write) ______ a letter to her friend in Texas.

8. Becky (buy) ______ a new dress at the mall.

10. The frightened cat (hide) ______ under the bed.

Story Time

Circle the **present-tense verbs** in the story. Then rewrite the highlighted sentences in the **past tense.** When you're done, circle all the **irregular verbs.**

Language Arts

Irregular verbs

Today I am going to soccer camp. We will drive four hours to get there. When I get there, I will catch up with my camp friends before dinner.

My camp routine is perfect. I eat breakfast in the mess hall and then spend the morning practicing drills. Then I eat lunch and go to an activity like art, music, or chorus. I always choose chorus and sing my heart out every afternoon. After activities we spend more time playing soccer.

On the last night of camp, we all play a joke on our coaches and wear our pajamas to the game. When it is time to say goodbye, we give each other hugs and promise to stay in touch.

Yesterday I went to soccer camp.

How, When, or Where

Underline the **verb** in each sentence. Circle the **adverb.** Then sort the adverbs on the cards below.

Shai plays soccer outside.

Samuel played the computer game skillfully.

Did it rain today?

There are mosquitoes everywhere.

The ballerina danced gracefully.

The boys waited patiently for their turn.

Kiko walked upstairs.

The rock star played his guitar yesterday.

Tomorrow, I will eat a burrito for lunch.

Brain Box

An **adverb** is a word that describes a verb. Adverbs tell **how, when,** or **where** an action happens. For example: The baby cried **loudly.** The adverb **loudly** tells **how** the baby cried.

Many adverbs end with the suffix **ly.**

70

Meet in the Middle

In each sentence, draw one line under the **subject** and two lines under the **predicate.**
Then circle all the **nouns.**

Language Arts

Subjects and predicates

The funny clown rode on a tiny bike.

The sandy beach was very crowded.

The mothers took their children to the park.

All of the dogs began to bark.

The Peterson family is going to the mountains tomorrow.

The grumpy man yelled at the noisy boys.

Christian likes to visit his grandparents.

Dawn won a ribbon at the horse show.

Brain Box

A sentence has two parts, a **subject** and a **predicate.**

The **subject** tells **who** or **what** the sentence is about.

The **predicate** tells **what** the subject is or does. The predicate often begins with the verb.

For example:

The shiny jet | took off from the airport.

subject | predicate

What's the Story?

Choose an **article, adjective,** and **noun** from the Word Boxes and create a **subject** for each sentence.

Articles	
a	those
an	our
the	my

Adjectives	
shy	sweet
silly	funny
old	crazy

Nouns	
owl	kangaroos
seal	comedian
rabbits	grandmother

Article	Adjective	Noun	
A	silly	seal	balanced a ball on its nose.
			built a nest in the tall tree.
			told a very hilarious joke!
			ran away when they saw us.
			couldn't wait to see us.
			knit me a warm sweater.

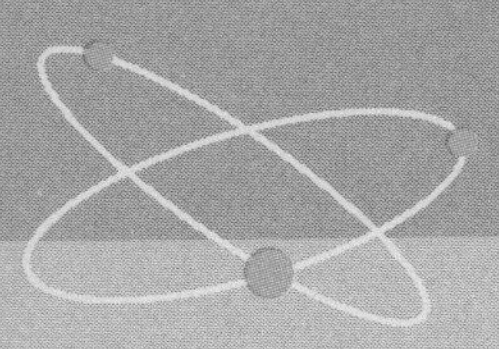

Picture This

Look at each picture. Complete each sentence with a **predicate.**

The space aliens want to travel to Earth.

I always ______________________.

Sometimes he ______________________.

The panda bear ______________________.

That roller coaster ______________________.

The audience ______________________.

The sun ______________________.

Language Arts

Predicates

It's in Its Den

Language Arts

It's and its

Circle the correct word in each sentence.

My horse won it's its first race today.

I hope it's its ready. I'm really hungry!

You should buy that sweater. It's Its color is perfect for you.

The elephant and it's its new baby can now be seen at the zoo.

It's Its time to leave for the movies.

That's a cute puppy. What is it's its name?

I wonder if it's its hot outside today.

Hurry up! It's Its going to rain soon.

What a pretty bird. It's Its feathers are a beautiful color.

Have you seen my book? It's Its not in it's its usual place on my desk.

Write two sentences about your favorite toy. Use **it's** in one sentence and **its** in the other.

____

____

____

____

Brain Box

It's and **its** have different meanings.

Its is a possessive pronoun. For example: **The lion licked its paw.**

It's is a contraction that means **it is.** For example: **It's my turn to pitch.**

The Three T's

Complete each sentence with **there, their,** or **they're.**

Language Arts

There, their, and they're

Please put the flowers ____________ .

Have you been ____________ before?

____________ going to the zoo tomorrow.

Have you seen ____________ new car?

I like swimming in pools when ____________ not too crowded.

Your pencil is over ____________ on the desk.

____________ house is right next to ours.

Will you go ____________ with me?

On Saturday, ____________ having a birthday party.

I just saw ____________ new lizard.

Now write one sentence for each T-word.

they're ____________________________

____

there ____________________________

____

their ____________________________

____

Brain Box

The three words **there, their,** and **they're** are often mixed up.

There tells **where something is.** Example: Put it over **there.**

Their means **belonging to them.** Example: That is **their** puppy.

They're is a contraction that means **they are.** Example: **They're** the best team.

The Wonderful W's

Language Arts

Where, were, and we're

Complete each sentence with **where, were,** or **we're.**

I don't know ____________ we are going on our vacation.

If ____________ late, he won't let us in.

What ____________ you buying in that store?

Tomorrow, ____________ going to canoe on the lake.

Do you remember ____________ Kelly said we should meet her?

We ____________ in Florida last winter.

____________ not singing in the school concert this year.

____________ is your new bicycle?

Do you remember ____________ you left your coat?

They ____________ the winning team in the relay race.

Now write one sentence for each W-word.

where ____

____

were ____

____

we're ____

____

Brain Box

Where tells or asks about **a place.** Example: **Where** is your house?

Were is the past tense of **are.** Example: We **were** going there yesterday.

We're is a contraction meaning **we are.**

Example: **We're** leaving now.

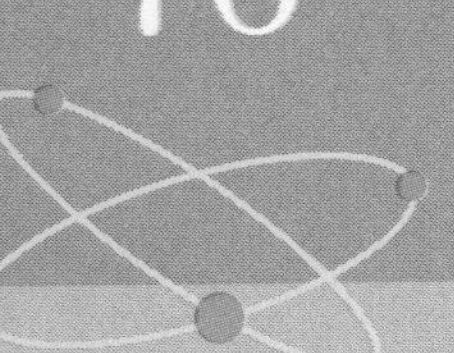

Language Arts

Homographs

Double Meaning

Write two different definitions for each **homograph.**

yard — a measurement of length

an outdoor play area

duck

fly

can

bat

ring

pitcher

light

Brain Box

Homographs are words that are spelled the same and sound the same but have different meanings.

Choose a pair of homographs and use both meanings in one sentence.

You Said It

Fix the punctuation in each sentence by adding **quotation marks.**

Kevin said, "Let's go to the zoo tomorrow."

Is that your new dress? asked Chitra.

Here we are at last! said Ari. I can't wait to see this movie!

I'm cooking spaghetti for dinner, said Rudi's father.

David asked, Why are you laughing so hard?

There was one third grader, said the teacher, who got every answer right.

You'd better wear your coat. It's very cold today, said Philip's grandfather.

I'm having my birthday party at the bowling alley, said Carlo.

Are you going to play soccer this year? asked Li.

Watch out! There's a car coming! yelled Alan.

Language Arts

Quotation marks

Brain Box

Quotation marks show what a person is saying. They go before the first word and after the final punctuation of the quotation. The first word of a quotation is always capitalized.

For example: Leslie said, **"We** are going to camp this summer."

On the Mark!

Add the correct **punctuation mark** to the end of each sentence.

My new dog has one black ear.

What time is your piano lesson

Where did you put your boots

That is so exciting

Julia and Jeffrey both live in North Carolina

Hurry, the bathtub is overflowing onto the floor

Oh no, our dinner is burning

How long will you be gone

That is so wonderful

Language Arts

Statements, questions, and exclamations

Brain Box

Declarative sentences are statements that tell about something. They end with a period. For example: I went fishing.

Interrogative sentences are questions that ask about something. They end with a question mark. For example: Do you have a bike?

Exclamatory sentences are exclamations that express strong feelings. They end with an exclamation point. For example: I hooked a big one!

Now write three sentences of your own—one **declarative,** one **interrogative,** and one **exclamatory.** Remember to use correct punctuation.

____

____

____

____

____

____

To the Letter

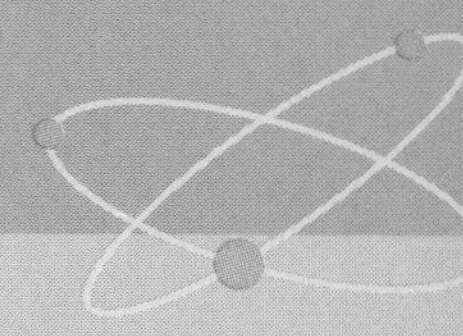

Add the missing **commas** and **periods** to this letter.

January 14, 2009

Dear Hernando,

I am so excited. We are now in our new home in Middletown Pennsylvania Our kitchen has a new stove refrigerator microwave and sink I have my own bedroom with a nice view

Middletown is a lot smaller than Philadelphia Pennsylvania where we used to live It is so different living in a smaller town

I can't wait to see you at camp this summer We'll sail boats go horseback riding swim and play tennis I hope we'll be in the same tent like we were last year!

Your friend

Neel

Language Arts

Punctuation

Brain Box

Commas are used to **separate words in a list** of three or more things. For example: My favorite fruits are apples, peaches, pears, and bananas.

Commas are used in **dates** to separate the date from the year. For example: He was born on June 3, 1774.

Commas are used to **separate the name of a city and a state.** For example: The fair was held in Chicago, Illinois.

Ben's Broken Keyboard

Language Arts

Capitals

The shift key on Ben's keyboard is broken, so he couldn't capitalize any words in his homework. Circle each word that should begin with a **capital letter.**

i watched the red sox play against the yankees last night.

sashiko lives in the united states, but she was born in japan.

is your uncle fred coming to your house for thanksgiving?

we swam in the pacific ocean on our vacation last year.

i can't wait for school to start in september.

have you read the new harry potter book?

chris was born in dallas.

we are going to disneyland on friday.

Sort the proper nouns from the sentences above and write them on the cards.

Brain Box

Always use a capital letter at the beginning of every sentence. Always **capitalize** proper nouns that name a specific person, place, date, holiday, or event.

Reading

A Native American Myth

Read the **story.**

Reading

Cause and effect

Coyote and the River

It was a beautiful day, and the sun was shining brightly. It was so lovely outdoors that Coyote decided to take a walk. Before long, though, Coyote began to feel hot. "I wish there was a cloud in the sky," said Coyote.

In time, a cloud appeared in the sky and made some shade for Coyote. "Just one cloud doesn't help me feel cooler," he said. "I wish there were more shade."

Soon there were more clouds, and the sky began to darken and look stormy. But Coyote was still hot. He wished for a way to become even cooler.

Suddenly, a small sprinkle of rain came down from the clouds. "I want much more rain," Coyote demanded. Before long, buckets of rain began to fall.

"That's better, but I wish I had a way to cool off my feet," Coyote said. In no time at all, a creek sprang up right beside him. Coyote waded in and cooled off his feet. "I wish the creek were deeper," he said.

All at once, the creek turned into a large, swirling river. Coyote was swept up by the water and nearly drowned. Frightened and sputtering, he was finally tossed onto a bank of this mighty river. Coyote was no longer hot, but he was very wet.

And that is how the Columbia River was created.

Fill in each missing **cause** and **effect.**

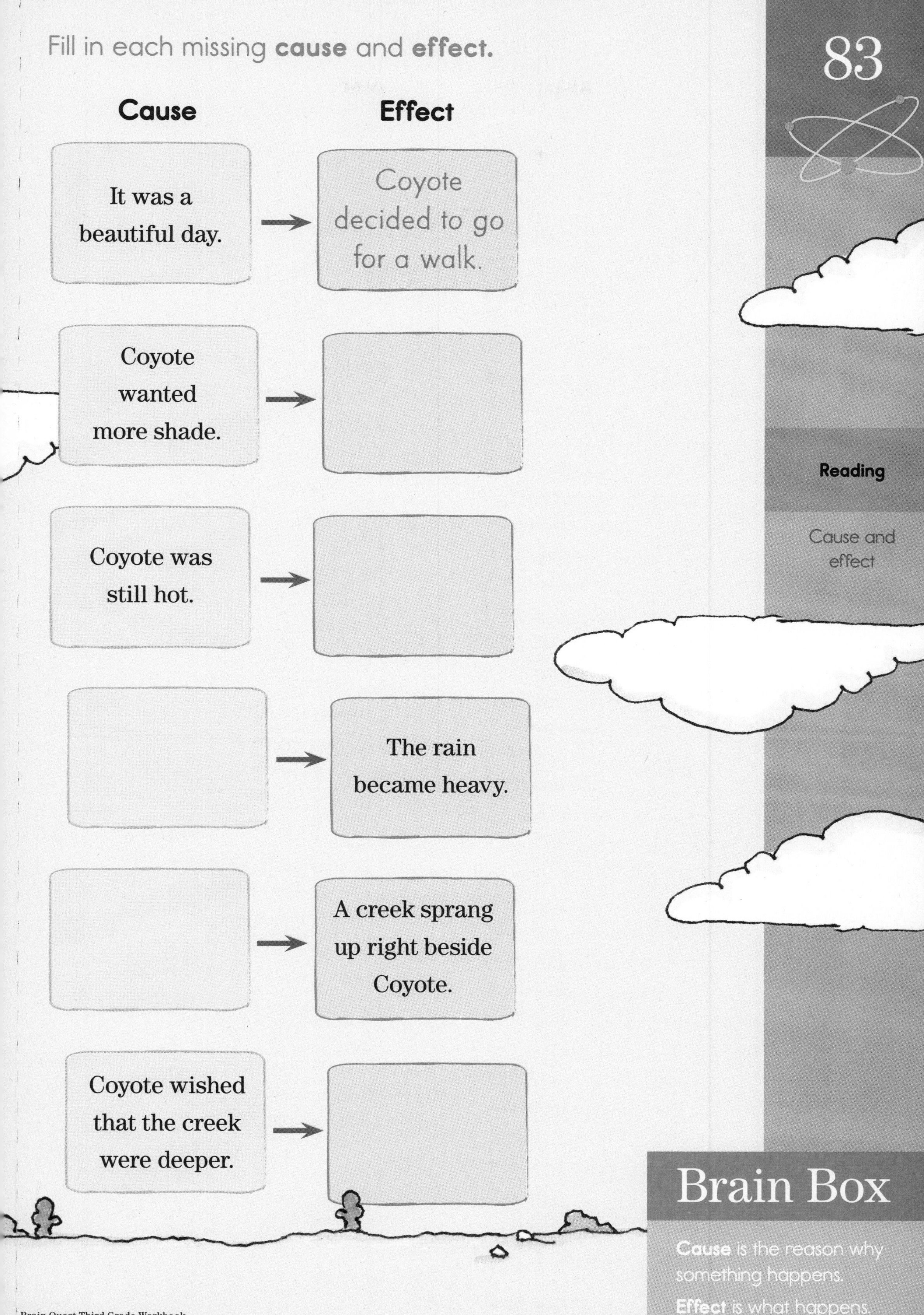

Cause		Effect
It was a beautiful day.	→	Coyote decided to go for a walk.
Coyote wanted more shade.	→	
Coyote was still hot.	→	
	→	The rain became heavy.
	→	A creek sprang up right beside Coyote.
Coyote wished that the creek were deeper.	→	

Reading

Cause and effect

Brain Box

Cause is the reason why something happens.

Effect is what happens.

A History

Read the **biography.**

Reading

Remembering facts and details

The Pharoah Queen

Long, long ago, a baby girl was born to Queen Ahmose, the wife of Pharaoh Tuthmosis I. The Pharaoh was the supreme ruler of ancient Egypt, which was a powerful and wealthy empire. Queen Ahmose named her daughter Hatshepsut, a name that meant "the foremost of noble ladies."

Young Hatshepsut lived in a palace and had many servants to care for her. During the day she played with her dolls in the nursery and sometimes visited her father's private zoo. As she grew older, Hatshepsut attended dinner parties with her parents where the guests were entertained by dancers, musicians, and acrobats. She also took part in religious festivals and watched special processions from the palace balconies.

When Hatshepsut's father died, her life changed dramatically. She was married to her half-brother Tuthmosis II, who had become the new pharaoh of Egypt. In time, Hatshepsut, now the Queen of Egypt, gave birth to a daughter, whom she named Neferure.

When Tuthmosis II died, Queen Hatshepsut became Egypt's pharaoh. Because it was unusual for a woman to become king, she was usually shown in wall paintings and carvings wearing a false beard and men's clothing.

During Hatshepsut's reign of about twenty-two years, she directed the building of many monuments and organized an ambitious expedition to a land far down the east coast of Africa. When she died, her mummified body was laid to rest in the Valley of the Kings instead of in the tomb that had originally been prepared for her when she was only a queen.

Answer the questions.

Which two adjectives are used in the first paragraph to describe Egypt at the time of Hatshepsut's birth?

As you read, Hatshepsut's name meant "the foremost of noble ladies." **Foremost** means **first.** Do you think this was a good name for Hatshepsut? Why?

When she was a young girl, what did Hatshepsut do that many young girls do today?

Who did Hatshepsut marry?

What was the name of Hatshepsut's daughter?

When Hatshepsut became pharaoh, how was she usually shown in paintings and carvings?

What was one of Hatshepsut's accomplishments when she was pharaoh?

Why do you think Hatshepsut wasn't buried in the tomb that had been prepared for her?

A Rhyming Poem

Read the **poem.**

Reading

Poetry

How the Little Kite Learned to Fly

Anonymous

"I never can do it," the little kite said,
As he looked at the others high over his head;
"I know I should fall if I tried to fly."
"Try," said the big kite; "only try!
Or I fear you will never learn at all."
But the little kite said, "I'm afraid I'll fall."

The big kite nodded: "Ah well, good-bye;
I'm off"; and he rose toward the tranquil sky.
Then the little kite's paper stirred at the sight,
And trembling he shook himself free for flight.
First whirling and frightened, then braver grown,
Up, up, he rose through the air alone,
Till the big kite looking down could see
The little one rising steadily.

Then how the little kite thrilled with pride,
As he sailed with the big kite side by side.
While far below, he could see the ground,
And the boys like small spots moving round.
They rested high in the quiet air,
And only the birds and the clouds were there.
"Oh, how happy I am!" the little kite cried;
"And all because I was brave, and tried."

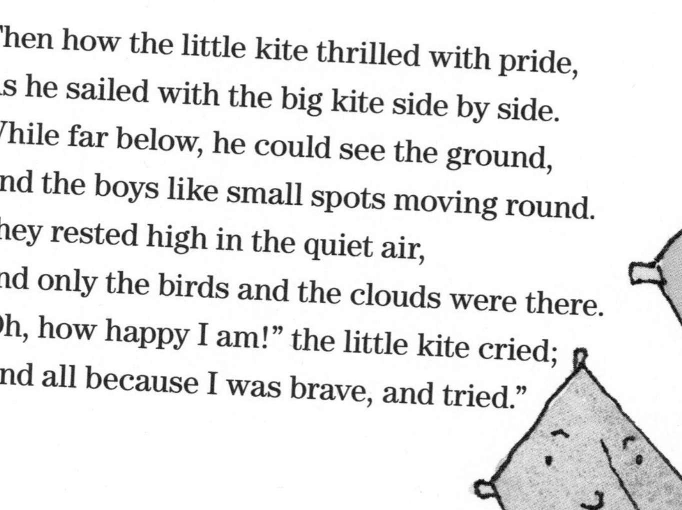

What is the first pair of rhyming words in this poem?

____

What adjective best describes how the little kite feels in the first stanza of this poem? Why?

____

Why are the boys described as “small spots” in the last stanza of this poem?

____

____

What two things are in the air with the big and little kite?

____

What adjective best describes how the little kite feels in the third stanza of this poem? Why?

____

____

What lesson was the big kite trying to teach the little kite?

____

____

An African Folktale

Read the **story.**

Reading

Reading comprehension

The Honeybird

Leza was a kind god who wanted the people he had created to have a happy life. That's why he decided to give them three special gourds. "Fly these gourds down to First People," he instructed the honeybird. "Tell them that the red gourd must not be opened. I will descend my spiderweb ladder and meet them on earth to explain its purpose."

The honeybird was eager to know what was inside the gourds. When it reached a clearing near First People's hut, the bird said, "What harm can there be in taking just a tiny peek?" It pecked a hole in the side of the green gourd. Out poured all kinds of seeds. Next, it pecked a hole in the yellow gourd. Out spilled metals, clay, and cloth. Without thinking, it then pecked a hole in the red gourd. Out burst biting insects, poisonous snakes, and rats with sharp teeth.

Just then Leza appeared. He was very angry. "Look what you've done!" he shouted at the honeybird. Leza tried to capture the creatures, but they had hurried away and hidden themselves in dark places.

With great patience, Leza showed First Woman how to plant and care for the seeds in the green gourd. He taught First Man how to make tools from the metals and pots from the clay. He explained how to live with the creatures that had escaped from the red gourd. Then he wished them well and returned to his home in the sky.

First People were alarmed by thoughts of the creatures that they were sure were nearby. "Why should we not live in the sky with Leza?" they asked each other. They began to climb up the spiderweb ladder, but they were too heavy and tumbled back down to earth in a tangle of spider silk.

The honeybird tried to make up for what it had done. Whenever it saw First Man and First Woman, it fluttered its tail feathers and led them with loud chirps to hidden combs of sweet golden honey. Even today, this bird can be heard in the trees where it lives. It calls, "This way! This way!" in hopes that one day it may be forgiven for the trouble it caused.

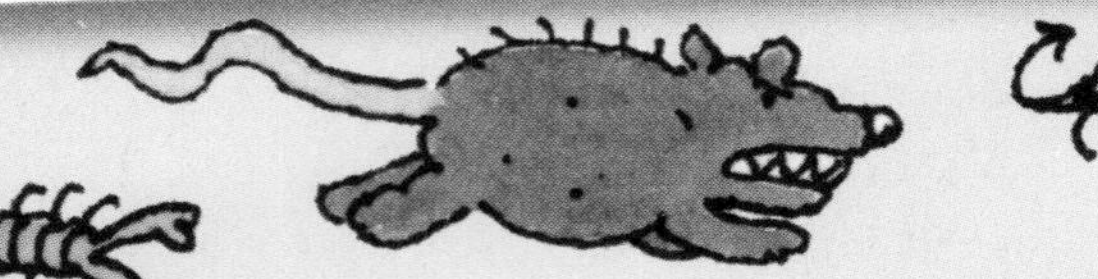

Answer the questions.

What word best describes the god named Leza? ______

a. grumpy b. curious c. kind d. frightened

What warning was the honeybird supposed to give to First People? ______

a. not to open any of the gourds

b. not to climb up the spiderweb ladder

c. not to eat honey

d. not to open the red gourd

The word "descend" is underlined in paragraph one. "Descend" means to ______

a. go up b. hang on to c. go down d. destroy

Which three things did Leza try to teach First Woman and First Man after the contents of the red gourd spilled?

____

____

Have you ever felt like the honeybird feels in this story? What made you feel this way?

____

____

What do you think is the moral of this story?

____

____

A Biography

Read the **biography.**

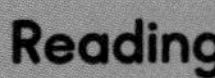

Reading

Remembering facts and interpreting language

Thomas Alva Edison

Young Thomas Edison was naturally curious. He was always asking questions and liked to experiment. Once, when he was very small, he even sat on some goose eggs to see if they would hatch.

As a young boy, Thomas had trouble sitting still in class, so his mother took him out of school and taught Thomas herself at home. He was a fast learner who loved looking for answers in books.

When Thomas was twelve, he started his first job. He sold newspapers, food, and candy on the train that traveled between Port Huron and Detroit. By the time he was fifteen, he was also selling his own weekly paper that he printed himself. It was full of news about the people who traveled or worked on the train.

In 1868, when he was twenty-one, Edison invented an automatic vote counter for which he received his first patent. (A patent, issued by the United States government, gives an inventor the sole right to make and sell his or her idea.) Unfortunately, the vote counter turned out to be a failure because no one wanted it. Edison vowed that, from that point on, he would invent only things that people wanted. When he was about thirty, Edison established a laboratory in Menlo Park, a small town in New Jersey. It was here that he invented the tinfoil phonograph and the electric lightbulb.

Edison was granted over a thousand U.S. patents during his life. As he became increasingly famous, he was called "The Wizard of Menlo Park." Edison felt, though, that his success was the result of hard work, not wizardry. "Genius," he once said, "is one percent inspiration and ninety-nine percent perspiration."

Answer the questions.

Why do you think young Thomas Edison sat on the goose eggs?

____

What job did Thomas have when he was twelve?

____

What is a patent? ______________________________

____

Why was Edison's automatic vote counter a failure?

____

____

What adjective do you think best describes Edison? Why?

____

Edison said, "Genius is one percent inspiration and ninety-nine percent perspiration." What did he mean when he said this?

____

____

Do you agree with Edison's quote about genius? Why or why not?

____

____

____

Reading

Remembering facts and interpreting language

Get Out the Griddle!

Read the **recipe.**

Reading

Following directions

Patty's Pancakes

Ingredients:

- 4 tablespoons of butter
- 1 cup of flour
- 3 tablespoons of sugar
- a pinch of salt
- 1 tablespoon of baking powder
- 1 cup of milk
- 2 eggs
- $\frac{1}{2}$ teaspoon of vanilla

1. Preheat the griddle to high.
2. Melt 4 tablespoons of butter over low heat on the stove.
3. While the butter is melting, mix the dry ingredients (flour, sugar, salt, and baking powder) together in a large mixing bowl.
4. Mix the wet ingredients (milk, eggs, melted butter, and vanilla) in a second bowl.
5. Slowly pour the wet ingredients into the bowl of dry ingredients and stir about 1 minute.
6. Use a small ladle to pour spoonfuls of batter onto the griddle, making each pancake about 3 inches in diameter.
7. When the top of the pancake starts to bubble, flip the pancake over and cook the other side.
8. The pancakes are done when both sides are brown. Serve them warm with syrup.

Answer the questions about the recipe.

How many tablespoons of butter do you need to melt? __________

What do you need more of: vanilla or baking powder?

____

Should you start melting the butter before or after you mix the dry ingredients? ______________________________

Reading

Following directions

Does the recipe say how you know when a pancake is done cooking? ______________________________

Which dry ingredients should be mixed in one bowl?

____

Which wet ingredients should be mixed in the other bowl?

____

How long should you stir when you blend the wet and dry ingredients together? ______________________________

How should the pancakes be served? ______________________________

____

What is your favorite meal? List the ingredients you need to make it. ______________________________

____

____

____

A Greek Myth

Read the myth.

Reading

Remembering details

Baucis and Philemon

A long time ago in a town in Greece, there lived a couple who loved each other dearly. Their names were Baucis and Philemon, and they were quite poor. One day, an old beggar appeared at their doorway. He had been turned away by all their neighbors, but when the couple saw him they were filled with pity. “Come inside,” they insisted. “We haven’t much, but what we have is yours.” All they had to eat was a loaf of bread, a few eggs, and a cabbage, but they set a plate before the old man and told him to eat until he was full. They filled his cup with the last bit of pomegranate juice they had. Then, after the old man had finished eating, they wrapped the warmest robe they owned around the old man’s shoulders. “We wish there were more to give you,” they said, “but, as you can see, we are poor folk. Our cupboards are empty.”

“Nay, look again,” said the beggar, smiling. Baucis and Philemon, not wishing to offend the old man, opened their cupboards. You can imagine their shock when they saw their cupboards full of all sorts of delicious foods to eat and fresh juices to drink! Before they could say anything, they realized they were no longer dressed in tattered clothes, but were wrapped in robes of fine linen. And the house that had only moments before been a hovel was now a great palace all around them. Most surprising of all, though, was the old beggar, for it was Zeus himself, king of all the gods, who stood before them now. “Your eyes do not deceive you,” said Zeus. “And for all your kindnesses you shall be rewarded. Ask whatever you want and you shall have your wish.”

“We’ve been poor our whole lives but we’ve been lucky,” they said, “for we have known love. Please grant that we may never have to live one without the other.”

The couple lived out the rest of their lives in luxury, and never knew hunger again. One day when they had become quite old, they were not at all surprised when suddenly they began to sprout leaves. They embraced each other as their arms became branches, and bark grew around them. “Thank you, Zeus,” they said as they turned into trees, for he had granted their wish.

Hundreds of years afterward people still marveled at the trees, for though one was a linden and the other was an oak, they both grew from a single trunk.

Answer the questions.

What kind of people were Baucis and Philemon? Use at least three adjectives to describe them.

What did Baucis and Philemon offer the old beggar to eat?

Why were Baucis and Philemon shocked?

Why did the couple consider themselves lucky?

What wish did Zeus grant them?

What was so special about the trees?

An Aesop Fable

Read the **fable.**

Reading

Sequence

A Farmer, His Son, and Their Donkey

One fine day, a farmer and his son were taking their donkey to market. They hoped to sell him for a good price. Before long, they met some women who were collecting water from a well.

"How very silly," said the women. "Those two are trudging along on foot when the donkey could be carrying one of them on its back."

Hearing this, the farmer lifted his boy onto the donkey's back and walked happily along by his son's side.

Presently an old man saw them and cried, "You should be ashamed of yourself, young man. Have you no respect for age? Your father should be riding, and you should be walking!" Red-faced with embarrassment, the son quickly got down and helped his father get up on the donkey.

They had gone only a little further when they came upon a group of young girls. "Have you no sense at all?" they laughed. "Both of you would easily fit on the donkey's back. Why should either one of you have to walk along the dusty road?" Feeling sure they were right, the farmer helped his son get behind him on the donkey's back.

As they neared the market they met a townsman. "How cruel you are!" he shouted. "That little poor animal has too heavy a load. You two are better able to carry him than he is to carry the two of you." Eager to do the right thing, the two got off the donkey. They tied the donkey's legs together, slung him onto a pole, and strained to carry him on their shoulders as they crossed the bridge near the entrance to the market.

Seeing this strange sight, the townspeople laughed and laughed. In fact, they laughed so loudly that they scared the donkey. The frightened animal kicked off the ropes that bound its legs, fell off the pole, and ran away.

"That will teach you," said an old woman who had followed them. "He who tries to please everyone, pleases no one."

Answer the questions.

What is the moral of the story? Describe it in your own words.

____

____

____

Place the pictures in the correct order by numbering them **1** through **5.**
Write a short descriptive caption below each picture.

____

____

____

____

____

____

____

____

____

____

Reading

Sequence

A Medieval Tale

Read the **story.**

The Sword in the Stone

fter the death of good king Uther, a miraculous stone appeared outside his castle. In the stone was a sword with the following words engraved upon its hilt:

I am Excalibur, the sword in the stone
Who pulls me free shall have the throne.

Many princes tried to pull the sword from the stone, and the strongest knights came from all over Britain to try. But no one could do it, and the Britons went without a king for a long time.

One day, all the best knights of the kingdom were assembled at the castle for a tournament. Sir Kay, a valiant and strong knight, broke his sword during a parry and sent his young squire, a boy named Arthur, to his house to retrieve another sword. Arthur, unable to find the sword he'd been sent to find, but afraid to return without a new sword, saw the hilt of Excalibur gleaming in the sunlight. Without stopping to read the words on the hilt, Arthur drew out the sword with great ease and brought it to Sir Kay.

All the knights at the tournament were astonished to see the boy with the sword Excalibur. "Tell us who gave you the sword so that we may proclaim a new king of Britain!" they demanded. When Arthur told them that he had pulled out the great sword himself, they laughed. Sir Kay, seeing the chance to become king, thrust the Excalibur back into the stone and went to retrieve it again, thinking that it would come free easily. But just as it had before, the sword stayed put. All the knights took a turn trying to loosen the sword. When each one of them failed, they brought little Arthur back to see what he could do. Then, before all their eyes, Arthur once again pulled the Excalibur from the stone.

"All hail King Arthur!" the knights proclaimed, and they all pledged their loyalty to the new King of Britain.

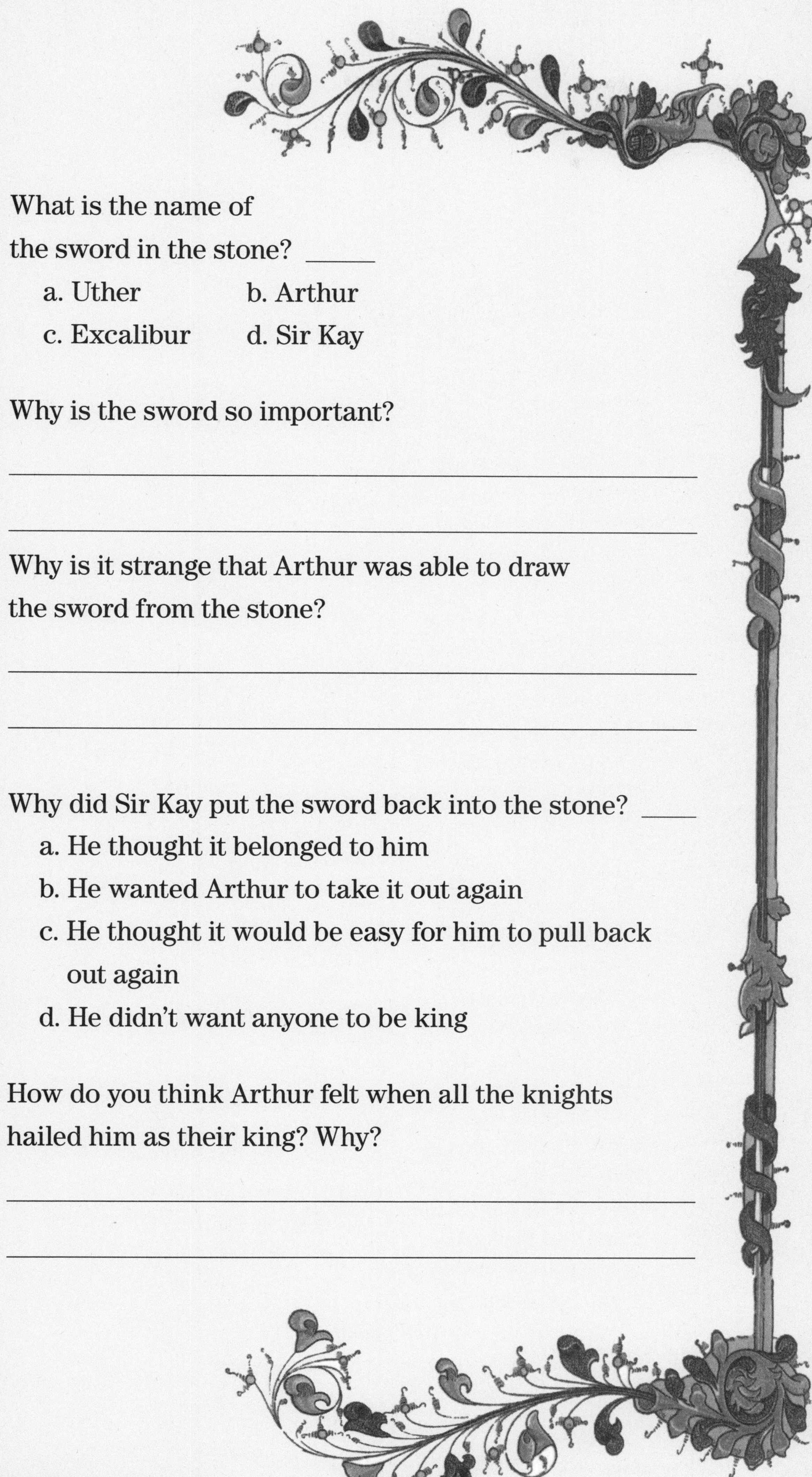

What is the name of the sword in the stone? _____

a. Uther   b. Arthur

c. Excalibur   d. Sir Kay

Why is the sword so important?

____

____

Why is it strange that Arthur was able to draw the sword from the stone?

____

____

Why did Sir Kay put the sword back into the stone? ____

a. He thought it belonged to him

b. He wanted Arthur to take it out again

c. He thought it would be easy for him to pull back out again

d. He didn't want anyone to be king

How do you think Arthur felt when all the knights hailed him as their king? Why?

____

____

A Baseball Legend

Read the **biography.**

Reading

Sequencing

Jackie Robinson

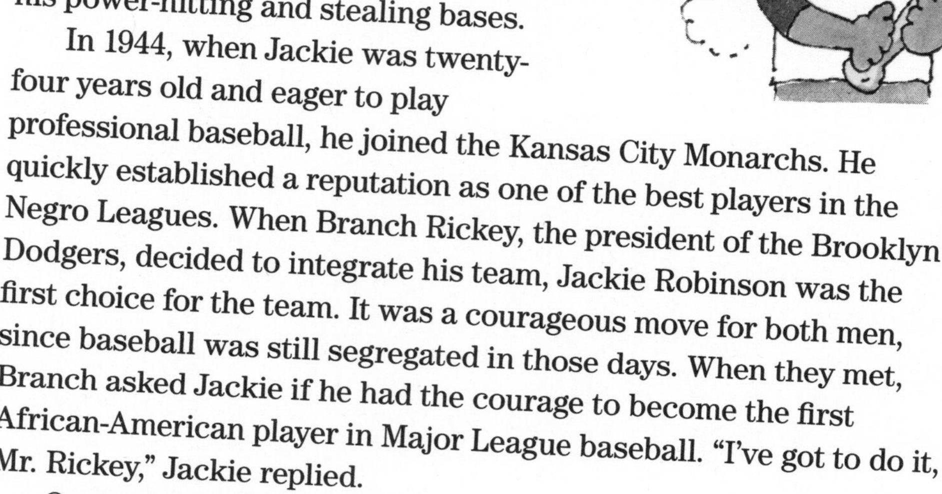

Young Jackie Robinson grew into a skilled athlete in every school sport he played. In high school, he earned letters in basketball, football, track, and baseball. In college, he established records in all those sports, as well. It was in baseball, though, that he really excelled. He was known for his power-hitting and stealing bases.

In 1944, when Jackie was twenty-four years old and eager to play professional baseball, he joined the Kansas City Monarchs. He quickly established a reputation as one of the best players in the Negro Leagues. When Branch Rickey, the president of the Brooklyn Dodgers, decided to integrate his team, Jackie Robinson was the first choice for the team. It was a courageous move for both men, since baseball was still segregated in those days. When they met, Branch asked Jackie if he had the courage to become the first African-American player in Major League baseball. "I've got to do it, Mr. Rickey," Jackie replied.

On April 9, 1947, Jackie officially joined the Brooklyn Dodgers. At first, he often heard boos and jeers. Soon, however, he began to gain the respect of the fans. In his first year, he led his league with twenty-nine stolen bases.

Jackie became a source of pride for African-Americans. He showed that he could prove himself on the field and that he had the courage to stand up for his rights. In 1949, he became the Most Valuable Player in the National League.

In 1955, when Jackie was thirty-six, the Dodgers won the World Series and Jackie got his first championship ring. By the time he retired in 1957, Jackie finished with a career .311 batting average, 1,518 hits, 947 runs scored, 137 home runs, and 197 stolen bases. In 1962, Jackie was voted into the National Baseball Hall of Fame. He was the first African-American to achieve that honor and has been a source of inspiration for players—and fans—ever since.

DODGERS

Number these sentences to show the order in which they happened.

- [ ] Jackie officially joined the Brooklyn Dodgers.
- [ ] Jackie was voted into the National Baseball Hall of Fame.
- [1] Jackie joined the Kansas City Monarchs.
- [ ] Jackie helped the Brooklyn Dodgers win the World Series.
- [ ] Jackie was named the Most Valuable Player in the National League.
- [ ] Jackie retired from baseball.

A Fairy Tale

Read the **story.**

Reading

Remembering facts and forming opinions

The Emperor's New Clothes

Many years ago, there lived an emperor who was very vain. He loved to show off his beautiful clothes, and he spent long hours proudly looking at himself in the mirror.

One day, two scoundrels arrived in the kingdom. They came to see the emperor and told him that they could make him a suit of the finest cloth ever imagined. "In fact," they told him, "this cloth will be so delicate that it will appear invisible to anyone who is not smart enough to appreciate it."

The emperor quickly agreed to have this suit made and gave them a large bag filled with gold. The men asked for a loom, the finest silk, and lots of gold thread. They then pretended to begin their work.

Every day, the emperor sent one of his ministers to check on the men's progress. Although they saw that nothing was being made, they were afraid to report this to the emperor. After all, they did not want him to think that they were not smart enough to see and appreciate the cloth. Instead, they told the emperor that his new suit would be magnificent.

At last, the two scoundrels announced that the suit was finished. "Tomorrow will be a holiday, and I will parade through the streets in my new suit," announced the emperor excitedly.

The next morning, the two men pretended to help the emperor put on his new suit. The ministers stood nearby, admiring the work. No one, including the emperor, was willing to admit that what they really saw was the emperor dressed only in his underwear.

The parade began, and crowds of people pushed and shoved to get a good look at the emperor and his new clothes. Because they, too, did not wish to seem less than smart, the people cheered and praised the beauty of his new suit. But then a young boy's voice was heard above the noise of the crowd. "Look," he shouted, "the emperor is wearing no clothes!"

Suddenly, everyone realized that the boy was right. As the crowd laughed and even the ministers chuckled, the foolish emperor rushed back to his palace as fast as he could go. The two scoundrels, of course, were nowhere to be found.

Reading

Remembering facts and forming opinions

Answer the questions.

In the first paragraph it says that the emperor was very vain. Circle the best definitive of **vain**.

a. quiet and shy

b. bold and adventurous

c. conceited and takes too much pride in his or her looks

d. smart and clever

What did the two men tell the emperor that they could do?

____

____

Why didn't the ministers tell the emperor they saw nothing being made?______________________________________

____

The two men are called scoundrels in this story. Circle the best definition of **scoundrel.**

a. someone who likes to do nice things for others

b. a skilled sewer of clothes

c. a tricky person who's up to no good

d. a person who travels from town to town looking for work

What lesson do you think the emperor learned from this experience?

____

____

Why do you think the scoundrels played this trick on the emperor? ______________________________

____

A Science Paper

Read the **essay.**

Reading

Remembering facts and details

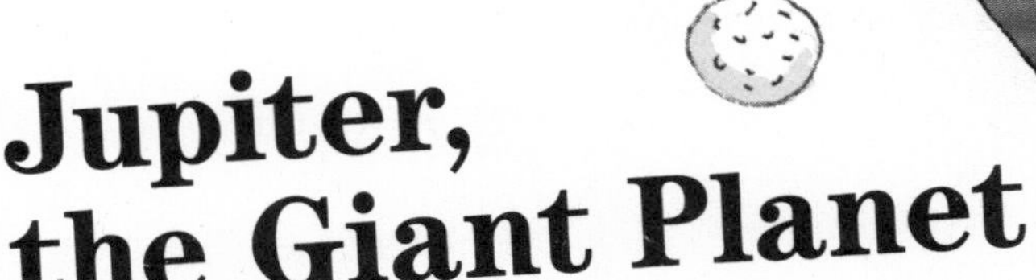

Jupiter, the Giant Planet

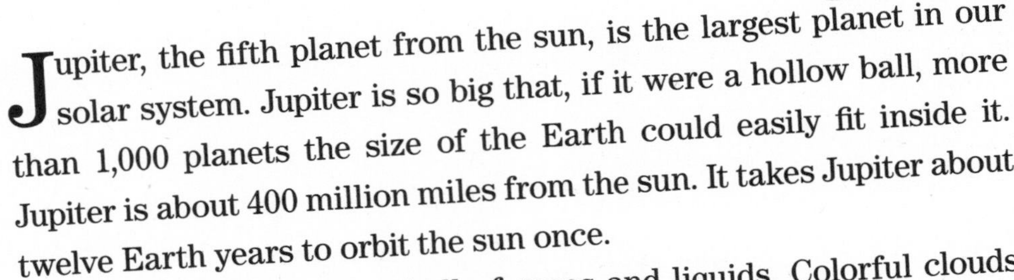

Jupiter, the fifth planet from the sun, is the largest planet in our solar system. Jupiter is so big that, if it were a hollow ball, more than 1,000 planets the size of the Earth could easily fit inside it. Jupiter is about 400 million miles from the sun. It takes Jupiter about twelve Earth years to orbit the sun once.

This giant planet is a ball of gases and liquids. Colorful clouds make up its outer atmosphere. These clouds are pushed by strong winds that can blow as hard as 400 miles an hour. That's much more forceful than the worst hurricanes on Earth!

Jupiter has sixty-four moons, though scientists are still evaluating recent discoveries and that number may change. The four largest moons are named Io, Europa, Ganymede, and Callisto. Io has active volcanoes. In fact, it has even more volcanic activity than the Earth. Europa is covered with ice. Many scientists believe that this layer of frozen water is more than 60 miles thick in some places. Callisto has more craters than any other moon in our solar system. Ganymede is Jupiter's largest moon. It is even bigger than the planet Mercury!

Much that we know about Jupiter has come from unmanned space probes. In 1973, *Pioneer 10* flew within 81,000 miles of Jupiter's cloud tops. It sent more than five hundred photographs back to Earth. *Voyager 1* flew by Jupiter in 1979, and the spacecraft *Galileo* began to orbit Jupiter in late 1995, sending back beautiful and detailed images of the planet until it finished its orbit in 2003.

Scientists believe that studying Jupiter and its moons may help us learn more about the early history of the Earth. The better we understand other planets in our universe, the better we will understand and appreciate our own planet.

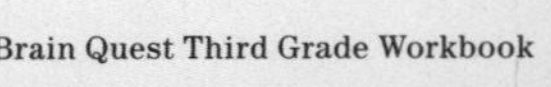

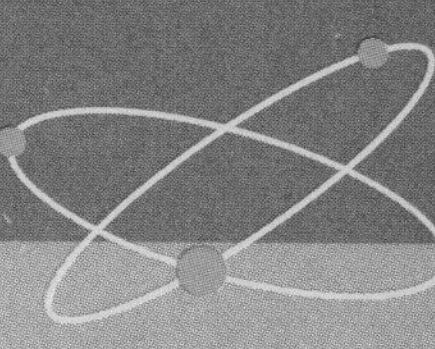

List five facts about Jupiter that you learned from the passage.

1. ______________________________

2. ______________________________

3. ______________________________

4. ______________________________

5. ______________________________

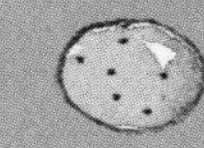

Why are scientists interested in studying Jupiter?

____

____

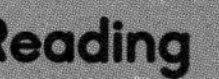

What does Callisto have more of than any other moon in our solar system?

____

____

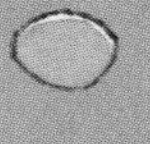

Why do you think the unmanned space probes have names like *Pioneer* and *Voyager*?

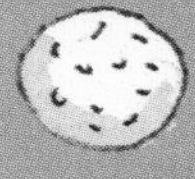

____

____

In what year did the first unmanned space probe get close to the surface of Jupiter? ______________

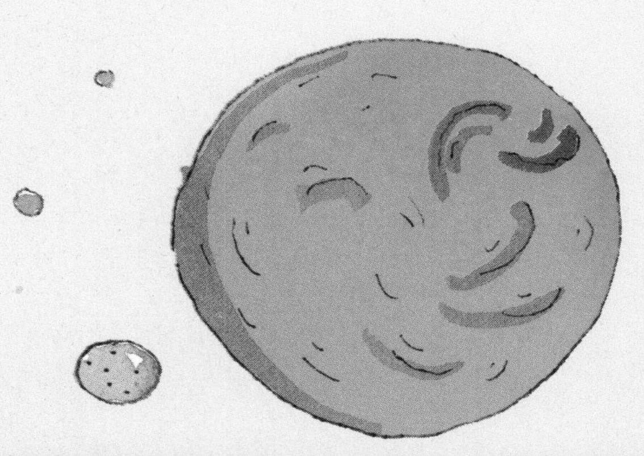

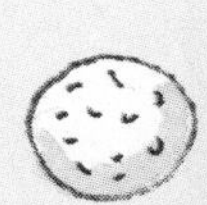

An Animal Essay

Read the **essay.**

Reading

Remembering facts and details

Emperor Penguins

The largest of all penguins, emperor penguins are the only animals that are able to survive the extreme cold of the Antarctic winter. They spend their summer feeding at sea. But shortly before the endless darkness of winter begins, they come ashore on the ice and travel many miles south to their breeding area. They move along by waddling on their feet or, at times, by lying on their bellies and pushing themselves forward with their flippers. Once they have reached their breeding ground, they gather together in a large crowd. They begin to court and eventually pair up and mate.

The female produces one large egg, which she places on top of her feet so that it won't freeze. Almost at once, her mate comes up, takes the egg from her, and moves it onto his own feet. There the egg is kept warm by a fold of feathered skin that hangs down from his stomach. Tired and in need of nourishment, the female now heads back to the sea.

For the next two months, the male penguins huddle closely together with the eggs on their feet. They try to keep warm in spite of fierce blizzards and howling winds. There is nothing to eat, and for nearly a month there is total darkness.

At last, sixty days after they were laid, the eggs hatch. The males are close to starvation, but the females almost immediately return and begin feeding the chicks with half-digested fish. Happily, the males are now free to return to the sea and find food for themselves.

After several weeks, the males return to their mates. For the remaining weeks of the winter, the parents take turns fishing and bringing back food for their chicks. At last, the long winter ends and the ice begins to break up. In a long procession of parents and young, all of the penguins trail down to the sea where they'll spend the short summer swimming and feeding.

What can emperor penguins do that no other animal can do?

____

Describe one of the ways the penguins move when they travel to their breeding ground.

____

____

How many eggs does each female emperor penguin lay?________

How does the male penguin keep the egg warm during the long, freezing winter? ______________________

____

How long does it take for an egg to hatch? ______________

Why are the males able to leave their chicks shortly after they have hatched?

____

What adjective would you use to describe the male penguin's time while the egg is on his feet? ______________

Why did you pick this adjective?______________________

____

Reading

Remembering facts and details

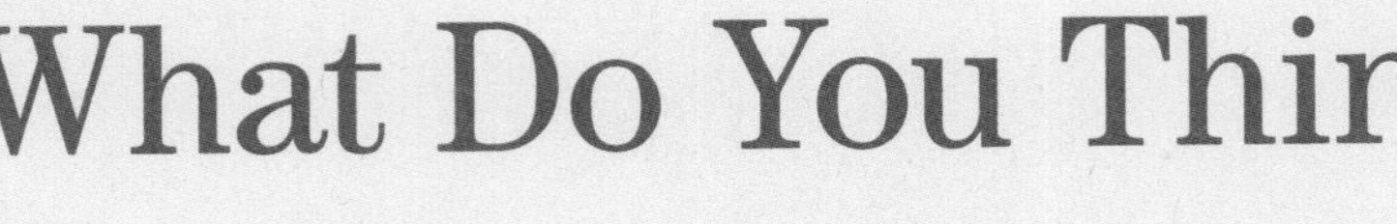

What Do You Think?

Read each paragraph carefully. Then circle the best **conclusion** based on what you have read.

Reading

Drawing conclusions

Mrs. Fussfrot always wears green dresses. She thinks they look wonderful with her green eyes. Yesterday, she went to Belle's Boutique to look for a new dress. They had every color of dress but green.

a. Mrs. Fussfrot bought two red dresses.

b. Mrs. Fussfrot didn't buy a dress yesterday at Belle's Boutique.

c. Mrs. Fussfrot will never go to Belle's Boutique again.

Dr. Drill is a good dentist, but his waiting room is always crowded with patients reading magazines. That's because Dr. Drill is always behind in his schedule. Some patients complain to his receptionist when they become impatient.

a. Dr. Drill has very good magazines.

b. Dr. Drill has a tiny waiting room.

c. If you decide to go to Dr. Drill, you should be prepared to wait.

The movie theater, Popcorn Cinema, has 150 seats. Tonight, the movie *Alien Attack* will start at 8:00 p.m. A crowd of 180 people is standing in line for tickets.

a. It should be a good movie.

b. Everyone will probably buy popcorn.

c. Not all the people in line will get a ticket for the 8:00 show.

Brain Box

A **conclusion** is a decision you make after thinking about all the facts you have read.

Writing

Tell Me More!

Think of **adjectives** and **adverbs** that make each sentence more interesting. Then write a new interesting sentence using these words.

The boy ran.

When? Yesterday

How? Very fast

Where? Around the track

Yesterday the boy ran very fast around the track.

Writing

Adding details

The girl played.

When?

What?

Where?

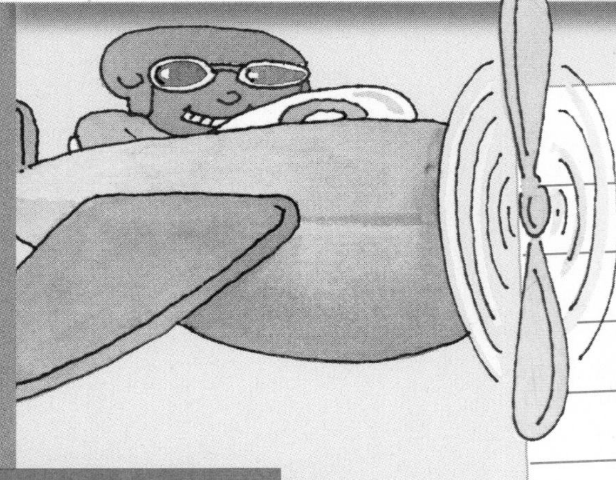

He traveled.

Who?

How?

Why?

When?

Where?

Brain Box

Interesting sentences give details about **when, what, how, why,** and **where.**
For example:
The dog **ran.** The dog **happily ran to the park with his owner.**

Rewrite each sentence by replacing the highlighted verb with a stronger and more specific **verb.**

The three friends played all day long.

The cook washed his pots and pans.

The car drove down the road.

Now write your own sentences using the **strong verbs** on the cards.

glisten

shriek

whirl

rejoice

Brain Box

You can make writing more interesting by using strong verbs that show the action. For example:
The horse **ran.** The horse **galloped.**

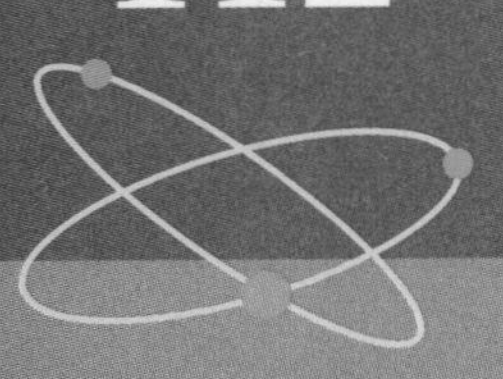

Read All About It!

You've been asked to write an article for the school paper. Choose an interesting, exciting, or funny event. Then answer the questions below.

Who was involved in the event?

What was the event and **what** happened during it?

When did the event take place?

Where did the event take place?

Why was the event interesting, exciting, or funny?

Writing

Who, what, when, where, and why

Who?
What?
When?
Where?
Why?

Brain Box

When you write about an event, it is important to answer these questions first:

Who? What? When? Where? Why?

Now use the information from the questions you answered to write your article.

Title

By

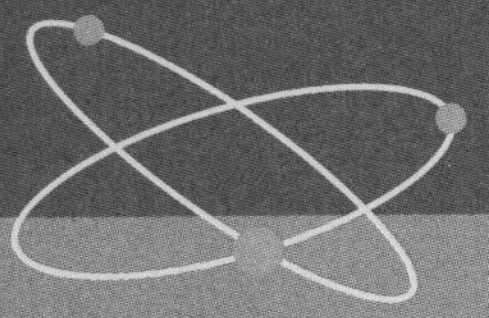

Say It with Details

Make the sentences more interesting by thinking of **adjectives** that tell about the highlighted nouns. Then rewrite each sentence using your new adjectives. Remember to change **a** to **an** if your adjective starts with a vowel.

A dragon flew over the forest.

An enormous dragon flew over the enchanted forest.

The teacher praised the girl.

____

Writing

Descriptive writing

A car drove down the street.

____

One day the girls went to a movie.

____

The man saw a bear.

____

The boy chased a pig.

____

The clown wore a wig.

____

The woman baked a cake.

____

Brain Box

Adding well-chosen, descriptive **adjectives** to sentences adds detail and interest to writing.

The king lived in a castle.

____

____

Write a sentence using the word on each card.
Use at least two adjectives per sentence.

magician The funny magician pulled a cute rabbit out of a hat.

children ______________________________

monster ______________________________

family ______________________________

party ______________________________

stranger ______________________________

lake ______________________________

Writing

Descriptive writing

116 Getting Together

Read each set of sentences. Circle the words that are used more than once. Then **combine** each set of sentences into one sentence, eliminating as many unnecessary words as possible.

When I go to the pool, I will swim. I will also dive off the diving board at the pool.

When I go to the pool, I will swim and dive off the diving board.

Everyone was having fun. Everyone was excited.

The boys put on their uniforms. The boys ran out onto the baseball field.

The fans were really excited. The fans at the soccer game cheered loudly for their team.

Writing

Combining sentences

Brain Box

Combining sentences can make your writing more interesting. Sometimes, one long smooth sentence is better than two or more short sentences that repeat similar information. Often, two sentences with the same subject can be combined into one sentence.

For example:

After school, Levi was tired. Levi was hungry. → After school, Levi was tired and hungry.

Combine these sentences to create an interesting paragraph.

We walked on the beach. We found lots of pretty shells. We put the shells in our buckets. Afterwards we went in the ocean. The ocean was cold. The sun was hot. The sun warmed us up. We went home. We put our seashells in a glass jar.

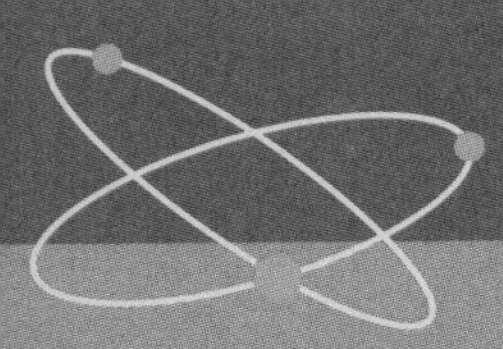

What's It All About?

Read the paragraph. Then color the card with the best **topic sentence** for the paragraph.

In the morning, we play a really fun family football game. I often score the winning touchdown. Then everyone goes inside and my older cousins build a fire in the fireplace to keep us warm in the cold November weather. I feel so happy as we sit around the house telling jokes and smelling all the yummy aromas from the kitchen. We all know the food will be delicious. My father always cooks a turkey with gravy and stuffing. My aunt makes sweet potatoes, and my grandmother brings three different kinds of pies. Her pumpkin pie is the best. While I love the meal, the best part of Thanksgiving is spending the day with my family. I look forward to the day all year.

There's no school on Thanksgiving.

Thanksgiving is in November.

Thanksgiving is my favorite holiday.

Writing

Writing topic sentences

Brain Box

A **topic sentence** tells a reader what a paragraph is about. It is usually the first sentence in a paragraph.

Read the paragraph. Then color the card with the best **topic sentence** for the paragraph.

They are shaped like seals or small whales and have large upper lips that look like mini elephant trunks. They swim at an average of three to five miles per hour. Sometimes manatees stand up straight in the water with bits of water plants on top of their heads. This makes it look like they have green hair. Most manatees are friendly and will play nearby while people swim. One thing is for sure, manatees are truly unique animals.

Manatees are endangered animals.

Manatees have many interesting characteristics and habits.

Manatees live in Florida.

Writing

Writing topic sentences

Now write your own topic sentence for this paragraph.

First, my uncle and I hung buckets on the sides of sugar maple trees. In a few days, after the buckets had filled with sap, we boiled the sap in large kettles until it turned into thick syrup. Then we cleaned the syrup and poured it into bottles. My uncle sold most of the maple syrup, but we kept some for ourselves. I felt very lucky to have helped make such a delicious part of breakfast!

120

Strong Foundations

Read the paragraph. Underline the **topic sentence** in red. Underline the **detail sentences** in blue. Underline the **concluding sentence** in green.

Katie had a great time at tennis practice this morning. First she practiced her forehand shot with her coach. Then she worked on her backhand with the ball machine. Once she was warmed up, Katie and her coach played a few practice games, so Katie could work on her serve. Katie was exhausted when she got home, but at least she felt ready for Saturday's tournament.

Writing

Paragraph structure

Brain Box

A **paragraph** is a group of sentences that talks about the same main idea. Paragraphs have three parts: a beginning, a middle, and an end.

The **beginning** of a paragraph usually has a **topic sentence.** It tells what the rest of the paragraph is about.

The **middle** of a paragraph contains **details about the main idea.**

The **concluding** of a paragraph usually **finishes the main idea** of the paragraph.

The first line of every paragraph is indented, which means the first word always begins a little bit to the right of the rest of the lines.

Summer Vacation

Organize the sentences on the cars into paragraphs. Number the sentences in the order that makes the most sense.

☐ We drove from California to New York.

☐ This summer, my family drove across the country for vacation.

☐ Along the way, we stopped in small towns and big cities.

☐ We had fun in each town and city.

☐ I was sad when we had to leave.

☐ While we were in Hot Springs, we spent most of our time in the national park.

☐ We hiked in the mountains and had a picnic by a creek.

☐ My favorite place was Hot Springs, Arkansas.

☐ My mom and dad had to be back at work, and I was starting to miss my dog, Baxter.

☐ Seven days later, we pulled up in our driveway.

☐ After four weeks of touring the United States, it was time to head home.

☐ I had a great time, but I was happy to be home.

All About Me

Finish the sentences.

PARAGRAPH 1

Four adjectives that describe me well are:

__________ __________ __________ __________

I live in a/an (describe the place you live) ____________________

I live there with ____________________

Writing

Narrative paragraphs

PARAGRAPH 2

My school is called ____________________

My favorite subject is ____________________

The best thing about school is ____________________

PARAGRAPH 3

After school, I like to ____________________

My hobbies are ____________________

Before I go to bed each night, I always ____________________

Use your answers from the previous page to write three paragraphs about yourself. Include a topic sentence, supporting details, and a concluding sentence in each paragraph. Don't forget to indent the first line.

Writing

Narrative paragraphs

That's the Point!

Read the **persuasive paragraph.** Then answer the questions.

Running is the most ideal exercise for staying healthy and fit. Unlike many other sports, running is something that just about anyone can do, and it isn't hard to get started. Running also burns calories while giving your heart and legs a great workout. You can either do it with a friend or you can go by yourself. Of course, the best part about running is you can do it anywhere. Whether you're in a gym, on the sidewalk, or at the beach, all you need is a pair of running shoes to get moving. If you've never run before, give it a try. You'll have fun and feel good after you do it!

Writing

Persuasive paragraphs

Brain Box

Persuasive writing tries to get the reader to agree with an opinion or point of view. Persuasive paragraphs contain three elements:

1) A **topic sentence**—a sentence that introduces the opinion

2) **Supporting facts**—details, facts, or reasons that support the opinion

3) **Conclusion**—a sentence that restates the opinion or finishes the argument

What is the main idea of the topic sentence?

____

Is the main idea a fact or an opinion? _______________

What are some of the reasons the writer gives to support his or her main idea? _______________________

____

____

____

Now it's your turn to write a **persuasive paragraph.** First, think about an issue you feel strongly about. Use some of the persuasive words from the Word Box to strengthen your writing.

necessary	surely	definitely	best
certainly	only	important	amazing

Write your opinion about the issue here.

List any facts, details, or reasons that support your opinion here. Be sure to include the details that would most likely convince someone else to agree with your opinions.

Restate your opinion from question #1, but state it in a different way.

Here's My Point!

Now, take your answers from the questions on the previous page and organize them into your own **persuasive paragraph.**

Writing

Persuasive paragraphs

Make sure you state your case clearly in your topic sentence, use the middle of the paragraph to support your opinion, and conclude by restating your opinion or finishing the argument.

All About Outlines

Read this **outline** for a short report about Halloween. Use the paragraph ideas in the boxes to help you fill in the blanks.

Making a jack-o'-lantern	Knocking on doors
Making a costume	How Halloween started

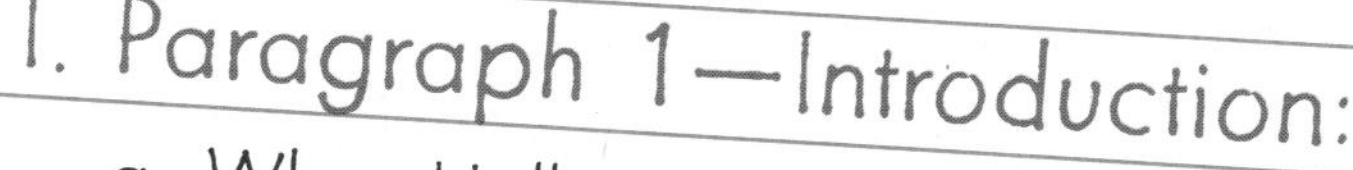

I. Paragraph 1—Introduction:

a. When Halloween is celebrated

b. Where Halloween is celebrated

c. ______________________________

d. Halloween traditions

Writing

Using outlines

II. Paragraph 2—Costumes:

a. Costume ideas

b. ______________________________

c. Buying a costume

III. Paragraph 3—Pumpkins:

a. Pumpkin picking

b. ______________________________

c. Roasting pumpkin seeds

IV. Paragraph 4—Trick-or-Treating:

a. Getting dressed

b. ______________________________

c. Sorting candy

Brain Box

An outline usually contains a list of ideas grouped together in the same order they will be presented in a report. Outlines are often broken down by paragraphs. Creating an **outline** is a great way to organize your thoughts before writing the report.

Time to Outline

Write an outline for a short report about your favorite holiday.

Writing

Using outlines

I. Paragraph 1—Introduction:

a.

b.

c.

a.

b.

c.

a.

b.

c.

IV. Paragraph 4—Main Idea:

a.

b.

c.

When writing a report, think about what kinds of details you would include. What points do you want to make? What facts are especially interesting?

Now use your outline to write a short report about your favorite holiday. Expand on the ideas you listed by using interesting language and details in your writing.

My Favorite Holiday:

What's Your Line?

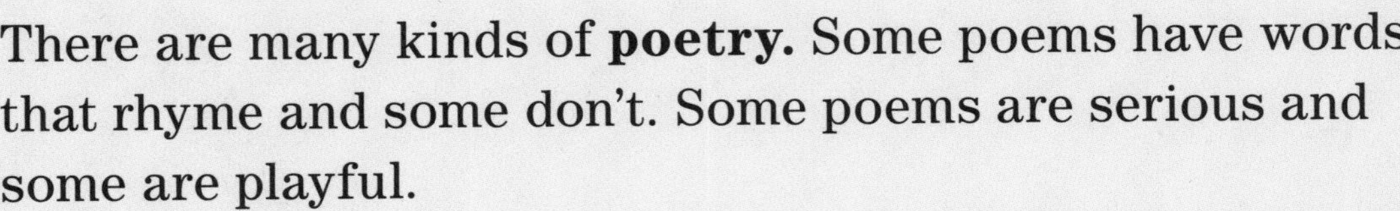

There are many kinds of **poetry.** Some poems have words that rhyme and some don't. Some poems are serious and some are playful.

Here's a short nonsense poem that ends with words that rhyme. Each line of this poem has five beats.

There once was a snake
Who liked to eat cake

Write a line with five beats to finish each of these poems. Look at the Word Box if you need ideas for rhyming words.

There once was a goat
Who rode in a boat.

There once was a flea
____

There once was a cat
____

There once was a crow
____

You Name It!

Write an **acrostic poem** using the letters in your name.

Writing

Poetry

Hello, My Name is
Fred

Brain Box

Acrostic poetry, uses the letters of a name to begin each line in the poem. For example:

Fred
Friendly and fun
Red hair
Energetic
Dynamic

The Proof Is in the Writing

Study the chart to learn how to use **proofreading marks.**

Symbol	What it means	Example
a (triple underline)	capitalize	The pacific Ocean is the largest ocean in the world.
A (slashed)	make lowercase	There are 25,000 Islands scattered throughout the ocean
^/m	insert letter to spell correctly	The Pacific Ocean is so wide it touches the coasts of Indonesia and Colobia.
^,	add a comma	It is home to incredible whales, sharks, and coral reefs.
⊙	add a period	The Pacific Ocean gets its name from the word for peaceful⊙ It isn't always peaceful, though.
(delete mark)	delete or take out	The area the Pacific Ocean covers is ~~bigger~~ larger than the area covered by all the dry land on Earth.
¶	start a new paragraph	The Pacific Ocean has the deepest trenches in the world.¶ The Indian Ocean is another beautiful Ocean.

Writing

Proofreading

Brain Box

Proofreading marks are used to edit a piece of writing. They are a handy way of marking errors for review or revision.

Use **proofreading marks** to mark the errors in this essay. Use a red pen.

If you travel to hawaii, don't forget to vsit the the Mauna Loa Volcano. Mauna Loa is the the biggest Volcano on earth, and one of the most active Tourists visit from all over the World to see hot red lava flowing from the volcano down into the Pacific Ocean below.

Mauna Loa is located on the the island of Hawaii, and it is part of Hawaii Volcanoes National park. The park is so big that it could take you several days just to drive arund and see all the sights. Be sure to pack your raincoat and boots, because it's often cool and cloudy rainy at the top of the volcino. Of course as soon as you drive down to sea level the weather gets warmer and sunnier that's Hawaii!

Writing

Proofreading

Check it Off!

Use this checklist to make sure your writing is as good and grammatically correct as possible.

✓	Did I read my writing to myself to make sure it made sense?
✓	Does my title fit what I wrote?
✓	Did I start each paragraph with a topic sentence?
✓	Did I use details and descriptive words to make my writing interesting and clear?
✓	Did I use strong verbs that show the action?
✓	Does each sentence begin with a capital letter and end with a period, question mark, or exclamation point?
✓	Did I use commas and quotation marks where needed?
✓	Did I use complete sentences?
✓	Did I check my spelling and make any necessary corrections?
✓	Did I capitalize all proper nouns?

Math Skills

How Very Odd

Circle the **even** numbers. Draw a square around the **odd** numbers.

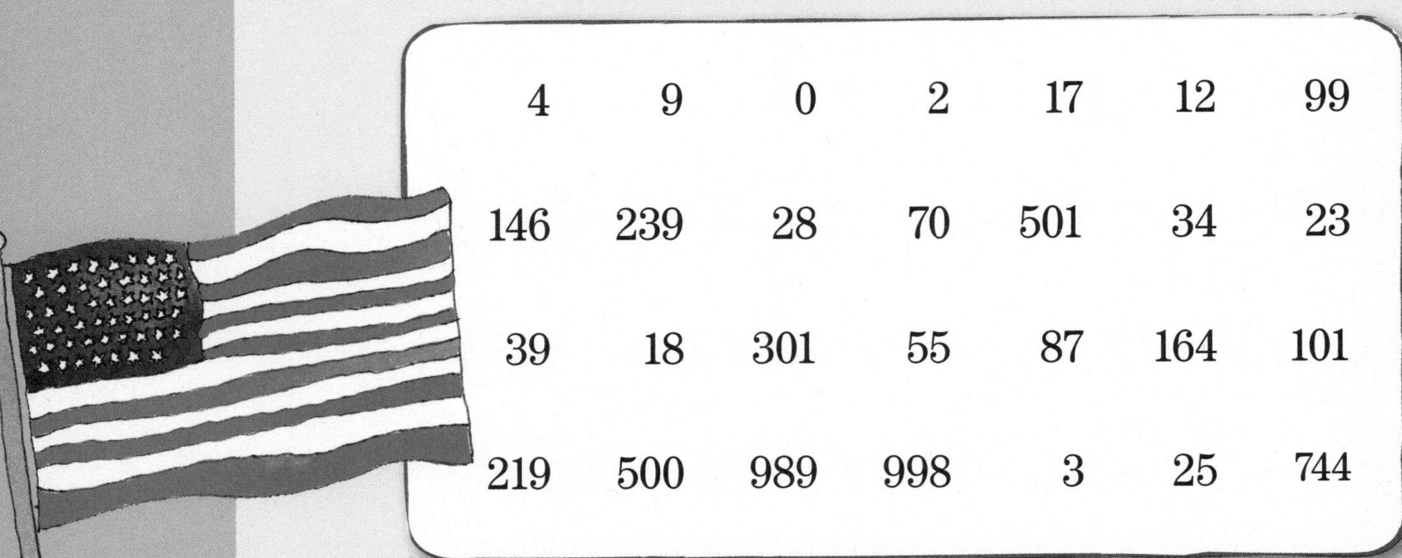

4	9	0	2	17	12	99
146	239	28	70	501	34	23
39	18	301	55	87	164	101
219	500	989	998	3	25	744

Math Skills

Odd and even numbers

Fill in the pattern on the card. Then circle all the even numbers and draw a square around the odd numbers.

8 ____ ____ 11 12 ____ 14 ____ ____ ____ 18

Brain Box

An **even** number is a whole number that ends in **0, 2, 4, 6,** or **8.**

An **odd** number is a whole number that ends in **1, 3, 5, 7,** or **9.**

When you add two even numbers, the answer is always even.

When you add two odd numbers, the answer is always even.

When you add one odd number and one even number, the answer is always odd.

Circle the correct answer.

When you add 34 and 18, two even numbers, the sum will be

odd even

When you add 24 and 13, the sum will be

odd even

When you add 21 and 42, the sum will be

odd even

Number Riddles

Solve the puzzles about **odd** and **even** numbers.

What even, 2-digit number is larger than 2 but smaller than 12?

10

What even number is greater than 6 and less than 18, and can be divided evenly by 6?

___

What odd number between 16 and 34 can be evenly divided by 5?

___

What odd number between 9 and 21 can be evenly divided by 3?

___

What even 2-digit number is a multiple of 9? It is smaller than 46 and larger than 20.

___

What odd 2-digit number between 20 and 30 has digits that add up to 7?

___

Math Skills

Odd and even numbers

What even 3-digit number between 75 and 150 has digits that add up to 1?

___

What odd 3-digit number has digits that are all the same and that add up to 9?

___

What's Its Value?

Answer the following questions about place value.

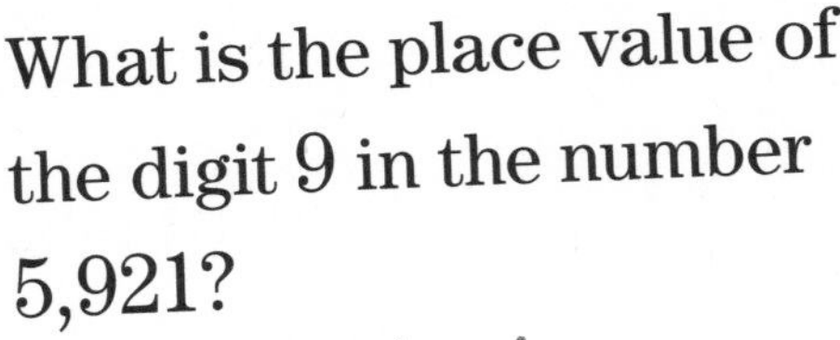

What is the place value of the digit 9 in the number 5,921?

hundreds

In the number 52,689, which digit is in the ten-thousands place?

____

What is the place value of the digit 6 in the number 86,542?

____

Which digit is in the tens place in the number 34,720?

____

Write the number seventy thousand, two hundred and eight.

____

Brain Box

You can use **place value** to figure out how much numerals are worth.
For example: **423,879**

hundred-thousands	ten-thousands	thousands	hundreds	tens	ones
4	2	3	8	7	9

The **4** tells us there are **4** hundred-thousands. The **2** tells us there are **2** ten-thousands. The **3** tells us there are **3** thousands. The **8** tells us there are **8** hundreds. The **7** tells us there are **7** tens. The **9** tells us there are **9** ones.

Write the number 48,567 using words.

____

____

What is the place value of the digit 3 in the number 526,310?

____

Write the number that has 2 hundred-thousands, 7 ten-thousands, 7 thousands, 5 hundreds, 3 tens, 9 ones.

____

Which digit is in the hundreds place in the number 59,216?

____

Write the number seventy-five thousand, two hundred, twenty-two.

____

What is the place value of the digit 4 in the number 34,890?

____

Write the number four thousand, six hundred, one.

____

In the number 305,678, which digit is in the hundred-thousands place?

____

Count Them Up

Answer the following questions about numbers. Use the extra space on the cards to do your calculating. Write the correct answer in the box on the card.

How many zeros does the number seven thousand, seven have?

7,007

2

I have seventy ones. What number am I?

I have eighty hundreds. What number am I?

How many zeros does the number one hundred thousand, ten have?

How many digits are in the number seven hundred thousand?

Math Skills

Number sense

What number is the same as sixteen tens?

I have ten tens and three ones. What number am I?

How many zeros does the number ten thousand, fifty have?

How many digits are in the number eighty one thousand?

What's My Line?

Identify each of these figures. Write **line, line segment,** or **ray** in the space beside the figure.

ray	C D (ray)
	W X (line)
	A B (ray)
	R D (line segment)

Math Skills

Lines, line segments, and rays

Brain Box

A **line** goes on and on in both directions forever. It is named by any two points (dots that show a certain location) on the line. For example:

G H = **line GH** or **line HG**

A **line segment** is part of a line that stops at both ends. A line segment is named by a point at each end, called an end point. For example:

M N = **line segment MN** or **line segment NM**

A **ray** has only one end point and continues on and on in the other direction. It is always named starting with its one end point. For example:

S T = **ray ST**

What's Your Angle?

Identify each of these angles by writing **right, acute,** or **obtuse** on the line below the angle.

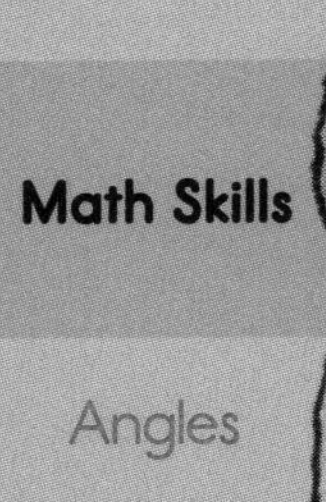

Math Skills

Angles

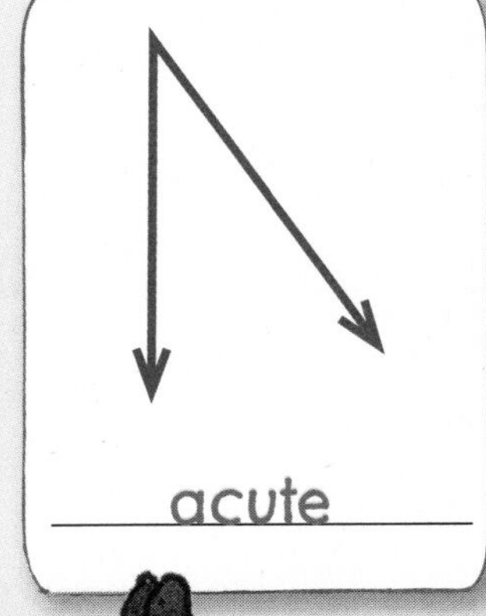

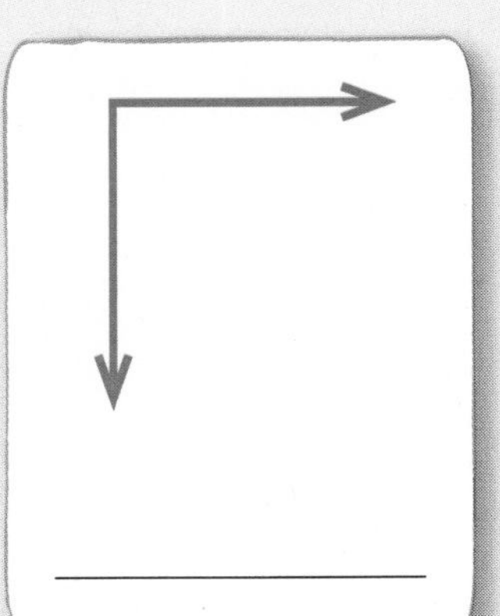
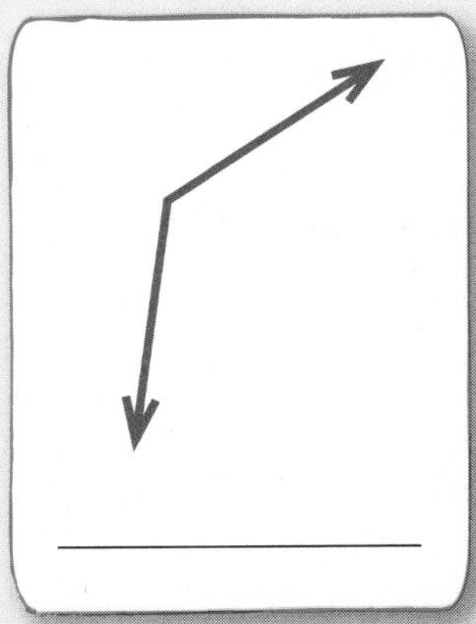
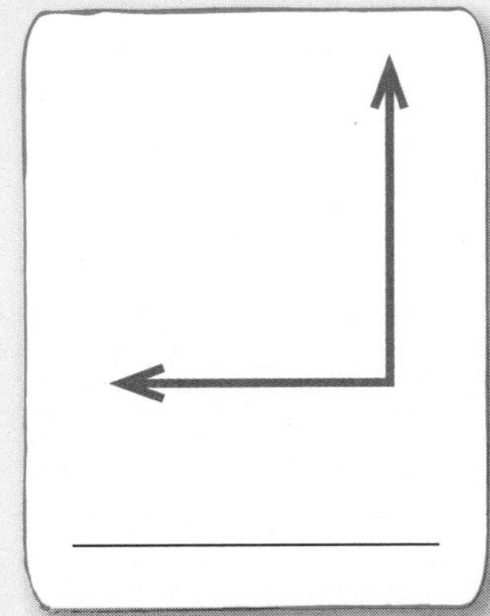
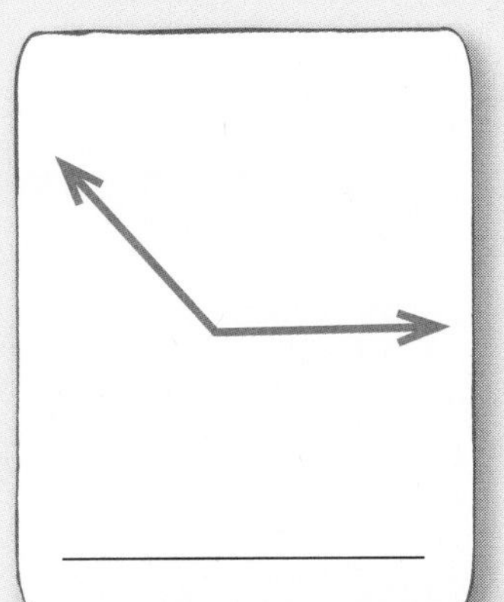
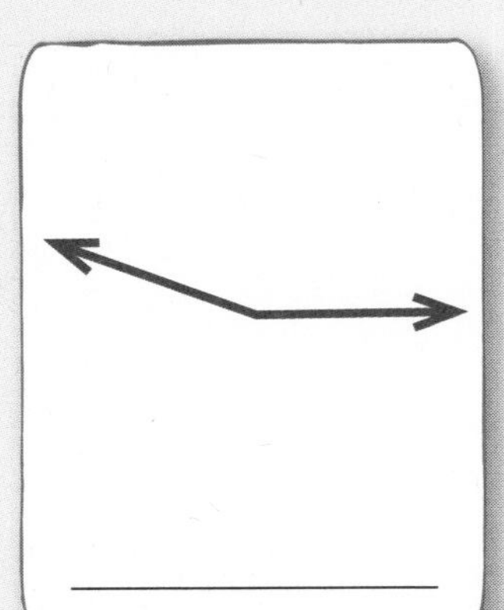
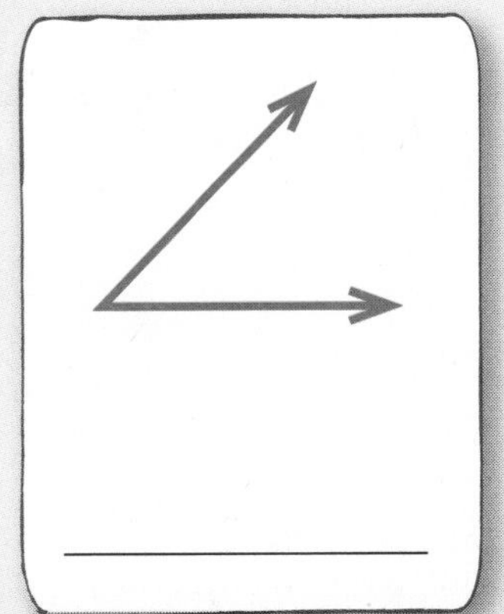

Brain Box

When two lines meet at one point they form an **angle.**

This is angle A. A

Angles can be different sizes. Some are wide and some are narrow.

A **right angle** forms a square corner.

An **acute angle** is less than a right angle.

An **obtuse angle** is greater than a right angle.

How many angles does a triangle have? ______

How many angles does an octagon have? _____

How many angles does a rectangle have? _____

Does a square have acute, right, or obtuse angles? _______

Draw an **acute angle, right angle,** and **obtuse angle** in the space below. Label each.

Shape Up

Draw a line to match each **solid figure** to its name.

sphere

cube

rectangular prism

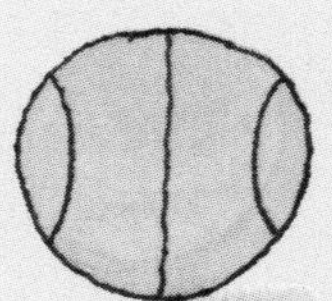

cylinder

cone

Math Skills

Three-dimensional geometric figures

Brain Box

Three-dimensional or **3-D** figures are often called **solid figures.**

A **sphere** is a **3-D** circle.

A **cube** is a **3-D** square.

A **rectangular prism** is a **3-D** rectangle.

A **cylinder** is a **3-D** figure with circles at either end.

A **cone** is a **3-D** figure with a circle on the bottom end and a point at the top.

What shape is each side of a cube? ______________________

What shape is the flat side of a cone? ______________________

How many faces does a rectangular prism have? ______

Circle the one that does not belong in this group:

cone, cylinder, cube, sphere, triangle.

Why doesn't it belong in the group?

____

How many angles does a sphere have? ______

What solid figure are dice? ______________________

How many flat faces does a cylinder have? ______

What shape is the top and the bottom of a cylinder?

____

Which solid figure is a bongo drum: a cylinder, a cube, a cone, or a rectangular prism? ______________________

What solid figure is a baseball? ______________________

Math Skills

Three-dimensional geometric figures

Brain Box

The flat sides of a 3-D figure are called **faces.**

What's Next?

What comes next in each of these **patterns?** Draw your answer in the box.

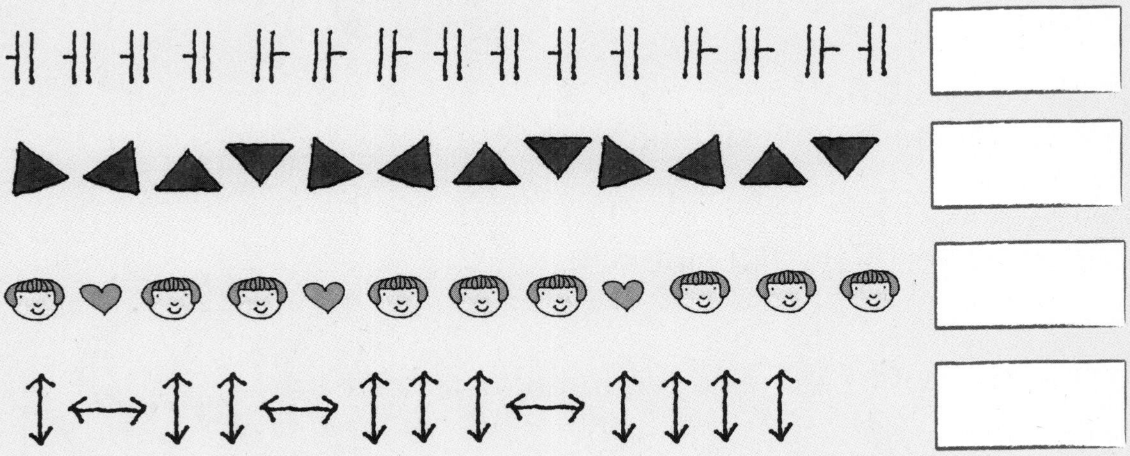

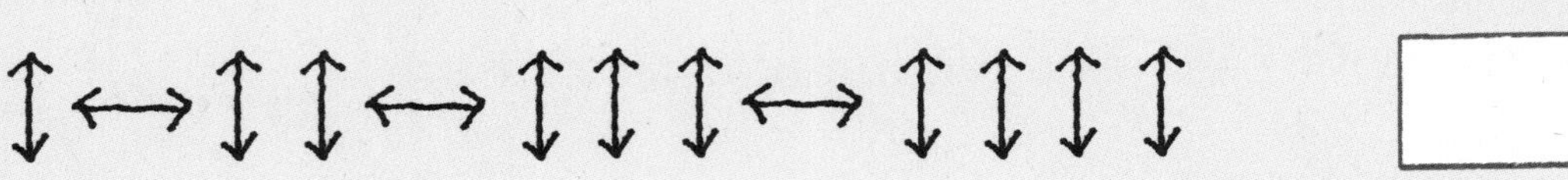

What two letters come next in each of these patterns?

A b c D e f G h i J k l M n ____ ____

z y x w v u t s r q p o ____ ____

a c e g i k m o q ____ ____

a z b y c x d w e v f u g t ____ ____

Math Skills

Identifying patterns

What two numbers come next in each of these series?

11 22 33 44 55 66 ______ ______

4 44 444 4,444 ______ ______

7 14 21 28 35 ______ ______

25 50 75 100 125 ______ ______

1 3 2 4 3 5 4 6 5 ______ ______

2 3 5 8 12 17 ______ ______

4 3 7 6 10 9 13 ______ ______

Math Skills

Identifying patterns

Brain Box

To figure out the pattern for a number series, look at the relationship between each number and the number that follows it in the series.

For example:

2 5 3 6 4 7 5

+3 −2 +3 −2 +3 −2

The pattern for this number series is (+ 3, − 2). The next two numbers would be **8** and **6.**

Round 'Em Up

Round these numbers to the nearest **ten.** If you round up, draw a circle around your answer. If you round down, draw a box around your answer.

58  11 _____ 26 _____ 83 _____

62 _____ 37 _____ 44 _____ 79 _____

17 _____ 74 _____ 19 _____ 24 _____

Round these numbers to the nearest **hundred.** If you round up, draw a circle around your answer. If you round down, draw a box around your answer.

Math Skills

Rounding numbers

487 _____ 833 _____ 729 _____ 596 _____

924 _____ 297 _____ 678 _____ 354 _____

324 _____ 198 _____ 109 _____ 247 _____

429 _____ 888 _____ 949 _____ 151 _____

Brain Box

Rounding to the nearest ten

If the **ones** number is **5** or greater, **round up** to the **nearest ten.** If the ones number is **4** or less, **round down** to the **nearest ten.**

Rounding to the nearest hundred

If the **tens** number is **5** or greater, **round up** to the **nearest hundred.** If the tens number is **4** or less, **round down** to the **nearest hundred.**

Now try rounding with larger numbers.

Alaska is our largest state. It is 587,878 square miles. Round 587,878 to the nearest ten thousand.

There are 56,803 poodles registered with the American Kennel Club. Round 56,803 to the nearest ten thousand.

Angel Falls, the world's largest waterfall, is 3,281 feet high. Round 3,281 to the nearest thousand.

Yellowstone National Park gets an average of 3,012,171 visitors each year. Round 3,012,171 to the nearest million.

Math Skills

Rounding numbers

The Earth's diameter at the equator is 7,926 miles. Round 7,926 to the nearest thousand.

Fenway Park, home of the Boston Red Sox, has seating for 35,695 people. Round 35,695 to the nearest ten thousand.

The population of Tulsa, Oklahoma, is 387,807. Round 387,807 to the nearest hundred thousand.

The diameter of Earth's moon is 2,160 miles. Round 2,160 to the nearest thousand.

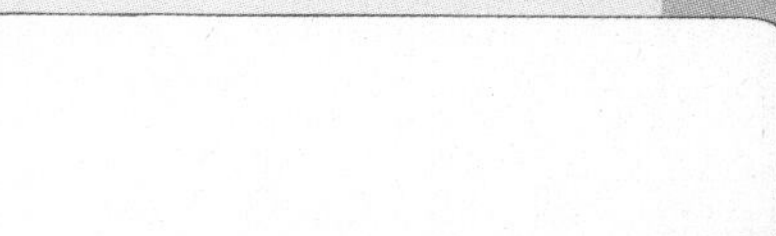

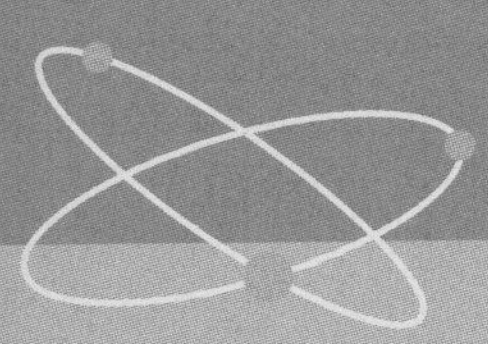

Close Enough

Estimate the sums by rounding each number to the nearest ten. Show your work.

77 → 80 + 24 → + 20 100	59 + 67	91 − 26
98 − 67	62 + 21	41 + 27
88 + 11	38 + 25	66 − 11
73 − 28	51 − 43	87 − 39

Math Skills

Estimating in number operations

Brain Box

To **estimate** means to make a good guess.

One way to estimate is to use **rounding**.

For example: **87 + 72**

Using rounding, this problem becomes 90 + 70

You can quickly guess that the answer is 160.

Solve the equations by rounding each number to the nearest 100.

$$\begin{array}{r} 876 \\ +\ 211 \\ \hline \end{array}$$

$$\begin{array}{r} 859 \\ +\ 611 \\ \hline \end{array}$$

$$\begin{array}{r} 729 \\ +\ 229 \\ \hline \end{array}$$

$$\begin{array}{r} 558 \\ +\ 307 \\ \hline \end{array}$$

$$\begin{array}{r} 285 \\ +\ 198 \\ \hline \end{array}$$

$$\begin{array}{r} 727 \\ +\ 254 \\ \hline \end{array}$$

$$\begin{array}{r} 651 \\ +\ 495 \\ \hline \end{array}$$

$$\begin{array}{r} 504 \\ +\ 386 \\ \hline \end{array}$$

$$\begin{array}{r} 437 \\ +\ 109 \\ \hline \end{array}$$

$$\begin{array}{r} 828 \\ +\ 751 \\ \hline \end{array}$$

$$\begin{array}{r} 939 \\ +\ 621 \\ \hline \end{array}$$

$$\begin{array}{r} 727 \\ +\ 158 \\ \hline \end{array}$$

Gone Fishing

Use the **bar graph** to answer the questions.

Math Skills

Reading a bar graph

Felix Flounder goes fishing every weekend from May through October. The bar graph shows how many fish he caught each month.

In which month did Felix catch the most fish? _______________

How many fish did Felix catch in June? _________

In which month did Felix catch the fewest fish? _______________

How many more fish did Felix catch in July than he did in June? _________

How many fish did Felix catch in May and June combined? ____

Show and Tell

Use the **graph** to answer the questions.

The third graders at Dwight Elementary School made a line graph showing how many of them own particular kinds of pets.

How many third graders own fish? ________

What kind of pet is owned by the greatest number of students?

____

What kind of pet is owned by the fewest number of students?

____

How many third graders own snakes? ________

Do more students own hamsters or lizards? ________

How many more third graders own dogs than cats? ________

Math Skills

Reading a line graph

Muscleville Medals

Use the **chart** to answer the questions.

Events	GOLD	SILVER	BRONZE
speed swimming events	3	4	2
diving events	5	5	2
relay races	2	4	1
running races	0	6	4
balance beam events	2	3	3
high and low jumps	1	5	0
hurdle races	4	4	3

Math Skills

Reading charts

Muscleville High School made a chart of all the medals they have won in the state sport championships.

How many gold medals did Muscleville High win in all? ______

How many silver medals did they win in all? ______

How many bronze medals did they win in all? ______

In what kind of events did they win the most medals?

____

In what kind of events did they win the least medals?

____

How many silver medals did they win in relay races and running races combined? ______

In what kind of events did they win the most gold medals? ______________________

First Things First

Solve each problem. Show your work.

$(6 + 4) \times 4 =$ 40

(10) × 4

$27 \div (4 + 5) =$ ______

$(3 + 2) \times (8 - 1) =$ ______

$(4 \times 7) \div 4 =$ ______

$(9 \div 3) - 3 =$ ______

$8 + (14 \div 2) =$ ______

$(8 - 2) + (6 - 3) =$ ______

$4 + (8 \times 7) =$ ______

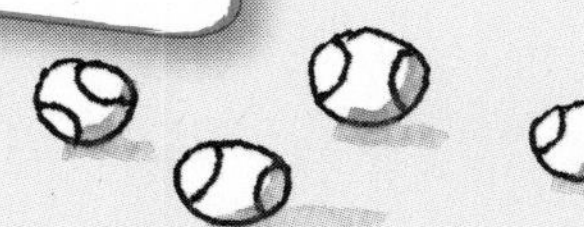

Math Skills

Math with multiple steps

Brain Box

Sometimes you have to solve a mathematical problem that involves more than one step. Always solve the part or parts in parentheses first. Then finish the rest of the problem.

Impress Your Friends

Do these mathematical tricks. Learn the steps by heart so you can amaze your friends.

The Number One Math Trick!

1. Pick a number from 1 to 100.
2. Multiply that number by 2.
3. Now add 2.
4. Next divide by 2.
5. Subtract the original number from the result of Step 4.
6. The number is always 1!

Math Skills

Mathematical tricks

The Magic Number Nine!

1. Write down your phone number without the dash or area code.
2. Arrange the digits to make the largest number possible.
3. Arrange the digits to make the smallest number possible.
4. Subtract the smaller number from the larger number.
5. Add up all the digits of the result.
6. Now add the two digits you ended up with.
7. The answer is 9!

Addition and Subtraction

Fact Families

Each triangle contains the numbers in a **fact family.** Add or subtract using the same three numbers.

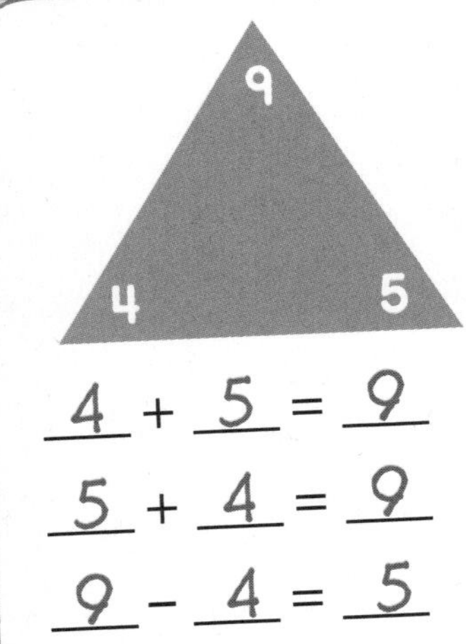

4 + 5 = 9
5 + 4 = 9
9 − 4 = 5
9 − 5 = 4

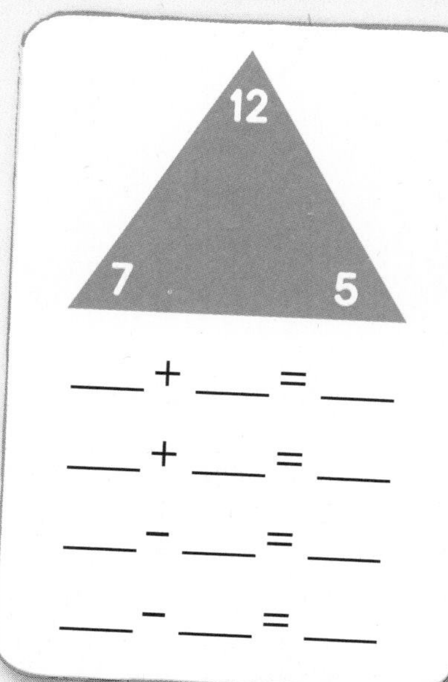

___ + ___ = ___
___ + ___ = ___
___ − ___ = ___
___ − ___ = ___

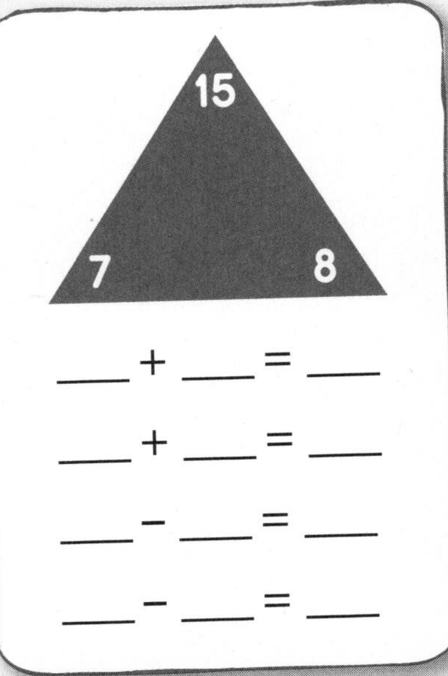

___ + ___ = ___
___ + ___ = ___
___ − ___ = ___
___ − ___ = ___

Addition and Subtraction

Fact families

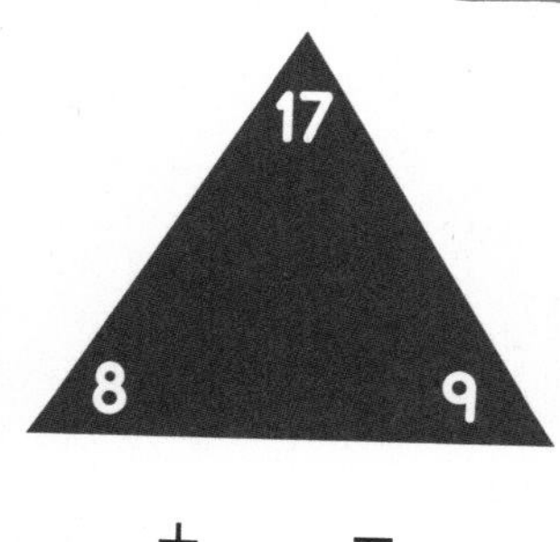

___ + ___ = ___
___ + ___ = ___
___ − ___ = ___
___ − ___ = ___

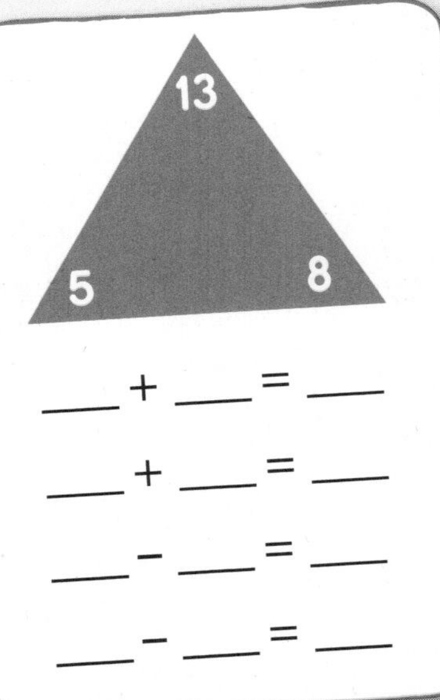

___ + ___ = ___
___ + ___ = ___
___ − ___ = ___
___ − ___ = ___

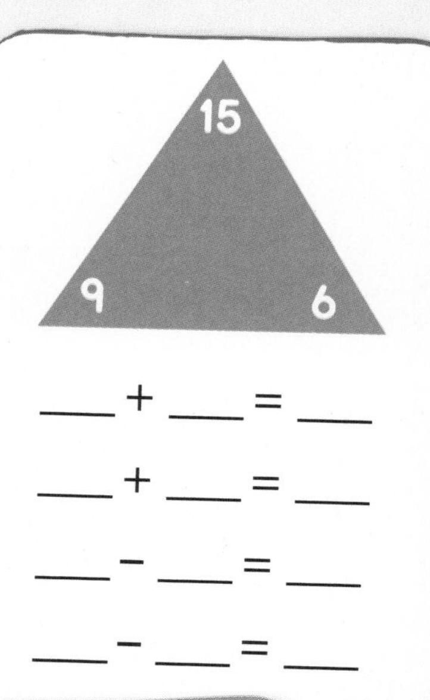

___ + ___ = ___
___ + ___ = ___
___ − ___ = ___
___ − ___ = ___

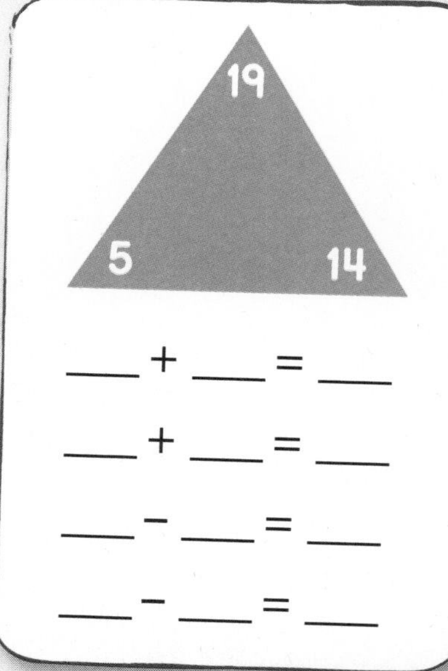

___ + ___ = ___
___ + ___ = ___
___ − ___ = ___
___ − ___ = ___

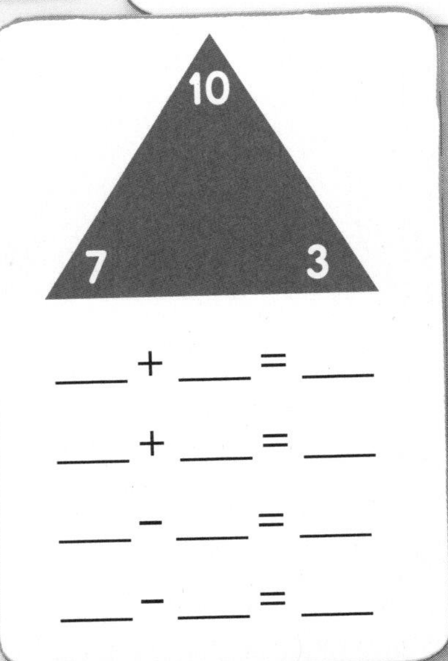

___ + ___ = ___
___ + ___ = ___
___ − ___ = ___
___ − ___ = ___

Brain Box

A **fact family** is a set of equations, each of which uses the same three numbers through addition and subtraction.

Add or subtract using the same three numbers.

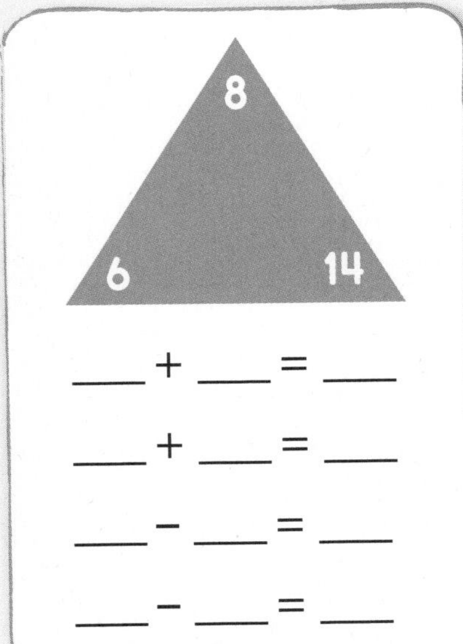

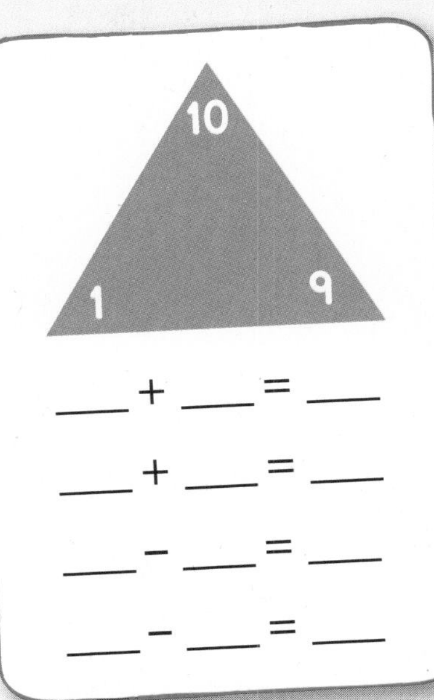

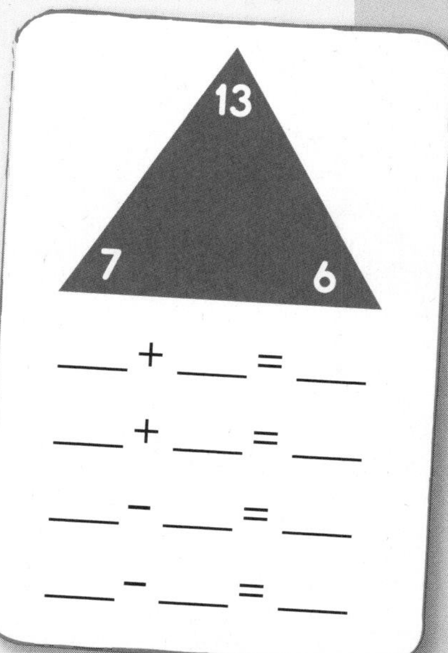

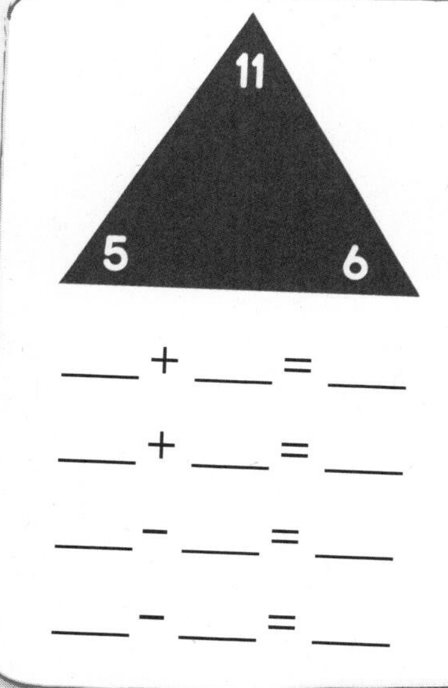

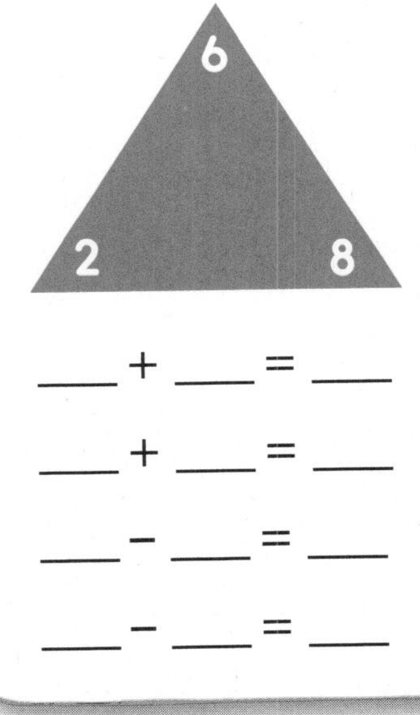

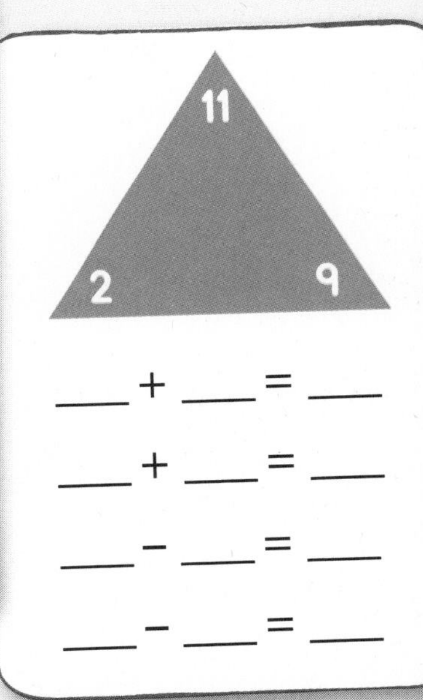

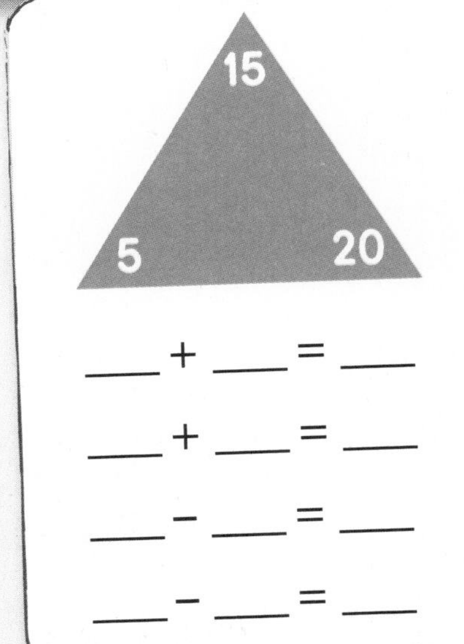

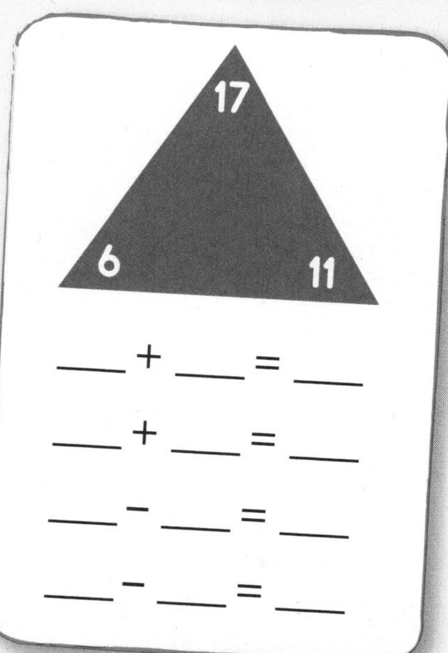

Addition and Subtraction

Fact families

Does It Add Up?

Add the numbers to find the **sum.**

37 + 12	235 + 542	87 + 11	628 + 171
77 + 22	625 + 324	354 + 544	65 + 13
27 + 61	544 + 323	899 + 100	731 + 247

Addition and Subtraction

Brain Box

Addition is when you put two or more numbers together. The numbers that are being added are called **addends.** The answer is called the **sum.**

This is how to add two-digit numbers:

Example: **54 + 23**

Step 1. Add the ones.

```
  5 4
+ 2 3
-----
    7
```

Step 2. Add the tens.

```
  5 4
+ 2 3
-----
  7 7
```

This is how to add three-digit numbers:

Example: **624 + 315**

Step 1. Add the ones.

```
  6 2 4
+ 3 1 5
-------
      9
```

Step 2. Add the tens.

```
  6 2 4
+ 3 1 5
-------
    3 9
```

Step 3. Add the hundreds.

```
  6 2 4
+ 3 1 5
-------
  9 3 9
```

Tall and Wide

Find the sum for each tall and wide addition problem.

4	2	3	6
4	8	3	2
2	5	3	3
3	3	3	1
5	1	5	4
1	1	3	4
+ 7	+ 9	+ 6	+ 10
______	______	______	______

3 + 2 + 7 + 7 + 2 + 3 + 3 = ________

6 + 6 + 1 + 3 + 3 + 3 + 4 = ________

10 + 8 + 3 + 5 + 5 + 4 + 6 = ________

8 + 5 + 7 + 6 + 2 + 1 + 3 = ________

4 + 1 + 6 + 9 + 4 + 4 + 2 = ________

7 + 5 + 2 + 3 + 4 + 5 + 2 + 1 + 6 = ________

9 + 0 + 4 + 3 + 3 + 7 + 2 + 3 + 5 = ________

What's the Difference?

Subtract the numbers to find the **difference.**

48 − 12	994 − 542	87 − 44	867 − 111
45 − 22	775 − 304	399 − 144	85 − 72
97 − 60	465 − 323	989 − 100	876 − 534

Addition and Subtraction

Brain Box

Subtraction is when you take one number away from another number. The answer to a subtraction problem is called the **difference.**

This is how to subtract two-digit numbers:

Example: **65 − 21**

Step 1. Subtract the ones.

$$\begin{array}{r} 65 \\ -\ 21 \\ \hline 4 \end{array}$$

Step 2. Subtract the tens.

$$\begin{array}{r} 65 \\ -\ 21 \\ \hline 44 \end{array}$$

This is how to subtract three-digit numbers:

Example: **978 − 342**

Step 1. Subtract the ones.

$$\begin{array}{r} 978 \\ -\ 342 \\ \hline 6 \end{array}$$

Step 2. Subtract the tens.

$$\begin{array}{r} 978 \\ -\ 342 \\ \hline 36 \end{array}$$

Step 3. Subtract the hundreds.

$$\begin{array}{r} 978 \\ -\ 342 \\ \hline 636 \end{array}$$

Mystery Numbers

Answer the number questions.

16 minus what mystery number equals 8?

16 − 8 = 8

8

When you subtract me from 24, the difference is 14. What number am I?

35 minus what mystery number equals 20?

My addends are 24 and 35. What is my sum?

21 plus what mystery number equals 36?

41 plus what mystery number equals 56?

My sum is 85. If one of my addends is 63, what is my other addend?

When you add me to 62, the sum is 84. What number am I?

MYSTERY NUMBER

Addition and Subtraction

Addition and subtraction

Magic Squares

Fill in the missing numbers so that every row (vertical, horizontal, and diagonal) in the **magic square** adds up to the number in the star.

4	3	8
9	5	1
2	7	6

		6
	9	
12	5	

	7	
6	11	

Addition and Subtraction

An addition challenge

Brain Box

In a **magic square,** every row (vertical, horizontal, and diagonal) adds up to the same sum. For example: In this magic square, every row adds up to 18.

9	2	7
4	6	8
5	10	3

Solve the **magic squares.**

13		
6	10	

	6	11
	8	

16		2	13
			8
	6	7	
4	15		1

14	9		2
	12		
4			16
17		10	5

Addition and Subtraction

An addition challenge

Time to Regroup

Regroup to find the **sum.** Show your work.

1 29 + 12 41	65 + 17	37 + 28
456 + 174	387 + 264	546 + 198
308 + 199	765 + 77	824 + 119

Addition and Subtraction

Regrouping in addition

Brain Box

Sometimes you need to **regroup** when you add two-digit numbers.

Example: 37 + 16

Step 1. Add the ones column. If the sum is greater than **9, carry** the **1** over to the tens column.

```
  1
  3 7
+ 1 6
    3
```

Step 2. Add the tens column, including the number you carried.

```
  1
  3 7
+ 1 6
  5 3
```

Regroup to find the **sum.** Show your work.

287 + 166	196 + 475	624 + 299
361 + 345	698 + 228	179 + 50
348 + 146	497 + 166	162 + 458
656 + 182	393 + 157	829 + 119

Brain Box

Sometimes you need to **regroup** when you add three-digit numbers.

Example:

```
  3 8 6
+ 1 8 5
```

Step 1. Add the ones column and carry the **1.**

```
    1
  3 8 6
+ 1 8 5
-------
      1
```

Step 2. Add the tens column, including the number you carried. If the sum is greater than **9, carry** the **1** to the hundreds column.

```
  1 1
  3 8 6
+ 1 8 5
-------
    7 1
```

Step 3. Add the hundreds column, including the number you carried.

```
  1 1
  3 8 6
+ 1 8 5
-------
  5 7 1
```

More Regrouping

Regroup to find the **difference.** Show your work.

3 14 ~~44~~ – 16 28	65 – 27	34 – 15
451 – 192	838 – 269	546 – 198
745 – 166	635 – 287	751 – 394

Addition and Subtraction

Regrouping in subtraction

Brain Box

Sometimes you need to **regroup** when you subtract two-digit numbers.

Example: 43 – 17

Step 1. Can you subtract **7** from **3?** No. You have to **borrow** from the tens column.	Step 2. Now you can subtract the ones column.	Step 3. Subtract the tens column, using the new number.
3 13 ~~4~~ ~~3~~ – 1 7	3 13 ~~4~~ ~~3~~ – 1 7 6	3 13 ~~4~~ ~~3~~ – 1 7 2 6

Regroup to find the **difference.** Show your work.

361 − 245	658 − 278	679 − 80
468 − 179	817 − 396	762 − 438
656 − 183	663 − 190	823 − 157
752 − 189	465 − 77	884 − 113

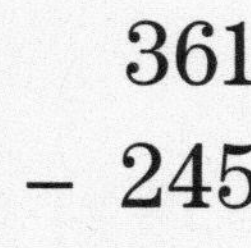

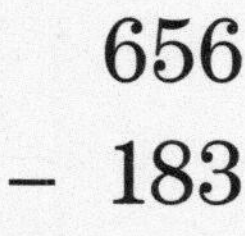

Addition and Subtraction

Regrouping in subtraction

Brain Box

Sometimes you need to **regroup** when you subtract three-digit numbers.

Example: 645 − 178

Step 1. Borrow from the tens column so you can subtract the ones column.

```
  3 15
6 4  5
-1 7 8
     7
```

Step 2. Borrow from the hundreds column so you can subtract the tens column.

```
5 13 15
6  4  5
-1 7  8
   6  7
```

Step 3. Subtract the hundreds column, using the new number.

```
5 13 15
6  4  5
-1 7  8
4  6  7
```

What About Zeros?

Regroup to find the **difference.** Show your work.

901 − 65	503 − 15	802 − 75
304 − 77	704 − 168	601 − 44
705 − 48	903 − 176	404 − 66

Addition and Subtraction

Regrouping in subtraction with zeros

Brain Box

In some subtraction problems, you have to **regroup across a zero.**

Example: 405 − 38

Step 1. To subtract the 8 from the 5 in the ones column, you would ordinarily borrow from the tens column. But since there are no tens to borrow from, you need to borrow from the hundreds column.

$$\begin{array}{r} \overset{3}{\cancel{4}}\,\overset{10}{0}\,5 \\ -\ \ 3\,8 \\ \hline \end{array}$$

Step 2. Now you have 10 in the tens column. You can borrow from the 10 to regroup for the ones column. Subtract.

$$\begin{array}{r} \overset{3}{\cancel{4}}\,\overset{\overset{9}{\cancel{10}}}{\cancel{0}}\,\overset{15}{\cancel{5}} \\ -\ \ 3\,8 \\ \hline 3\,6\,7 \end{array}$$

Double Zero

Regroup to find the **difference.** Show your work.

9 6 10 10 700 – 531 169	900 – 87	400 – 33
300 – 168	800 – 245	601 – 374
200 – 36	900 – 132	500 – 57

Addition and Subtraction

Regrouping in subtraction with zeros

Not Exactly

Estimate the sum by rounding each **addend** to the **nearest hundred.** Show your work.

554 → 600 + 210 → + 200 800	398 → + 475 → + ____
702 → + 613 → + ____	449 → + 279 → + ____
848 → + 137 → + ____	486 → + 256 → + ____
666 → + 312 → + ____	187 → + 624 → + ____
209 → + 288 → + ____	512 → + 434 → + ____
377 → + 391 → + ____	617 → + 218 → + ____

Addition and Subtraction

Estimating in addition by rounding

Just About

Estimate the difference by rounding each number to the **nearest hundred.** Show your work.

809 → – 462 → – ______	678 → – 127 → – ______
939 → – 258 → – ______	749 → – 252 → – ______
268 → – 99 → – ______	435 → – 186 → – ______
544 → – 489 → – ______	677 → – 268 → – ______
322 → – 185 → – ______	777 → – 679 → – ______
568 → – 141 → – ______	999 → – 876 → – ______

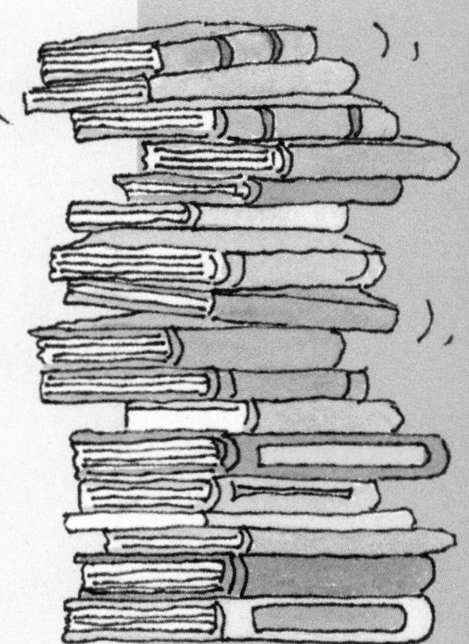

Addition and Subtraction

Estimating in subtraction by rounding

Missing Signs

These equations are missing the **plus** and **minus** signs. Write the correct sign in each box.

Addition and Subtraction

Addition or subtraction

9 □ 11 = 20

11 □ 5 = 6

3 □ 6 = 9

125 □ 75 = 50

37 □ 2 = 35

68 □ 12 = 80

12 □ 12 □ 24 = 0

150 □ 100 □ 14 = 64

22 □ 12 □ 11 = 21

21 □ 33 □ 3 = 57

33 □ 11 □ 10 = 34

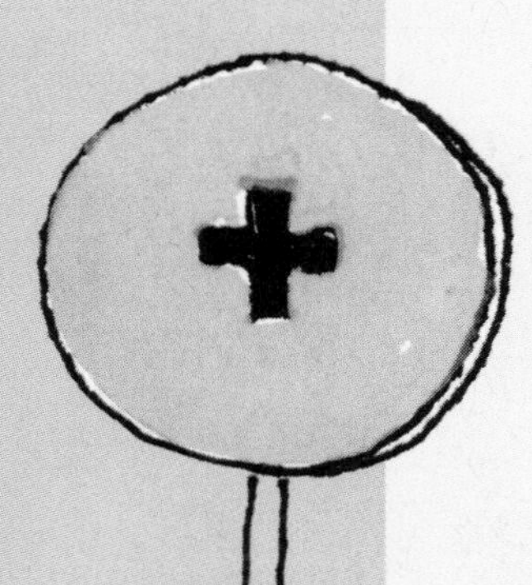

47 □ 15 □ 3 = 29

Sum Time

Find the **sum** for each addition problem. Some may require regrouping.

$$\begin{array}{r} 277 \\ +\ 111 \\ \hline \end{array} \qquad \begin{array}{r} 254 \\ +\ 269 \\ \hline \end{array} \qquad \begin{array}{r} 833 \\ +\ 144 \\ \hline \end{array}$$

$$\begin{array}{r} 666 \\ +\ 224 \\ \hline \end{array} \qquad \begin{array}{r} 156 \\ +\ 222 \\ \hline \end{array} \qquad \begin{array}{r} 752 \\ +\ 60 \\ \hline \end{array}$$

$$\begin{array}{r} 378 \\ +\ 167 \\ \hline \end{array} \qquad \begin{array}{r} 844 \\ +\ 235 \\ \hline \end{array} \qquad \begin{array}{r} 161 \\ +\ 428 \\ \hline \end{array}$$

$$\begin{array}{r} 672 \\ +\ 153 \\ \hline \end{array} \qquad \begin{array}{r} 500 \\ +\ 266 \\ \hline \end{array} \qquad \begin{array}{r} 708 \\ +\ 188 \\ \hline \end{array}$$

$$\begin{array}{r} 338 \\ +\ 116 \\ \hline \end{array} \qquad \begin{array}{r} 453 \\ +\ 71 \\ \hline \end{array} \qquad \begin{array}{r} 330 \\ +\ 169 \\ \hline \end{array}$$

Take It Away

Find the **difference** for each subtraction problem. Some may require regrouping.

$$\begin{array}{r} 756 \\ -\ 111 \\ \hline \end{array} \quad \begin{array}{r} 330 \\ -\ 119 \\ \hline \end{array} \quad \begin{array}{r} 807 \\ -\ 335 \\ \hline \end{array}$$

$$\begin{array}{r} 669 \\ -\ 226 \\ \hline \end{array} \quad \begin{array}{r} 763 \\ -\ 152 \\ \hline \end{array} \quad \begin{array}{r} 842 \\ -\ 60 \\ \hline \end{array} \quad \begin{array}{r} 752 \\ -\ 116 \\ \hline \end{array}$$

$$\begin{array}{r} 500 \\ -\ 176 \\ \hline \end{array} \quad \begin{array}{r} 864 \\ -\ 424 \\ \hline \end{array} \quad \begin{array}{r} 876 \\ -\ 234 \\ \hline \end{array}$$

$$\begin{array}{r} 703 \\ -\ 162 \\ \hline \end{array} \quad \begin{array}{r} 847 \\ -\ 146 \\ \hline \end{array} \quad \begin{array}{r} 900 \\ -\ 188 \\ \hline \end{array}$$

$$\begin{array}{r} 756 \\ -\ 71 \\ \hline \end{array} \quad \begin{array}{r} 752 \\ -\ 711 \\ \hline \end{array}$$

Multiplication and Division

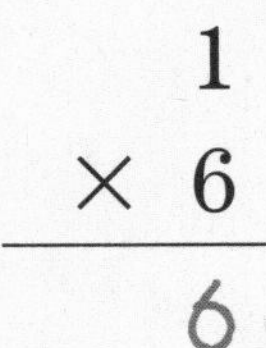

Multiplying by One

Find the **product** of each multiplication problem.

$1 \times 6 = 6$	7×1	1×5	8×1
1×0	1×3	2×1	1×1
4×1	1×4	9×1	1×2
10×1	6×1	5×1	1×7

QUICK FACT: When you multiply any number by 0, the product is 0.

QUICK FACT: When you multiply any number by 1, the product is the other number.

Multiplication and Division

Multiplication

Fill in the multiplication chart.

×	1	2	3	4	5	6	7	8	9	10
1	1									

Brain Box

Multiplication is a quick way of adding the same number a certain amount of times. The **product** is the number resulting from the multiplication of two or more numbers.

Multiplying by Two

Find the **product.**

2×1	3×2	2×6	7×2
2×5	2×4	5×2	2×8
10×2	2×2	2×9	6×2
2×3	4×2	9×2	2×0

Fill in the multiplication chart.

×	1	2	3	4	5	6	7	8	9	10
2										

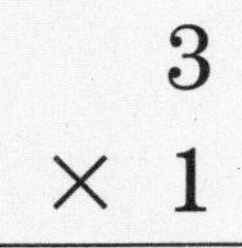

Multiplying by Three

Find the **product.**

$$\begin{array}{r} 3 \\ \times\ 1 \\ \hline \end{array} \quad \begin{array}{r} 3 \\ \times\ 7 \\ \hline \end{array} \quad \begin{array}{r} 0 \\ \times\ 3 \\ \hline \end{array} \quad \begin{array}{r} 3 \\ \times\ 4 \\ \hline \end{array}$$

$$\begin{array}{r} 10 \\ \times\ 3 \\ \hline \end{array} \quad \begin{array}{r} 3 \\ \times\ 3 \\ \hline \end{array} \quad \begin{array}{r} 3 \\ \times\ 6 \\ \hline \end{array} \quad \begin{array}{r} 2 \\ \times\ 3 \\ \hline \end{array}$$

$$\begin{array}{r} 9 \\ \times\ 3 \\ \hline \end{array} \quad \begin{array}{r} 3 \\ \times\ 5 \\ \hline \end{array} \quad \begin{array}{r} 7 \\ \times\ 3 \\ \hline \end{array} \quad \begin{array}{r} 5 \\ \times\ 3 \\ \hline \end{array}$$

$$\begin{array}{r} 4 \\ \times\ 3 \\ \hline \end{array} \quad \begin{array}{r} 3 \\ \times\ 8 \\ \hline \end{array} \quad \begin{array}{r} 6 \\ \times\ 3 \\ \hline \end{array} \quad \begin{array}{r} 3 \\ \times 10 \\ \hline \end{array}$$

Fill in the multiplication chart.

×	1	2	3	4	5	6	7	8	9	10
3										

Multiplying by Four

Find the **product.**

$\begin{array}{r} 2 \\ \times\ 4 \\ \hline \end{array}$ $\begin{array}{r} 8 \\ \times\ 4 \\ \hline \end{array}$ $\begin{array}{r} 4 \\ \times\ 6 \\ \hline \end{array}$ $\begin{array}{r} 3 \\ \times\ 4 \\ \hline \end{array}$

$\begin{array}{r} 4 \\ \times\ 5 \\ \hline \end{array}$ $\begin{array}{r} 10 \\ \times\ 4 \\ \hline \end{array}$

$\begin{array}{r} 9 \\ \times\ 4 \\ \hline \end{array}$ $\begin{array}{r} 4 \\ \times\ 1 \\ \hline \end{array}$

$\begin{array}{r} 7 \\ \times\ 4 \\ \hline \end{array}$ $\begin{array}{r} 4 \\ \times\ 2 \\ \hline \end{array}$ $\begin{array}{r} 4 \\ \times\ 9 \\ \hline \end{array}$ $\begin{array}{r} 6 \\ \times\ 4 \\ \hline \end{array}$

$\begin{array}{r} 4 \\ \times\ 3 \\ \hline \end{array}$ $\begin{array}{r} 4 \\ \times\ 4 \\ \hline \end{array}$ $\begin{array}{r} 5 \\ \times\ 4 \\ \hline \end{array}$ $\begin{array}{r} 0 \\ \times\ 4 \\ \hline \end{array}$

Fill in the multiplication chart.

×	1	2	3	4	5	6	7	8	9	10
4										

Multiplying by Five

Find the **product.**

$$\begin{array}{r} 5 \\ \times\ 4 \\ \hline \end{array} \quad \begin{array}{r} 5 \\ \times\ 5 \\ \hline \end{array} \quad \begin{array}{r} 2 \\ \times\ 5 \\ \hline \end{array} \quad \begin{array}{r} 7 \\ \times\ 5 \\ \hline \end{array}$$

$$\begin{array}{r} 9 \\ \times\ 5 \\ \hline \end{array} \quad \begin{array}{r} 0 \\ \times\ 5 \\ \hline \end{array} \quad \begin{array}{r} 10 \\ \times\ 5 \\ \hline \end{array} \quad \begin{array}{r} 5 \\ \times\ 8 \\ \hline \end{array}$$

$$\begin{array}{r} 1 \\ \times\ 5 \\ \hline \end{array} \quad \begin{array}{r} 5 \\ \times\ 2 \\ \hline \end{array} \quad \begin{array}{r} 5 \\ \times\ 9 \\ \hline \end{array} \quad \begin{array}{r} 6 \\ \times\ 5 \\ \hline \end{array}$$

$$\begin{array}{r} 5 \\ \times\ 3 \\ \hline \end{array} \quad \begin{array}{r} 4 \\ \times\ 5 \\ \hline \end{array} \quad \begin{array}{r} 8 \\ \times\ 5 \\ \hline \end{array} \quad \begin{array}{r} 3 \\ \times\ 5 \\ \hline \end{array}$$

Fill in the multiplication chart.

×	1	2	3	4	5	6	7	8	9	10
5										

Multiplying by Six

Find the **product.**

$$\begin{array}{r} 2 \\ \times\ 6 \\ \hline \end{array} \quad \begin{array}{r} 6 \\ \times\ 0 \\ \hline \end{array} \quad \begin{array}{r} 5 \\ \times\ 6 \\ \hline \end{array} \quad \begin{array}{r} 7 \\ \times\ 6 \\ \hline \end{array}$$

$$\begin{array}{r} 3 \\ \times\ 6 \\ \hline \end{array} \quad \begin{array}{r} 6 \\ \times\ 4 \\ \hline \end{array} \quad \begin{array}{r} 6 \\ \times\ 2 \\ \hline \end{array} \quad \begin{array}{r} 6 \\ \times\ 8 \\ \hline \end{array}$$

$$\begin{array}{r} 9 \\ \times\ 6 \\ \hline \end{array} \quad \begin{array}{r} 6 \\ \times\ 6 \\ \hline \end{array} \quad \begin{array}{r} 6 \\ \times\ 5 \\ \hline \end{array} \quad \begin{array}{r} 6 \\ \times\ 3 \\ \hline \end{array}$$

$$\begin{array}{r} 6 \\ \times 10 \\ \hline \end{array} \quad \begin{array}{r} 4 \\ \times\ 6 \\ \hline \end{array} \quad \begin{array}{r} 6 \\ \times\ 9 \\ \hline \end{array} \quad \begin{array}{r} 1 \\ \times\ 6 \\ \hline \end{array}$$

Fill in the multiplication chart.

×	1	2	3	4	5	6	7	8	9	10
6										

Multiplying by Seven

Find the **product.**

$7 \times 6 =$	$1 \times 7 =$	$5 \times 7 =$	$7 \times 7 =$
$3 \times 7 =$	$7 \times 4 =$	$8 \times 7 =$	$0 \times 7 =$
$7 \times 1 =$	$9 \times 7 =$	$7 \times 2 =$	$10 \times 7 =$
$7 \times 5 =$	$4 \times 7 =$	$7 \times 9 =$	$7 \times 8 =$

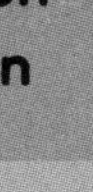

Fill in the multiplication chart.

×	1	2	3	4	5	6	7	8	9	10
7										

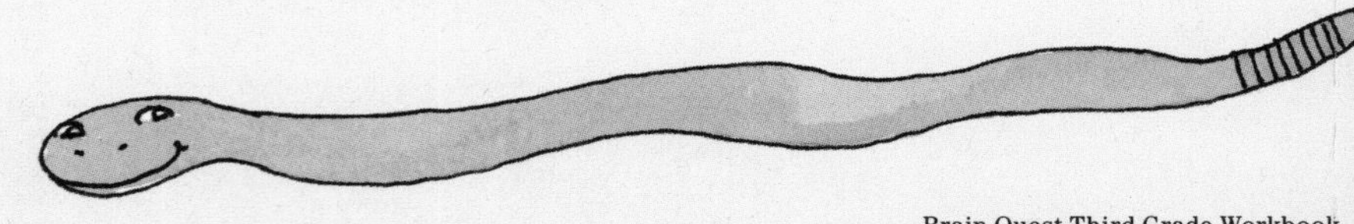

Multiplying by Eight

Find the **product.**

7×8	8×6	8×4	10×8
8×5	8×7	0×8	3×8
9×8	2×8	8×8	8×2
6×8	5×8	8×10	1×8

Fill in the multiplication chart.

×	1	2	3	4	5	6	7	8	9	10
8										

Multiplying by Nine

Find the **product.**

$$\begin{array}{r} 1 \\ \times\ 9 \\ \hline \end{array} \quad \begin{array}{r} 9 \\ \times\ 7 \\ \hline \end{array} \quad \begin{array}{r} 5 \\ \times\ 9 \\ \hline \end{array} \quad \begin{array}{r} 9 \\ \times\ 9 \\ \hline \end{array}$$

$$\begin{array}{r} 3 \\ \times\ 9 \\ \hline \end{array} \quad \begin{array}{r} 6 \\ \times\ 9 \\ \hline \end{array} \quad \begin{array}{r} 9 \\ \times\ 2 \\ \hline \end{array} \quad \begin{array}{r} 9 \\ \times\ 0 \\ \hline \end{array}$$

$$\begin{array}{r} 9 \\ \times\ 6 \\ \hline \end{array} \quad \begin{array}{r} 4 \\ \times\ 9 \\ \hline \end{array} \quad \begin{array}{r} 9 \\ \times\ 8 \\ \hline \end{array} \quad \begin{array}{r} 10 \\ \times\ 9 \\ \hline \end{array}$$

$$\begin{array}{r} 9 \\ \times\ 5 \\ \hline \end{array} \quad \begin{array}{r} 8 \\ \times\ 9 \\ \hline \end{array} \quad \begin{array}{r} 7 \\ \times\ 9 \\ \hline \end{array} \quad \begin{array}{r} 9 \\ \times\ 4 \\ \hline \end{array}$$

Fill in the multiplication chart.

×	1	2	3	4	5	6	7	8	9	10
9										

Helping Hands

Do you have trouble multiplying by 9?
Here's an easy trick to help you.

- Hold up both of your hands with your fingers spread apart.
- Let's use 9 × 3 as an example.
  Bend down your third finger from the left.
  You'll see 2 fingers to the left of your bent finger and 7 fingers to the right of your bent finger.
  The answer to 9 × 3 is 27.
- Try it again to find the answer to 9 × 6.
  Bend down your sixth finger from the left.
  You'll see 5 fingers to the left of your bent finger and 4 fingers to the right of your bent finger.
  The answer to 9 × 6 is 54.
- This works for 9 × 1 through 9 × 10.
  Isn't it a handy trick?

Use the trick you just learned to solve each problem.

$9 \times 4 =$ ________ $9 \times 3 =$ ________

$9 \times 8 =$ ________ $9 \times 9 =$ ________

$9 \times 6 =$ ________ $9 \times 1 =$ ________

$9 \times 2 =$ ________ $9 \times 7 =$ ________

$9 \times 5 =$ ________

Multiplying by Ten

Find the **product.**

$$10 \times 1$$

$$4 \times 10$$

$$10 \times 8$$

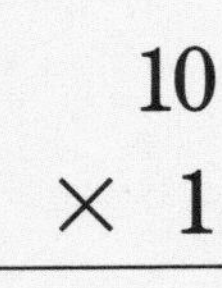

$$10 \times 7$$

$$10 \times 9$$

$$6 \times 10$$

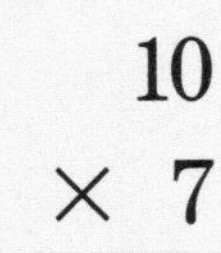

$$5 \times 10$$

$$10 \times 10$$

$$10 \times 4$$

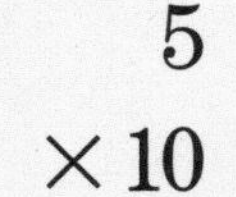

$$3 \times 10$$

$$10 \times 2$$

$$7 \times 10$$

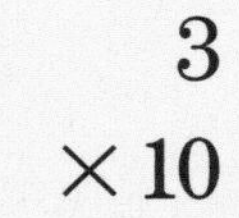

Fill in the multiplication chart.

×	1	2	3	4	5	6	7	8	9	10
10										

Brain Box

When you multiply by 10, simply multiply the number by 1 and add a zero to the answer.

Times Table to Twelve

Find the **product.**

$$\begin{array}{r} 1 \\ \times\ 1 \\ \hline \end{array} \quad \begin{array}{r} 2 \\ \times\ 2 \\ \hline \end{array} \quad \begin{array}{r} 3 \\ \times\ 3 \\ \hline \end{array} \quad \begin{array}{r} 4 \\ \times\ 4 \\ \hline \end{array}$$

$$\begin{array}{r} 5 \\ \times\ 5 \\ \hline \end{array} \quad \begin{array}{r} 6 \\ \times\ 6 \\ \hline \end{array} \quad \begin{array}{r} 7 \\ \times\ 7 \\ \hline \end{array} \quad \begin{array}{r} 8 \\ \times\ 8 \\ \hline \end{array}$$

$$\begin{array}{r} 9 \\ \times\ 9 \\ \hline \end{array} \quad \begin{array}{r} 10 \\ \times 10 \\ \hline \end{array} \quad \begin{array}{r} 11 \\ \times 11 \\ \hline \end{array} \quad \begin{array}{r} 12 \\ \times 12 \\ \hline \end{array}$$

Multiplication and Division

Multiplication

Fill in the multiplication charts.

×	1	2	3	4	5	6	7	8	9	10
11										

×	1	2	3	4	5	6	7	8	9	10
12										

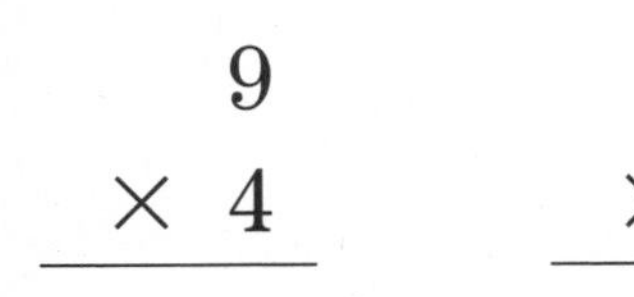

Practice Problems

Find the **products** of each multiplication problem.

$$\begin{array}{r} 9 \\ \times\ 4 \\ \hline \end{array} \qquad \begin{array}{r} 4 \\ \times\ 9 \\ \hline \end{array} \qquad \begin{array}{r} 8 \\ \times\ 3 \\ \hline \end{array} \qquad \begin{array}{r} 3 \\ \times\ 8 \\ \hline \end{array}$$

$$\begin{array}{r} 7 \\ \times\ 8 \\ \hline \end{array} \qquad \begin{array}{r} 8 \\ \times\ 7 \\ \hline \end{array} \qquad \begin{array}{r} 2 \\ \times\ 7 \\ \hline \end{array} \qquad \begin{array}{r} 7 \\ \times\ 2 \\ \hline \end{array}$$

$$\begin{array}{r} 5 \\ \times\ 4 \\ \hline \end{array} \qquad \begin{array}{r} 4 \\ \times\ 5 \\ \hline \end{array} \qquad \begin{array}{r} 6 \\ \times\ 5 \\ \hline \end{array} \qquad \begin{array}{r} 5 \\ \times\ 6 \\ \hline \end{array}$$

Multiplication and Division

Commutative property

Brain Box

The product of two or more numbers will always be the same, no matter in which order you multiply them. This is called the **commutative property of multiplication.** For example: **9 × 3 = 27** and **3 × 9 = 27**

Using the rule in the Brain Box, try this problem.

$$\begin{array}{r} 998 \\ \times\ 730 \\ \hline 728{,}540 \end{array} \qquad \begin{array}{r} 730 \\ \times\ 998 \\ \hline \end{array}$$

Hop, Skip, and Jump

In each row, **skip count** by the number shown in the star.

You can use multiplication facts to help.

4 8 12 16 20 24 28 32 36 40

5 ___ ___ ___ ___ 30 ___ ___ ___ 50

6 ___ ___ 24 ___ ___ ___ 48 ___ 60

___ ___ 21 ___ 35 ___ ___ 56 ___ ___

8 ___ ___ ___ 40 ___ ___ 64 ___ 80

Multiplication and Division

Skip counting for multiplication

Brain Box

Skip counting is when you count forward (or backward) by a number other than ten.

Missing Numbers

Complete each equation by writing the missing number in the box.

$2 \times \boxed{4} = 8$

$\square \times 7 = 42$

$\square \times 8 = 64$

$5 \times 7 = \square$

$\square \times 9 = 36$

$\square \times 8 = 48$

$3 \times 7 = \square$

$9 \times \square = 0$

$4 \times 7 = \square$

$1 \times 10 = \square$

$4 \times 8 = \square$

$2 \times \square = 12$

$7 \times \square = 49$

$\square \times 9 = 72$

$\square \times 3 = 18$

$\square \times 2 = 10$

$\square \times 9 = 54$

$9 \times \square = 27$

Multiplication and Division

Multiplication challenge

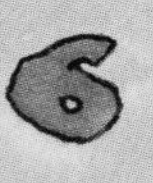
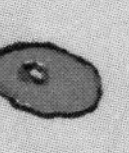

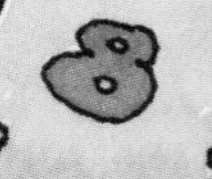

The Product Finder

Complete the **multiplication table** by filling in the missing numbers.

×	0	1	2	3	4	5	6	7	8	9	10	11	12
0	0												
1		1											
2			4										
3				9		15						33	
4													48
5	0							35					
6										54			
7							42						
8													
9													
10													
11													
12													144

Brain Box

You can use a **multiplication table** to help find the product in a multiplication problem. Just find one of the factors along the top row, and the other factor along the left column. The product of the two numbers can be found where the row and column with your factors meet!

Double Digit!

Find the **product.**

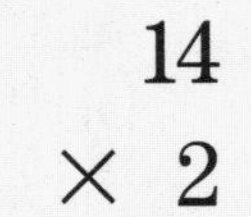

$\begin{array}{r} 14 \\ \times\ 2 \\ \hline \end{array}$	$\begin{array}{r} 62 \\ \times\ 3 \\ \hline \end{array}$	$\begin{array}{r} 31 \\ \times\ 5 \\ \hline \end{array}$	$\begin{array}{r} 52 \\ \times\ 4 \\ \hline \end{array}$
$\begin{array}{r} 12 \\ \times\ 7 \\ \hline \end{array}$	$\begin{array}{r} 80 \\ \times\ 9 \\ \hline \end{array}$	$\begin{array}{r} 61 \\ \times\ 8 \\ \hline \end{array}$	$\begin{array}{r} 73 \\ \times\ 3 \\ \hline \end{array}$
$\begin{array}{r} 98 \\ \times\ 1 \\ \hline \end{array}$	$\begin{array}{r} 44 \\ \times\ 2 \\ \hline \end{array}$	$\begin{array}{r} 52 \\ \times\ 3 \\ \hline \end{array}$	$\begin{array}{r} 60 \\ \times\ 9 \\ \hline \end{array}$

Multiplication and Division

Two-digit multiplication

Brain Box

This is how to multiply 2-digit numbers.

Example: $\begin{array}{r} 43 \\ \times\ 2 \\ \hline \end{array}$

Step 1. Multiply the ones.

$\begin{array}{r} 43 \\ \times\ 2 \\ \hline 6 \end{array}$

Step 2. Multiply the tens.

$\begin{array}{r} 43 \\ \times\ 2 \\ \hline 86 \end{array}$

Regroup It!

Find the **product.** Show your work.

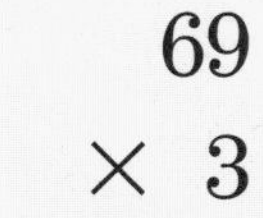

69×3	36×8	78×4
45×5	82×7	26×3
52×8	66×9	85×7
94×6	37×5	48×8

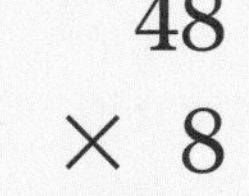

Brain Box

Sometimes, when you multiply the ones in a two-digit number, you have to regroup.

Example: 18×5

Step 1. Multiply the ones. Since the product is greater than 9, carry the **4** to the tens column.

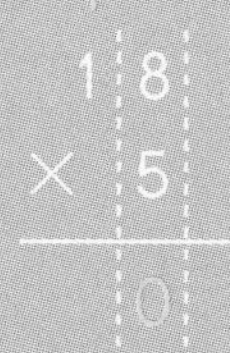

Step 2. Multiply the tens. Then add the number you carried to the product.

Legs on a Snake?

Solve each multiplication problem.

Multiply the number of wheels on 5 bicycles by the number of eyes on a dog. What's the product?

5 × 2 = 10
10 × 2 = 20

Multiply the number of letters in the alphabet by the number of noses on a rabbit. What's the product?

Multiply the number of legs on a snake by the number of hours in a day. What's the product?

Multiply the number of fingernails on two hands by the number of days in a week. What's the product?

Multiply the number of tusks on three elephants by the number of wings on three eagles. What's the product?

Multiplication and Division

Multiplication practice

Multiply the number of wheels on a tricycle by the number of months in a year. What's the product?

Multiply the number of pennies in a nickel by the number of nickels in a quarter. What's the product?

Multiply the number of hooves on a horse by the number of states in the United States. What's the product?

Multiply the number of bases on a baseball diamond by the number of sides on a triangle. What's the product?

Multiply the number of doughnuts in a dozen by the number of paws on a lion. What's the product?

Finding Quotients

Find the **quotient.**

$16 \div 2 = \boxed{8}$ $\quad 2\overline{)16}$ → $\boxed{8}$

HINT:
Find the anwer by using your multiplication facts.

2 × ? = 16

The answer is 8.

$9 \div 3 = \square$ $\quad 3\overline{)9}$

$12 \div 4 = \square$ $\quad 4\overline{)12}$

$6 \div 2 = \square$ $\quad 2\overline{)6}$

Division terms and basic rules

Multiplication and Division

Brain Box

Division is the process of finding out how many times one number will fit into another number. The number being divided is called the **dividend**. The number being divided into it is called the **divisor.** The answer to a division problem is called the **quotient.**

Example: 5 ← quotient
divisor → 3) 15 ← dividend

The Missing Divisors

Find the **quotient.**

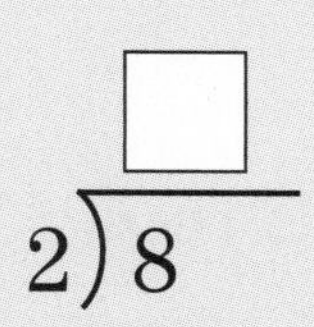 2) 8	3) 6	2) 12	3) 15
5) 10	2) 20	8) 16	2) 22
8) 32	7) 21	6) 24	6) 36
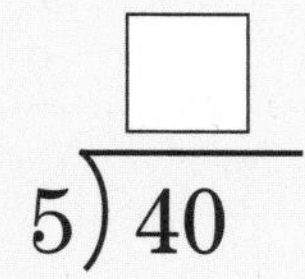 5) 40	2) 14	4) 8	1) 9
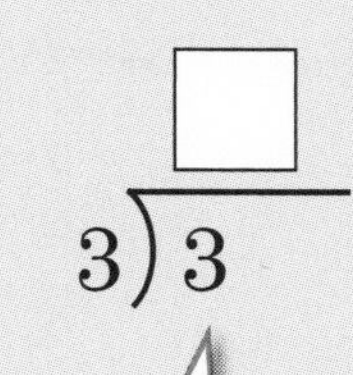 3) 3	2) 18	3) 27	3) 30

QUICK FACT:
Any number divided by 1 is the same number.

QUICK FACT:
Any number except zero divided by itself is always 1.

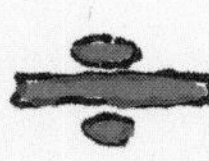

So Many Toes!

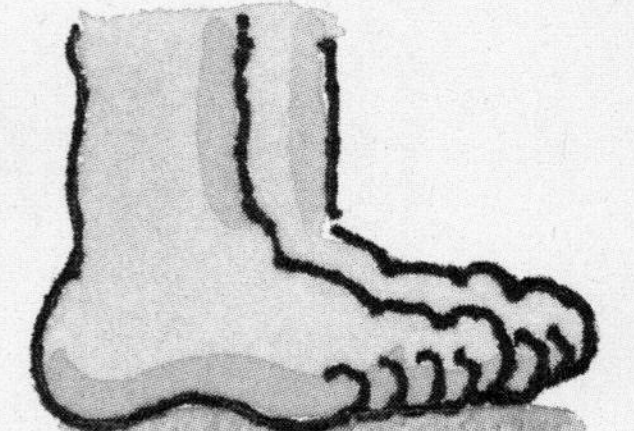

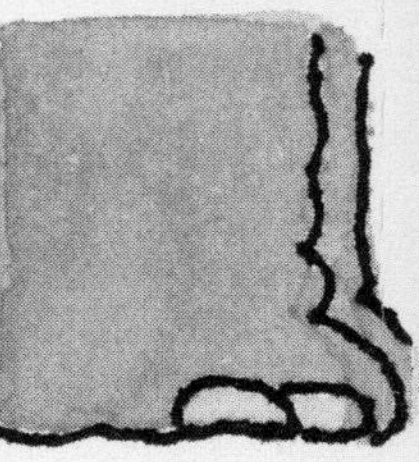

Find the **quotient.**

There were 100 toes in the pool. A person has 10 toes. How many people were in the pool?

100 ÷ 10 = ☐

Nicholas counted 12 rhino toes at the zoo. One rhino has a total of 6 toes. How many rhinos did he see?

☐ ÷ ☐ = ☐

There were 24 octopus arms in the aquarium tank. One octopus has 8 arms. How many octopuses were in the tank?

24 ÷ ☐ = ☐

There were 30 ladybug legs on the window. All ladybugs have 6 legs. How many ladybugs were on the window?

30 ÷ ☐ = ☐

Multiplication and Division

Division problems

Samantha saw 10 deer ears in the woods. A deer has 2 ears. How many deer did she see?

☐ ÷ ☐ = ☐

There were 21 tricycle wheels in the driveway. A tricycle has 3 wheels. How many tricycles were in the driveway?

☐ ÷ ☐ = ☐

Jay saw 40 hippo toes when he was on an African safari. One hippo has a total of 8 toes. How many hippos did he see?

☐ ÷ ☐ = ☐

Every kid in Matt's class raised his or her hand to answer the teacher's question. There were 75 fingers in the air. How many kids were in Matt's class?

☐ ÷ ☐ = ☐

Magaly counted 88 bicycle wheels in the park. A bicycle has 2 wheels. How many bicycles were in the park?

☐ ÷ ☐ = ☐

Joe counted 33 eggs in the nests near his house. Each nest had exactly 3 eggs. How many nests were near Joe's house?

☐ ÷ ☐ = ☐

Sadie needed 35 invitations for her party. Each box of cards came with 7 cards. How many boxes did she need to buy?

☐ ÷ ☐ = ☐

Math House

Only **fact families** live in this house. Write the four facts for the fact family in each room of the house.

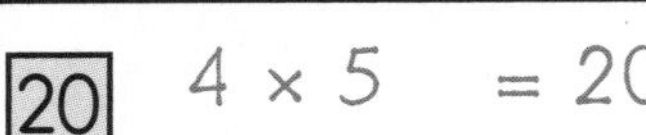

20	4 × 5 = 20
5	5 × 4 = 20
4	20 ÷ 4 = 5
	20 ÷ 5 = 4

12
3
4

32
8
4

35
7
5

28
7
4

45
9
5

Multiplication and Division

Fact families

Brain Box

A multiplication and division **fact family** is a set of facts, each of which relates the same three numbers through multiplication and division.

For example, the fact family for **2, 7,** and **9** is:

2 × 7 = 14 7 × 2 = 14

14 ÷ 2 = 7 14 ÷ 7 = 2

Math Building

Only **fact families** live in this building.
Write down the four facts for the fact family in each room of the building.

Multiplication and Division

Fact families

Watch the Signs!

Complete each equation with a **multiplication** or **division** sign.

8 ÷ 8 = 1

6 ☐ 5 = 30

64 ☐ 8 = 8

8 ☐ 2 = 4

8 ☐ 8 = 64	18 ☐ 9 = 2	12 ☐ 3 = 4
7 ☐ 9 = 63	7 ☐ 2 = 14	3 ☐ 7 = 21
32 ☐ 4 = 8	27 ☐ 3 = 9	49 ☐ 7 = 7
9 ☐ 5 = 45	6 ☐ 8 = 48	2 ☐ 4 = 8
6 ☐ 3 = 2	9 ☐ 3 = 3	56 ☐ 7 = 8

Multiplication and Division

Multiplication and division signs

Practice!

Multiply or **divide.**

9×3	4×9	$3\overline{)21}$	7×4
$6\overline{)24}$	$8\overline{)32}$	7×7	9×7
9×6	$7\overline{)28}$	3×8	$9\overline{)45}$
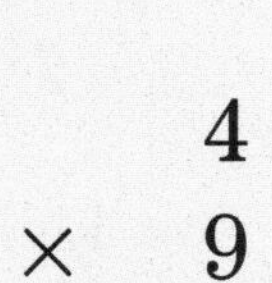 4×9	3×9	6×7	$4\overline{)12}$
65×3	5×5	4×4	$9\overline{)81}$

Practice!

Multiply or **divide.**

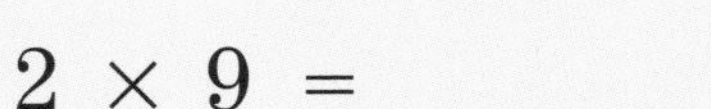

$2 \times 9 =$ ______

$4 \times 4 =$ ______

$28 \div 4 =$ ______

$24 \div 4 =$ ______

$14 \div 7 =$ ______

$3 \times 7 =$ ______

$6 \times 6 =$ ______

$14 \div 2 =$ ______

$8 \times 2 =$ ______

$5 \times 3 =$ ______

$9 \times 9 =$ ______

$6 \times 5 =$ ______

$48 \div 8 =$ ______

$8 \times 4 =$ ______

$64 \div 8 =$ ______

$4 \times 9 =$ ______

Fractions and Decimals

Hello Fractions!

Answer the questions about **fractions.**
Write your answers in the colored boxes.

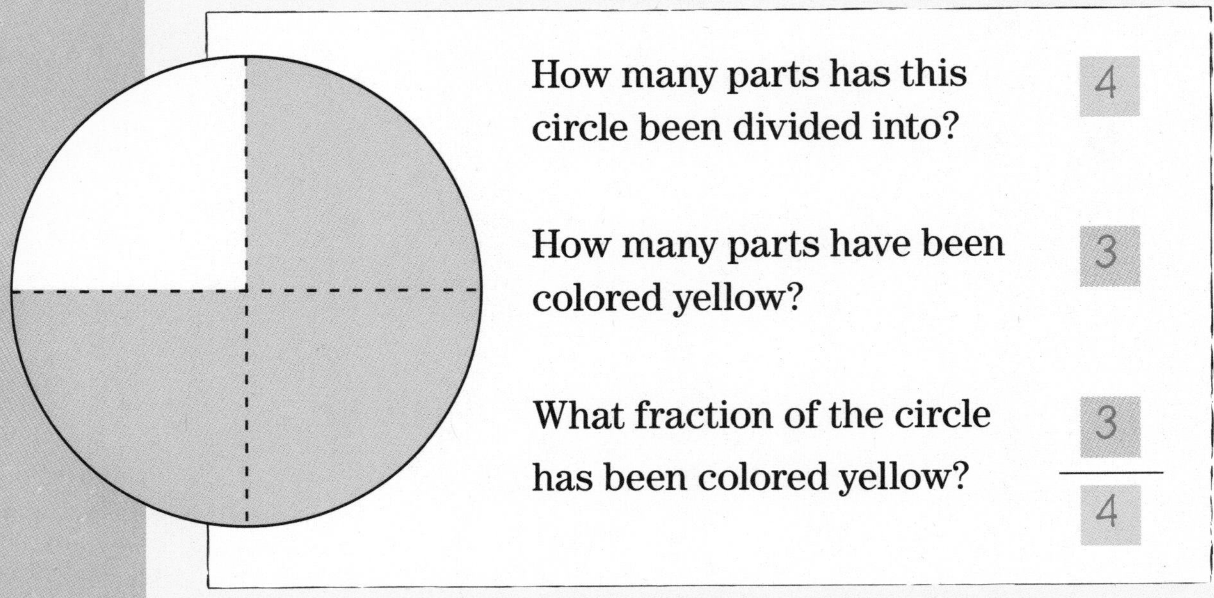

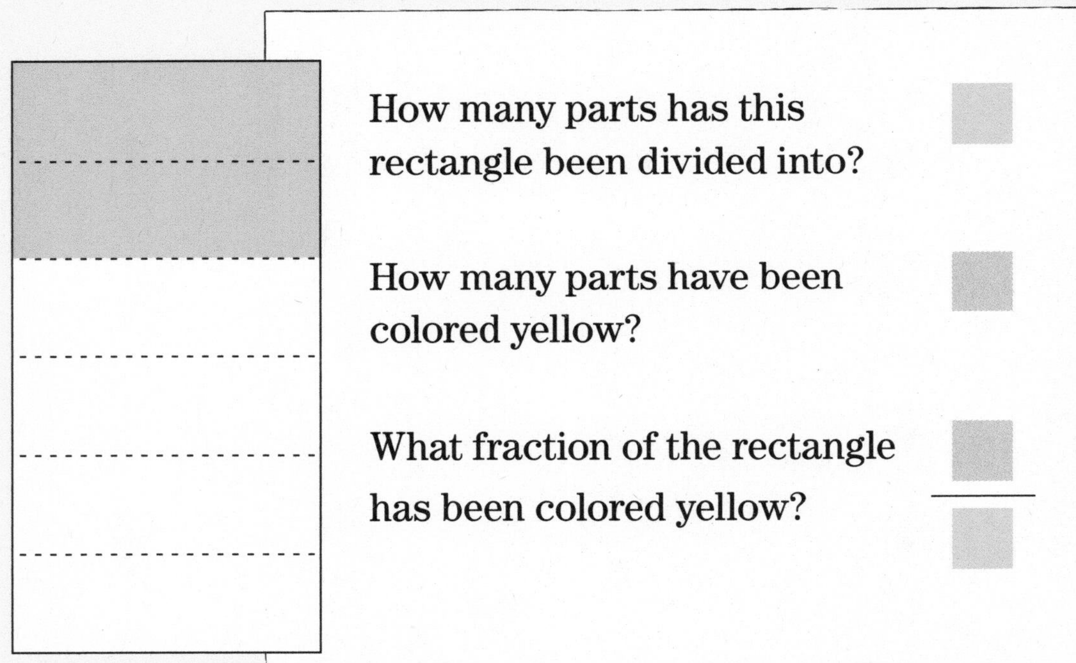

Fractions and Decimals

Fraction basics

Brain Box

A **fraction** represents one or more parts of a whole.

A fraction is made up of two numbers. The top number is called the **numerator.** The bottom number is called the **denominator.**

Answer the questions about **fractions.**

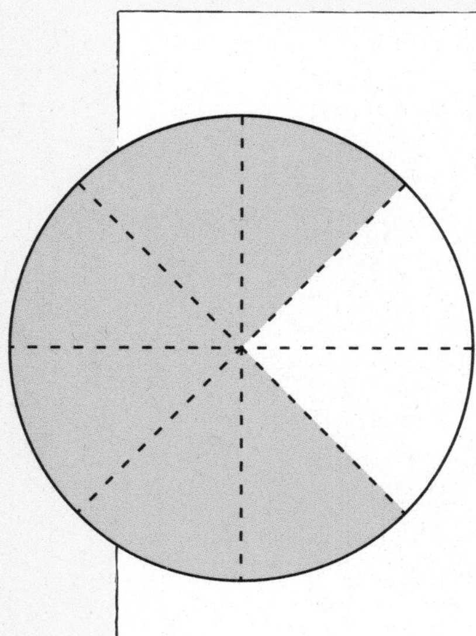

How many parts has this circle been divided into?

How many parts have been colored yellow?

What fraction of the circle has been colored yellow?

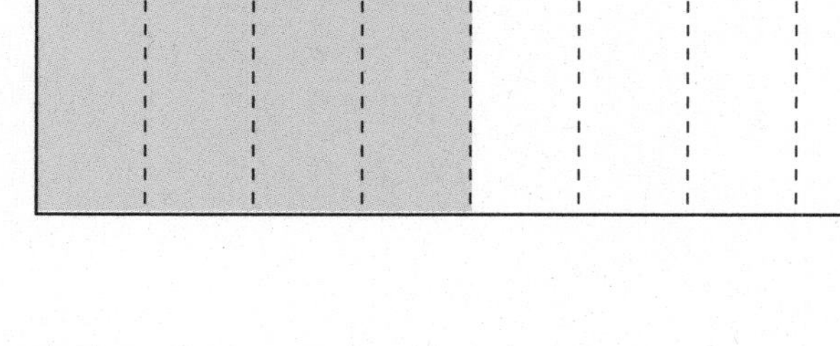

How many parts has this rectangle been divided into?

How many parts have been colored yellow?

What fraction of the rectangle has been colored yellow?

Brain Box

The **numerator** tells us how many parts of the whole we are counting. The **denominator** tells us the total number of parts in the whole.

Example: $\frac{3}{4}$ ← numerator / ← denominator

This fraction tells us there are three out of four parts.

Fraction Action

What **fractions** of these shapes have been colored? Write the correct fractions under the shapes.

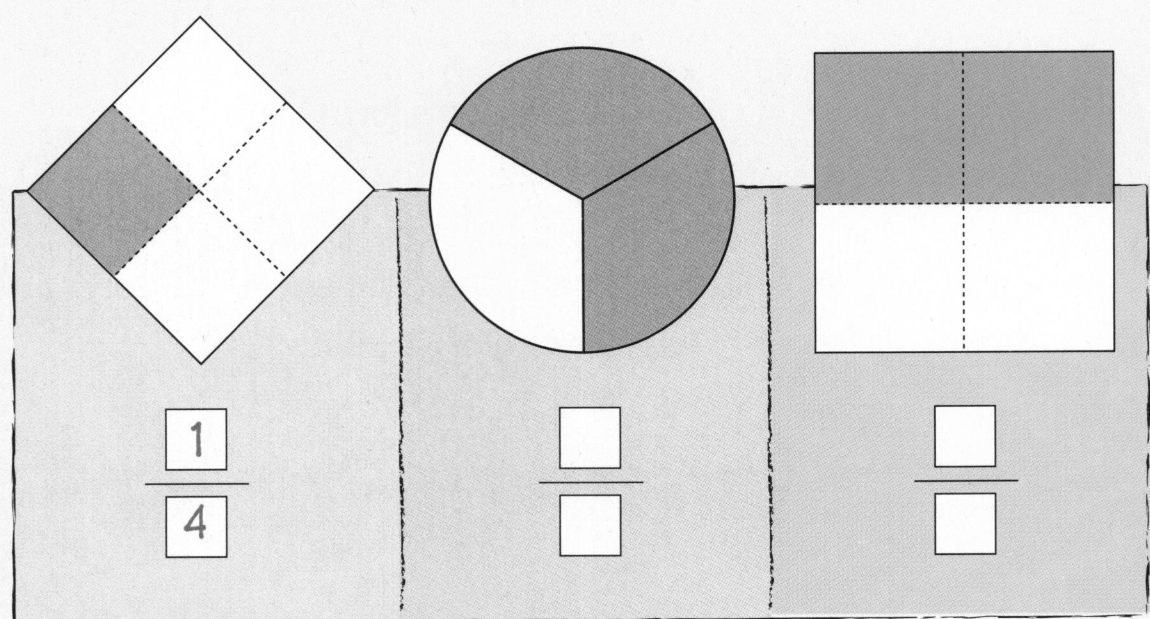

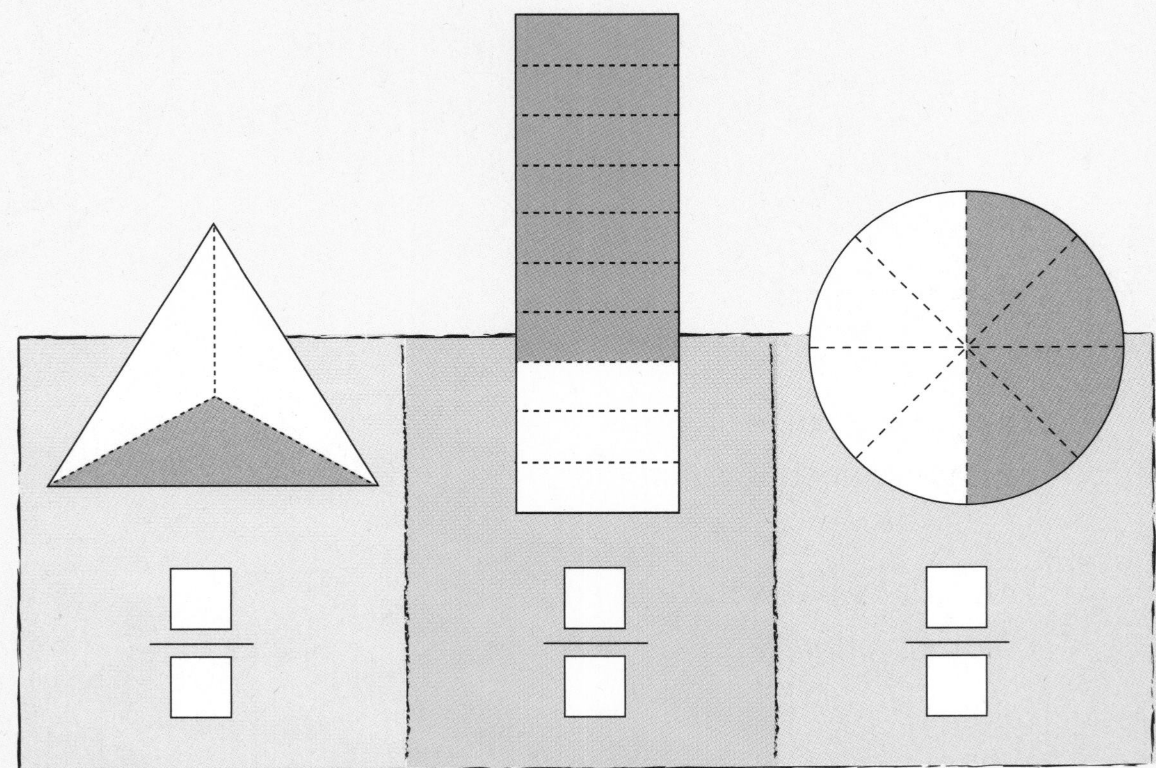

Fractions and Decimals

Fraction basics

Color the shapes.

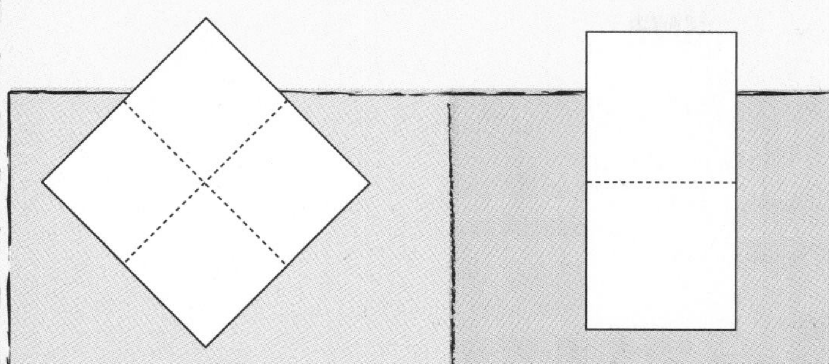

Color $\frac{3}{4}$ of this diamond red.

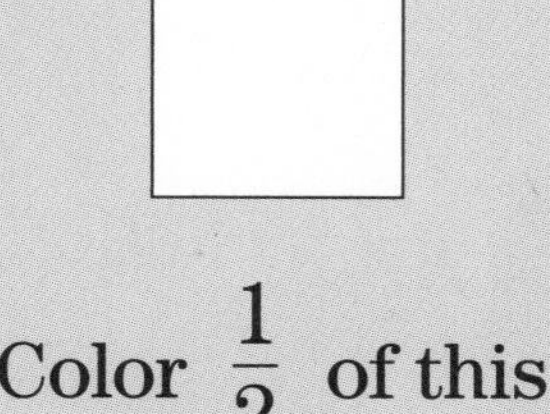

Color $\frac{1}{2}$ of this rectangle orange.

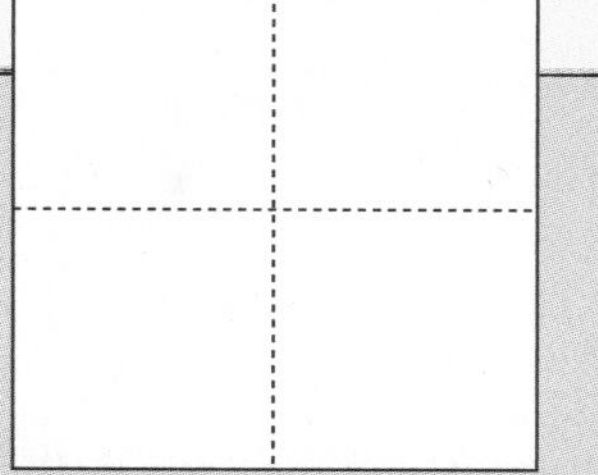

Color $\frac{1}{4}$ of this square blue.

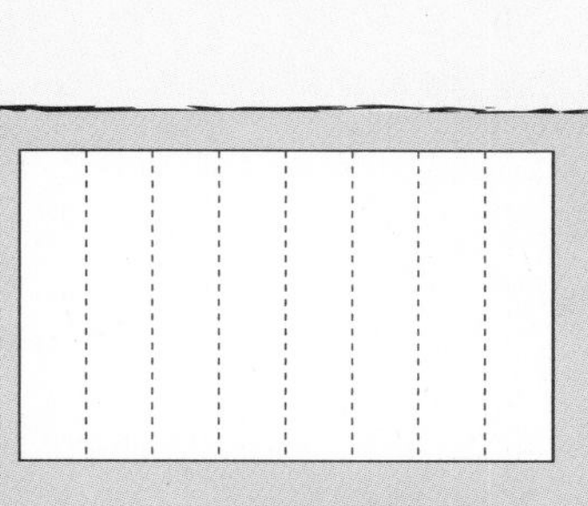

Color $\frac{2}{8}$ of this rectangle green.

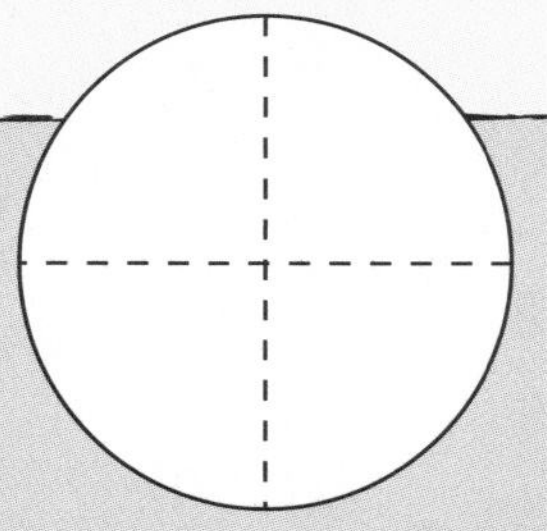

Color $\frac{2}{4}$ of this circle purple.

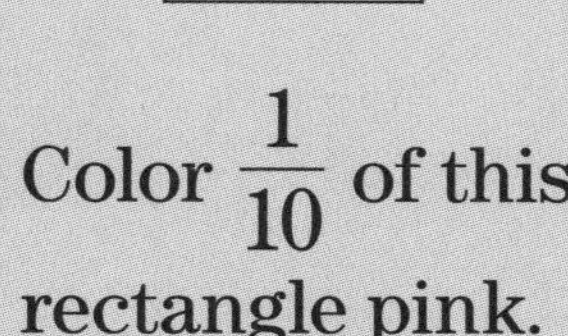

Color $\frac{1}{10}$ of this rectangle pink.

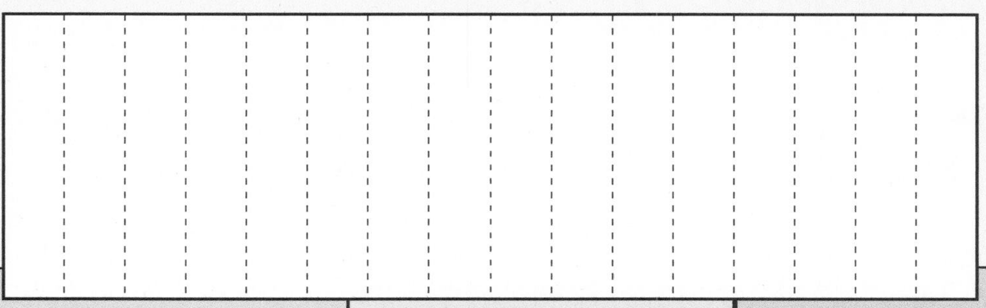

Color $\frac{1}{16}$ of this rectangle red.

Color $\frac{2}{16}$ of this rectangle blue.

Color $\frac{4}{16}$ of this rectangle purple.

Color $\frac{3}{16}$ of this rectangle orange.

Color $\frac{5}{16}$ of this rectangle green.

What fraction of the rectangle is left white? $\frac{\square}{\square}$

Fractions and Decimals

Fraction basics

The Dog Show

Use the picture to answer the questions.

What fraction of the dogs are spotted? $\frac{3}{10}$

What fraction of the dogs are brown?

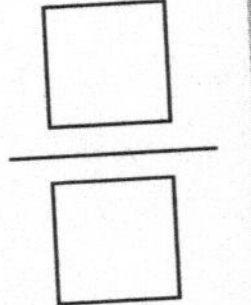

What fraction of the dogs are black?

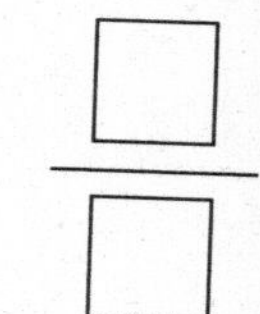

What fraction of the dogs have a bone?

What fraction of the dogs are standing?

Be Fair!

Answer the following **fraction** problems.

Mr. Johnson has 9 dollar bills. He wants to divide them equally and give an equal number to each of his 3 sons. Divide the dollars into 3 equal parts by circling each part.

Ms. Mathias has 10 cookies to hand out to her students. She has 5 children in her class. Divide the cookies evenly so that each student receives the same amount of cookies.

Tammy has 16 strawberries. She wants to divide them evenly between herself and her 3 friends. Divide the strawberries into 4 equal parts by circling each part.

Rosie's Restaurant

Read each **fraction** problem. Write the equation in the box. Then write your answer on the line.

Rosie's Restaurant has 20 tables. $\frac{1}{4}$ of the tables are empty. How many of the tables are empty?

20 ÷ 4 = 5

$\frac{1}{4}$ of 20 = 5

There are 6 diners at one of the tables. $\frac{1}{2}$ of those 6 diners have ordered chicken. How many have ordered chicken?

÷ =

$\frac{1}{2}$ of 6 = ____

10 diners are sitting at a corner table. $\frac{1}{5}$ of them have ordered peach pie. How many have ordered peach pie?

÷ =

$\frac{1}{5}$ of 10 = ____

There is a group of 8 people waiting to be seated. $\frac{1}{2}$ of those people are men. How many in that group are men?

÷ =

$\frac{1}{2}$ of 8 = ____

Fractions and Decimals

Dividing whole numbers into fractions

Brain Box

When dividing whole numbers into fractions, look at the numerator of a fraction. If the numerator is 1, divide the whole number by the **denominator.**

Solve the **fraction** problems.

At a table with 4 diners, $\frac{1}{2}$ have ordered baked potatoes. How many have ordered baked potatoes?

__ ÷ __ = __

$\frac{1}{2}$ of 4 = _____

There are 15 different desserts on the menu. $\frac{1}{3}$ of them are cakes. How many of the desserts are cakes?

__ ÷ __ = __

$\frac{1}{3}$ of 15 = _____

There are 16 burgers on the grill. $\frac{1}{2}$ of them have cheese on them. How many are cheeseburgers?

__ ÷ __ = __

$\frac{1}{2}$ of 16 = _____

At a table in the back there are 15 diners. $\frac{1}{5}$ of them have ordered spare ribs. How many have ordered spare ribs?

__ ÷ __ = __

$\frac{1}{5}$ of 15 = _____

At a table near the door, a couple had ordered a large pizza that was cut in 12 slices. They left $\frac{1}{6}$ of it uneaten because they were too full. How many slices didn't they eat?

__ ÷ __ = __

$\frac{1}{6}$ of 12 = _____

Exactly the Same

Color $\frac{1}{2}$ of this rectangle yellow.

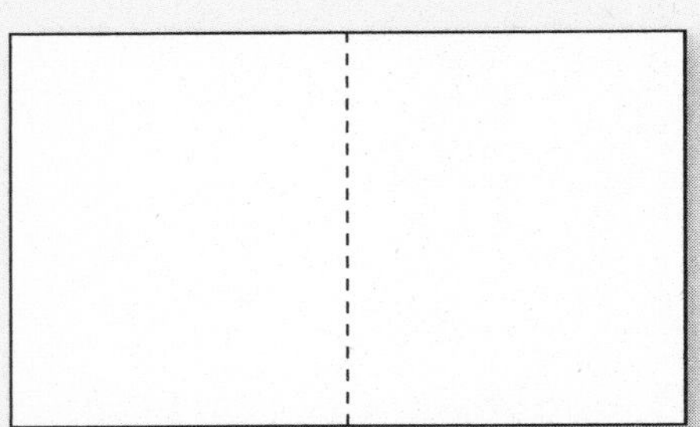

Color $\frac{2}{4}$ of this rectangle yellow.

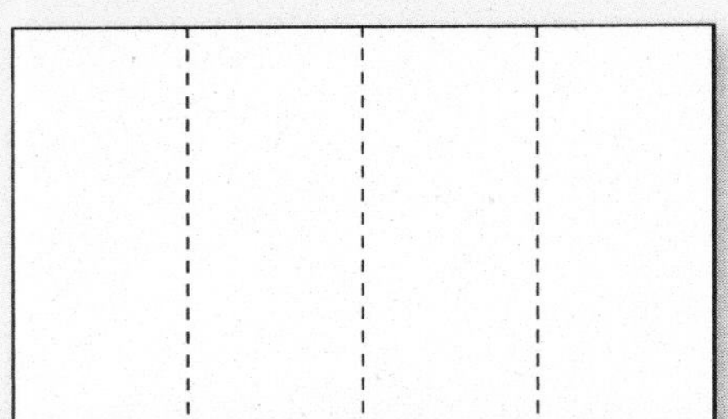

$\frac{1}{2}$ and $\frac{2}{4}$ both equal the same parts of the whole.

They are **equivalent fractions.**

Write the equivalent fractions for each figure.

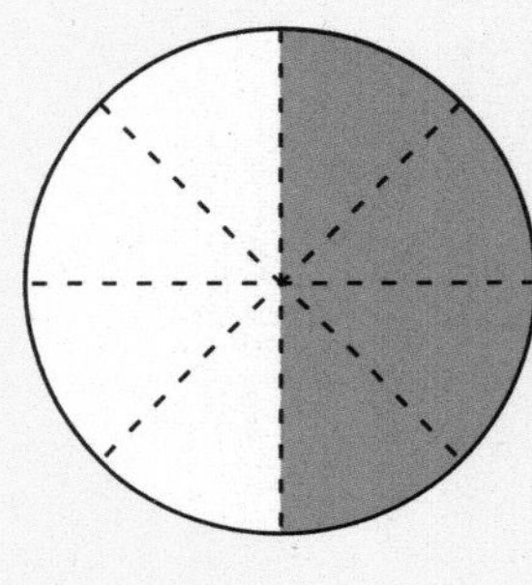

$\frac{4}{8}$

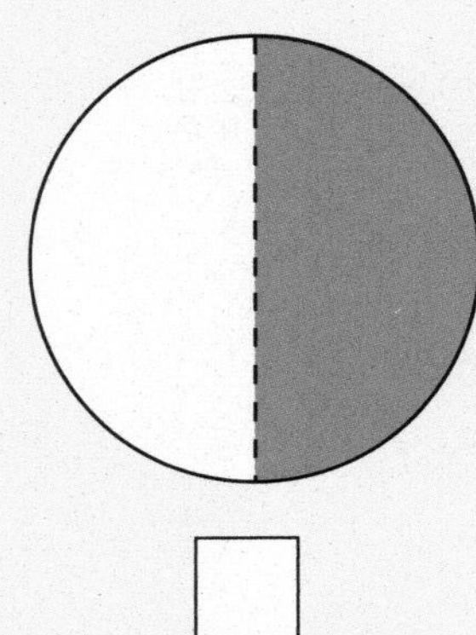

$\frac{\square}{\square}$

Fractions and Decimals

Equivalent fractions

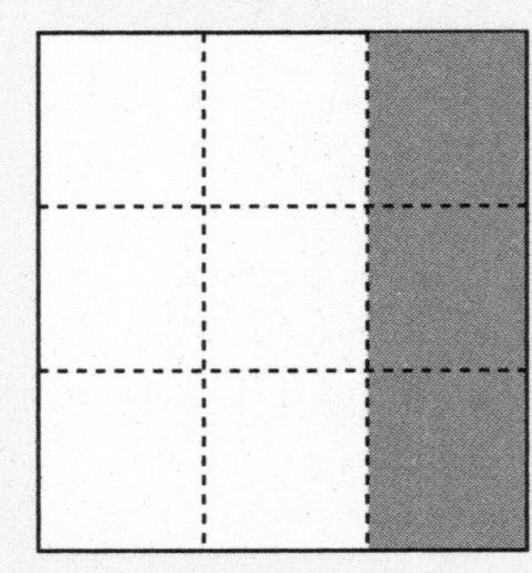

$\frac{3}{9}$

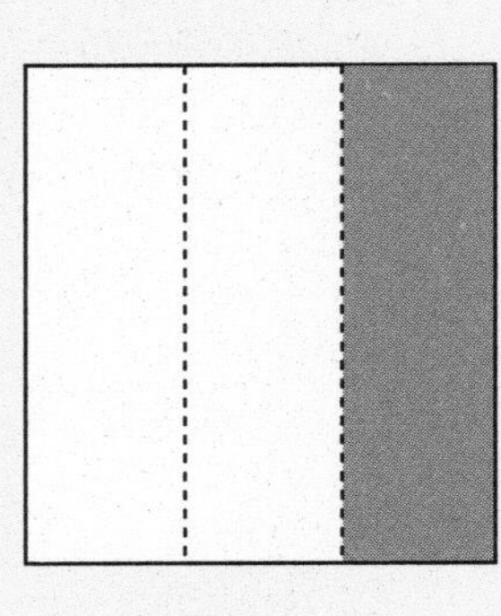

$\frac{\square}{\square}$

Adding Fractions

Add the fractions.

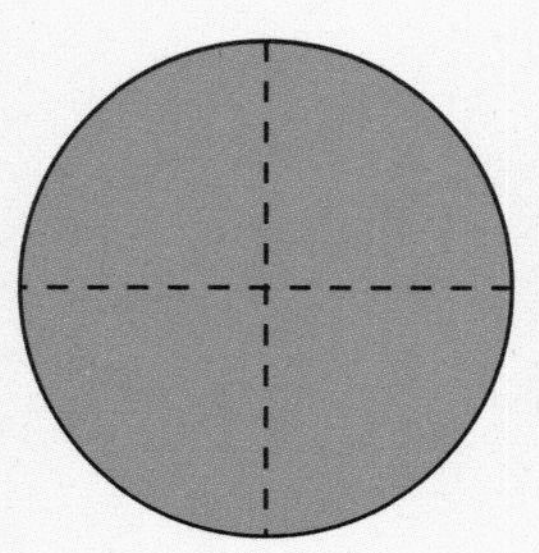

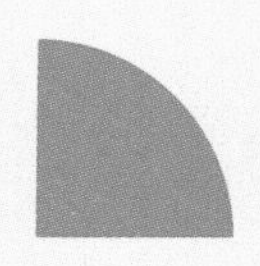

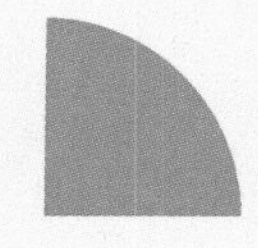

$\frac{1}{4} + \frac{1}{4} = \frac{2}{4}$

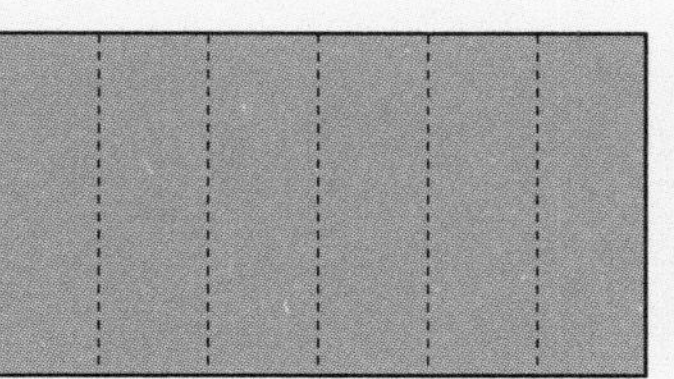

$\frac{2}{6} + \frac{3}{6} = \frac{\square}{\square}$

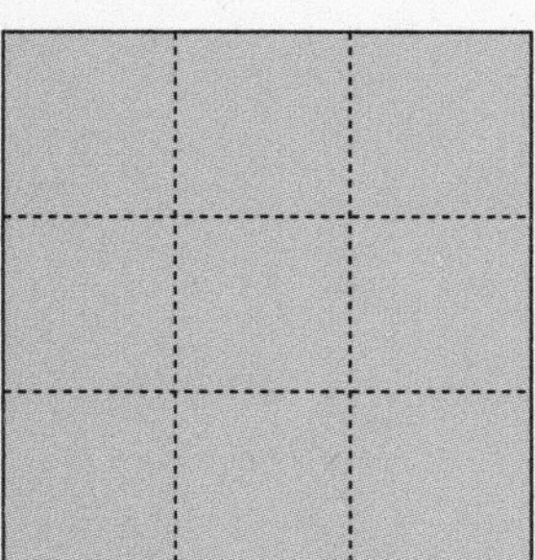

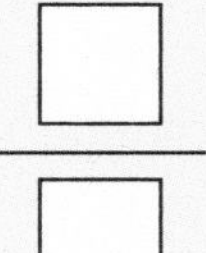

$\frac{1}{9} + \frac{3}{9} = \frac{\square}{\square}$

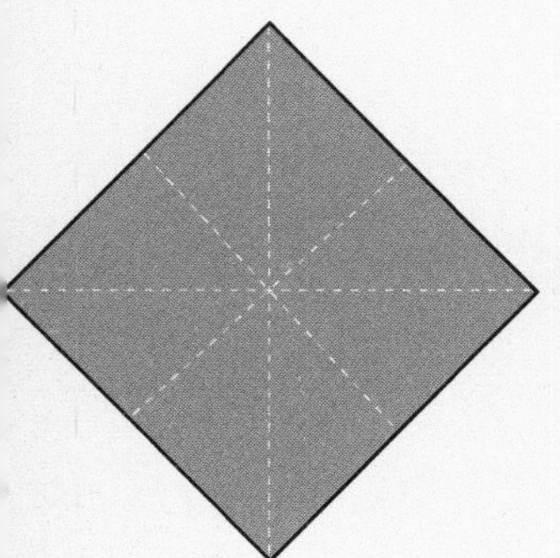

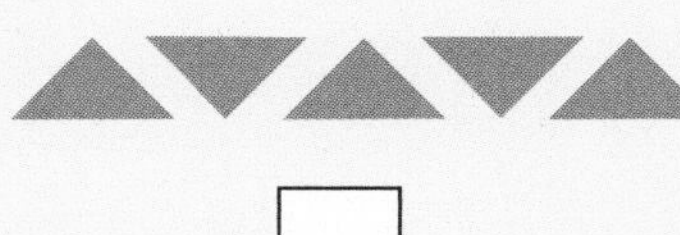

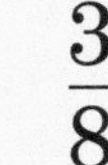

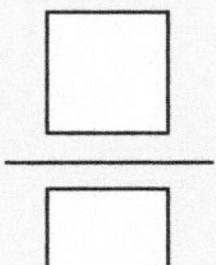

$\frac{3}{8} + \frac{2}{8} = \frac{\square}{\square}$

Brain Box

To **add fractions** that have the same denominator, simply add the numerators. The denominator remains the same.

Adding Fractions

Add the fractions.

$\frac{1}{3} + \frac{1}{3} = \frac{2}{3}$

$\frac{1}{5} + \frac{3}{5} = \frac{\square}{\square}$

$\frac{1}{4} + \frac{3}{4} = \frac{\square}{\square}$

$\frac{2}{4} + \frac{1}{4} = \frac{\square}{\square}$

$\frac{8}{10} + \frac{1}{10} = \frac{\square}{\square}$

$\frac{3}{6} + \frac{1}{6} = \frac{\square}{\square}$

$\frac{8}{12} + \frac{1}{12} = \frac{\square}{\square}$

$\frac{3}{8} + \frac{4}{8} = \frac{\square}{\square}$

Jared and Derek each ate $\frac{1}{5}$ of a pie.
What fraction of the pie was eaten altogether?

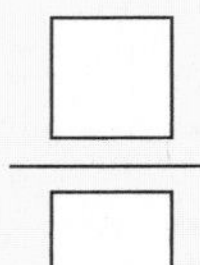

Jen poured $\frac{1}{4}$ cup of flour into the cake mix.
Her mother poured in another $\frac{1}{4}$ cup.
How much flour was in the cake mix?

Subtracting Fractions

Subtract the fractions.

$\frac{5}{6} - \frac{1}{6} = \frac{4}{6}$

$\frac{4}{5} - \frac{2}{5} = \frac{\square}{\square}$

$\frac{8}{7} - \frac{4}{7} = \frac{\square}{\square}$

$\frac{3}{4} - \frac{1}{4} = \frac{\square}{\square}$

$\frac{8}{12} - \frac{1}{12} = \frac{\square}{\square}$

$\frac{3}{8} - \frac{1}{8} = \frac{\square}{\square}$

$\frac{5}{10} - \frac{2}{10} = \frac{\square}{\square}$

$\frac{8}{9} - \frac{4}{9} = \frac{\square}{\square}$

Stephen and his brother Mark make up $\frac{2}{5}$ of the children in their family. What fraction do the other children in the family make up?

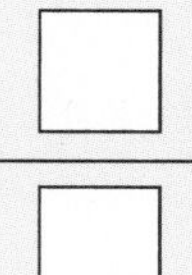

Diana picked $\frac{3}{6}$ of the apples from the tree. What fraction of the apples were left for Shareena to pick?

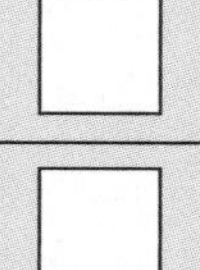

Brain Box

To **subtract fractions** that have the same denominators, simply subtract the numerators. The denominator remains the same.

Bits and Pieces

Write the fractions described by the words.

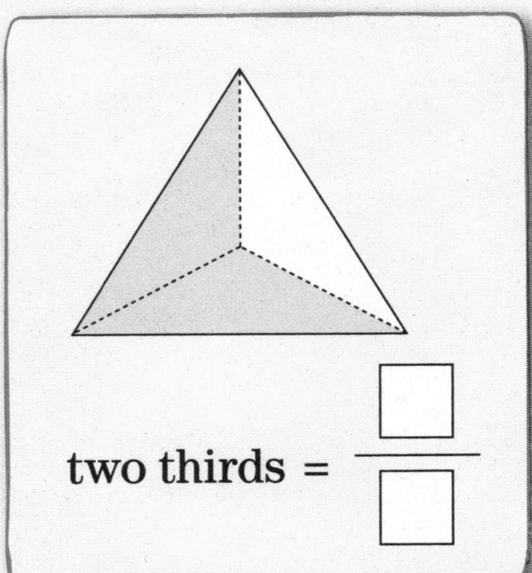

two thirds = $\frac{\square}{\square}$

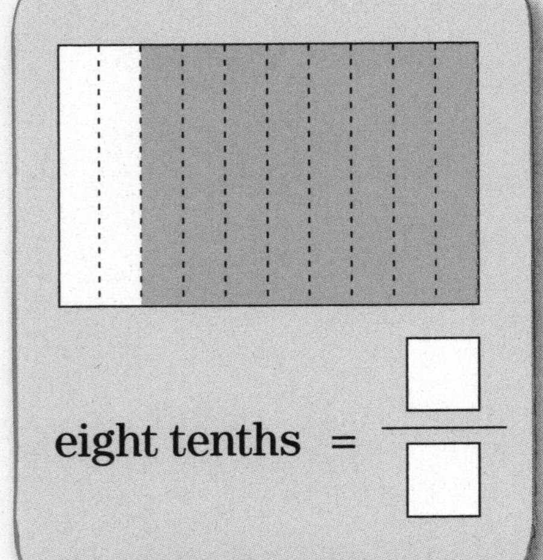

eight tenths = $\frac{\square}{\square}$

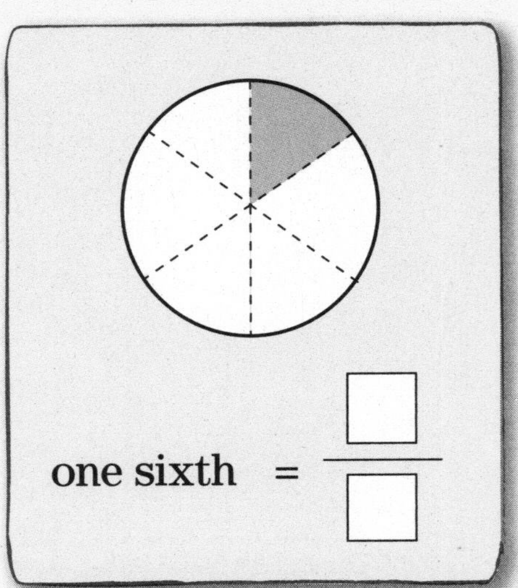

one sixth = $\frac{\square}{\square}$

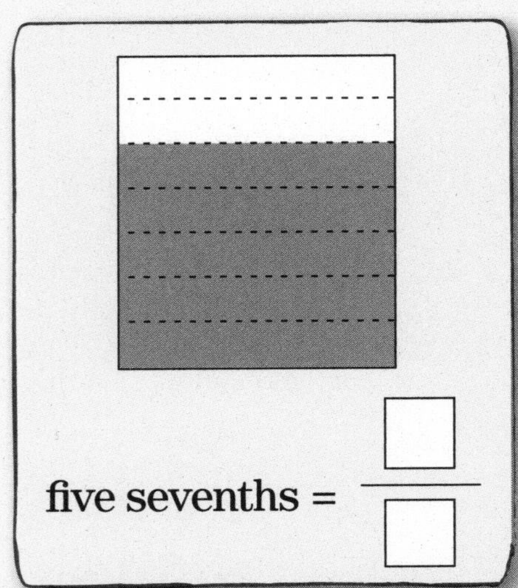

five sevenths = $\frac{\square}{\square}$

Answer each question. Show your work.

How much is $\frac{1}{3}$ of 21? 7

21 ÷ 3 = 7

How much is $\frac{1}{8}$ of 16? ____

How much is $\frac{1}{2}$ of 18? ____

How much is $\frac{1}{10}$ of 20? ____

How much is $\frac{1}{4}$ of 24? ____

Fractions and Decimals

Fractions review

Answer each question.

Jasmine ate $\frac{3}{8}$ of the raisins. What fraction of the raisins were left? $\frac{\square}{\square}$

Sean ate $\frac{3}{10}$ of the walnuts. Josh ate $\frac{4}{10}$ of the walnuts. What fraction of the walnuts were left? $\frac{\square}{\square}$

What whole number is equal to $\frac{7}{7} + \frac{7}{7}$? _____

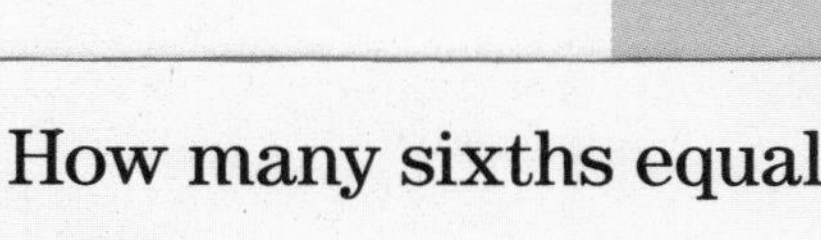

How many sixths equal one? _____

Draw a line from each fraction in the left column to the equivalent fraction in the right column.

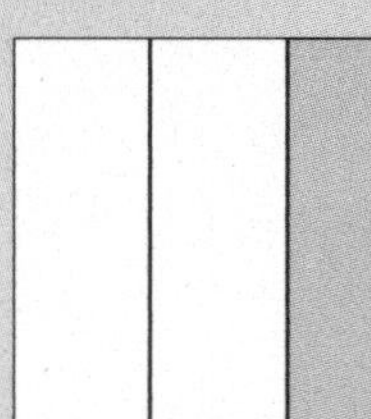

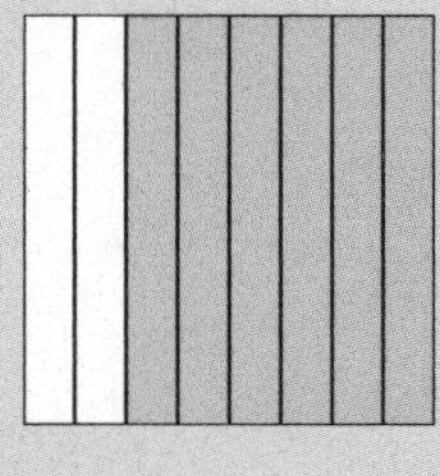

REMEMBER:
When a fraction has the same numerator and denominator, the fraction equals 1.

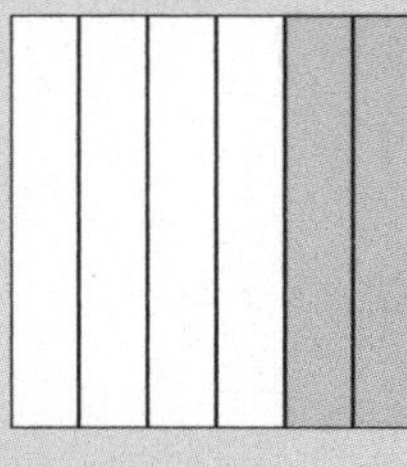

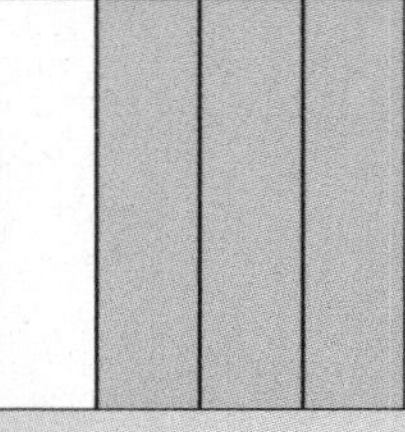

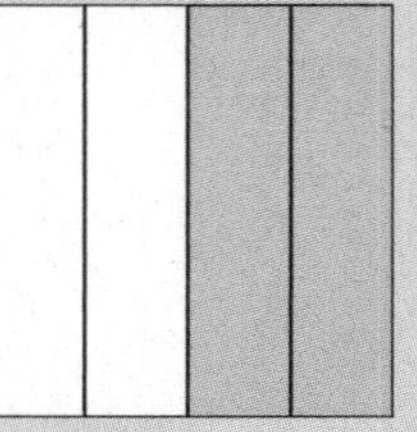

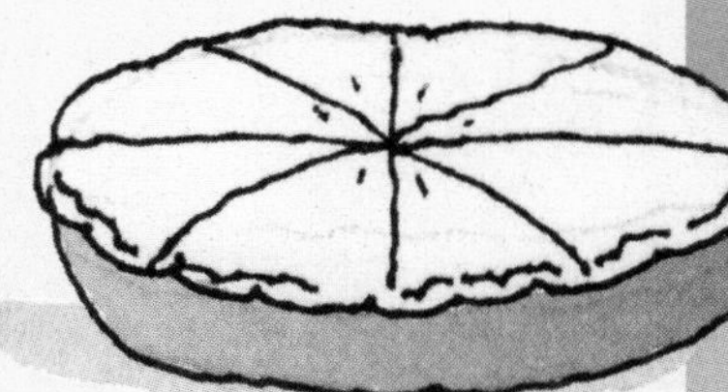

Juanita ate $\frac{1}{2}$ of the pie at lunch and the other $\frac{1}{2}$ after school. What fraction of the pie did she eat? $\frac{\square}{\square}$

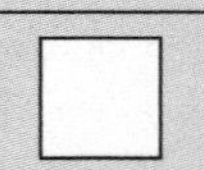

What's the Point?

What fraction of each shape is shaded?
Write the fraction and its **decimal** equivalent.

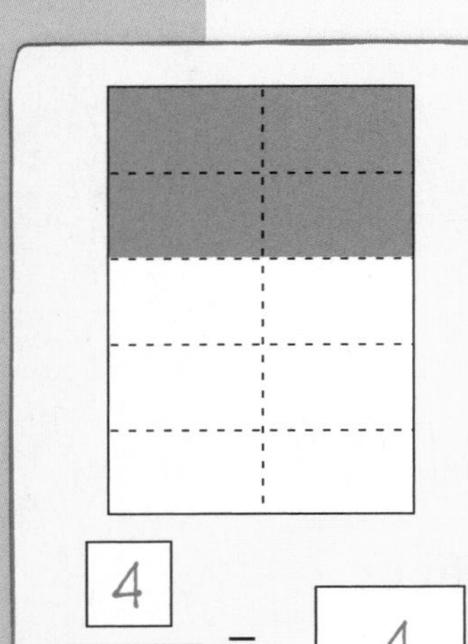

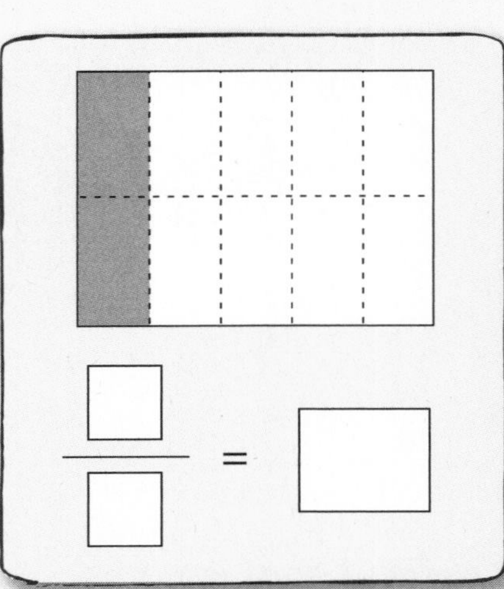

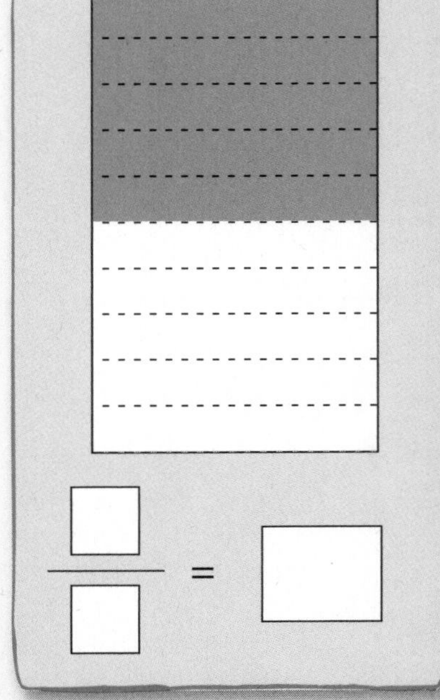

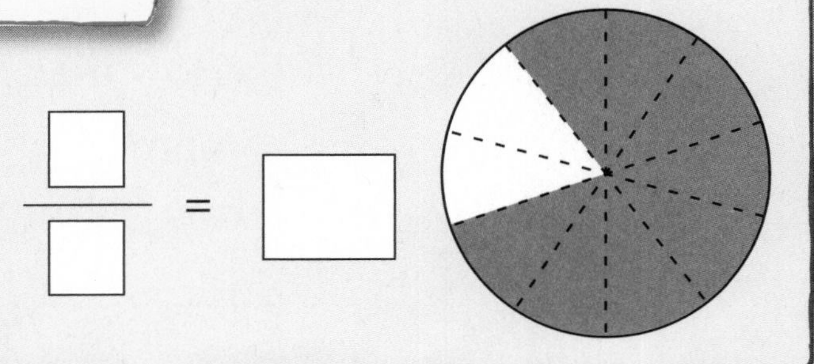

Convert each fraction to a decimal.

$\frac{9}{10}$ = ____

$\frac{1}{10}$ = ____

$\frac{4}{10}$ = ____

$\frac{2}{10}$ = ____

$\frac{5}{10}$ = ____

$\frac{7}{10}$ = ____

Fractions and Decimals

Brain Box

A **decimal** is a number that contains a decimal point followed by a number or numbers to the right of the point.

The first decimal to the right of the decimal point is in the **tenths place.**

Example: **.8** (tenths; decimal point)

.8 tells us there are **8 tenths** or $\frac{8}{10}$

Convert each decimal to a fraction.

.6 = $\frac{\square}{\square}$

.8 = $\frac{\square}{\square}$

.1 = $\frac{\square}{\square}$

This square has 100 equal parts.

What fraction of the square is shaded in?

Write your answer as a decimal. _____

Convert each fraction to a decimal.

$\frac{3}{100}$ = .03

$\frac{2}{100}$ = _____

$\frac{5}{100}$ = _____

$\frac{9}{100}$ = _____

$\frac{8}{100}$ = _____

$\frac{6}{100}$ = _____

Convert each decimal to a fraction.

.09 = $\frac{\square}{\square}$

.01 = $\frac{\square}{\square}$

.04 = $\frac{\square}{\square}$

Fractions and Decimals

Brain Box

The second digit to the right of the decimal point is in the **hundredths place.**

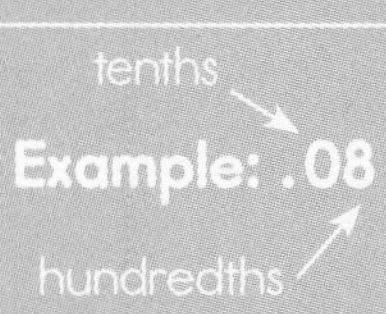

.08 tells us there are **8** hundredths or $\frac{8}{100}$

More to the Point

Answer the questions using the information on the card.

What is the place value of the **9** in the number above?

____

Fractions and Decimals

Decimal place values

Which digit is in the hundredths place? ____________________

Which digit is in the tens place? ____________________

What is the place value of the **5**? ____________________

Write the number as a mixed fraction. ____________________

Thousandths

Answer each question.

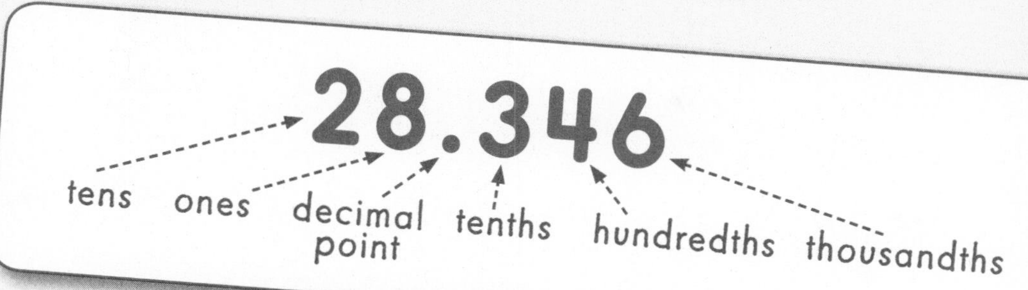

What is the place value of the **6** in the number above?

____

Write the number that says 8 tens, 5 ones, 3 tenths, 4 hundredths, 1 thousandth. ____________

Which numeral is in the thousandths place in the number 3.862? ____________

Write the number that says 3 tens, 2 ones, 4 tenths, 7 hundredths, 9 thousandths. ____________

Write the decimal number for three and one hundredth.

____

Write the number that says 4 tens, 0 ones, 0 tenths, 0 hundredths, 1 thousandth. ____________

Write the decimal number for five and one thousandth.

____

Fractions and Decimals

Decimal place values

Decimal Sums

Find the **sum.** Show your work.

5.6 + 1.2 6.8	7.3 + 6.6	3.7 + 2.8
8.17 + 2.3	9.14 + 3.73	4.25 + 3.71
4.85 + 3.22	6.38 + 2.17	8.49 + 2.45
5.33 + 6.27	9.75 + 1.82	7.64 + 1.85

Fractions and Decimals

Adding decimals

Brain Box

To **add decimals,** make sure that the decimal points are lined up. Add the numbers the same way you would in an ordinary equation. Then carry the decimal point directly down into your answer.

Example:

```
   1
  5.63
+ 4.85
 10.48
```

Decimal Differences

Find the **difference.** Show your work.

4.8 – 1.6 3.2	7.3 – 5.1	3.99 – 3.63
6.78 – 2.33	8.17 – 3.04	3.88 – 1.29
9.71 – 4.52	7.77 – 2.83	6.55 – 3.29
5.81 – 1.77	9.63 – 4.82	4.78 – 2.96

Brain Box

To **subtract decimals,** make sure that the decimal points are lined up. Subtract the numbers the same way you would in an ordinary equation. Then carry the decimal point directly down into your answer.

Example:
```
  4.36
- 2.14
  2.22
```

Connecting the Dots

Connect each **fraction** in the left column with an equivalent **decimal** in the right column.

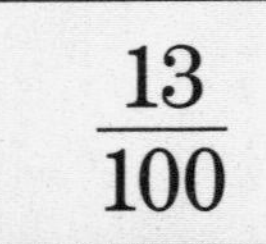 $\frac{13}{100}$	0.06
$\frac{6}{100}$	0.5
$\frac{5}{10}$	0.03
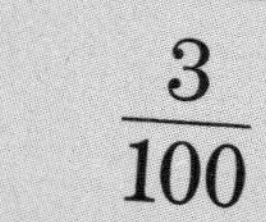 $\frac{3}{100}$	0.4
$\frac{4}{10}$	0.13
$\frac{1}{10}$	0.1
$\frac{1}{100}$	0.11
$\frac{7}{100}$	0.07
$\frac{6}{10}$	0.01
$\frac{11}{100}$	0.6

Fractions and Decimals

Equivalent decimals and fractions

Measurement

Is Your Foot a Foot Long?

Answer the questions about measuring **length.** Use the measurement cards to help with your calculations.

12 inches (in.) = **1 foot (ft.)**

36 inches (in.) or 3 feet (ft.) = **1 yard (yd.)**

1,760 yards (yds.) or 5,280 feet (ft.) = **1 mile (mi.)**

Which unit of measurement would you use to measure:

- the length of your big toe ____________
- the distance between two airports ____________
- the height of a man ____________

Circle the best measurement for each.

the length of a worm

3 inches	3 feet	3 yards

the height of a giraffe

15 inches	15 feet	15 miles

the width of a house

7 inches	7 feet	7 yards

the height of a door

7 inches	7 feet	7 miles

the length of a football field

100 inches	100 feet	100 yards

Measurement

Standard linear measurements

Brain Box

Inches, feet, yards, and **miles** are the standard units of measurement for **length** used in the United States.

Write =, >, or < to show the relationship between each pair of measurements.

20 inches ☐ 2 feet

2 yards ☐ 72 inches

6 feet ☐ 3 yards

10 feet ☐ 120 inches

1 mile ☐ 5,000 feet

Answer each question.

How many inches is 3 feet? ________

How many feet is 10 yards? ________

How many yards is 36 inches? ________

How many inches is $1\frac{1}{2}$ feet? ________

How many yards is 12 feet? ________

How many feet are in 2 miles? ________

Brain Box

To show that two things have the same value, use the **equal** sign.

Example: 12 inches = 1 foot

To show that a value is greater than another value, use the **greater than** sign.

Example: 3 feet > 2 feet

To show that a value is less than another value, use the **less than** sign.

Example: 8 inches < 12 inches

How Long Is That Ant?

Answer the questions about measuring length using the metric system.

100 centimeters (cm) = **1 meter (m)**

1,000 meters (m) = **1 kilometer (km)**

HINT: A kilometer is kind of like the metric equivalent of a mile: it measures long distances.

Which unit of measurement would you use to measure:

- the length of a finger? ____________
- the distance a plane travels? ____________
- the height of a door? ____________

Circle the best measurement for each.

the length of a long distance race:

41 centimeters | 41 meters | 41 kilometers

HINT: A meter is kind of like the metric equivalent of a yard.

the height of a basketball player:

2 meters | 2 centimeters | 2 kilometers

the length of a paper clip:

3 centimeters | 3 meters | 3 kilometers

the length of a rattlesnake:

$1\frac{1}{2}$ centimeters | $1\frac{1}{2}$ meters | $1\frac{1}{2}$ kilometers

HINT: A centimeter is kind of like the metric equivalent of an inch: it measures small things.

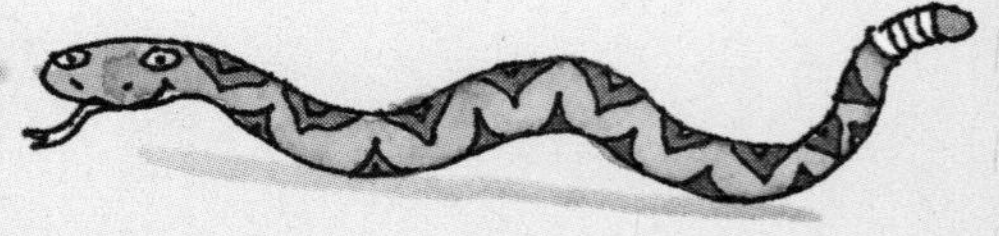

Measurement

Metric linear measurements

Brain Box

The **metric system** is based on the number 10. **Centimeters, meters,** and **kilometers** are the units of length in the metric system.

American vs. Metric

Cut out the ruler at the bottom of the page. Use it to measure the following items. Write the answers using the standard unit of measurement and the metric system.

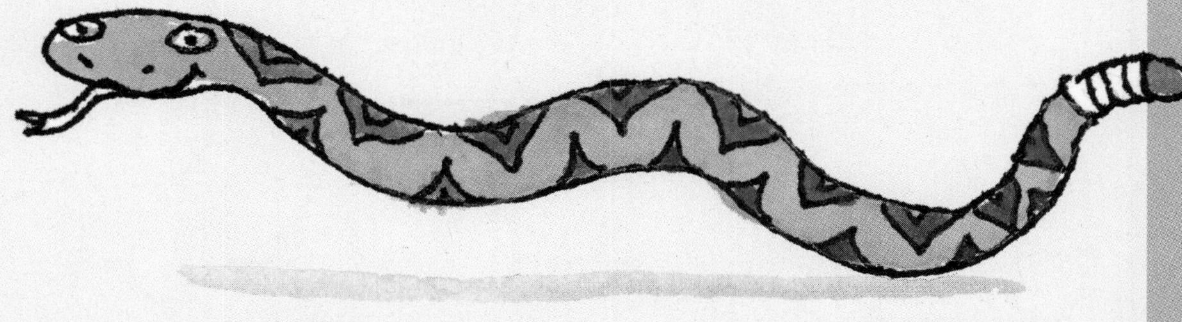

_____________ inches _____________ centimeters

_____________ inches _____________ centimeters

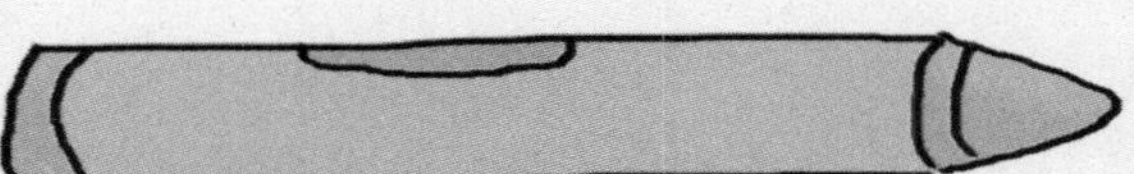

_____________ inches _____________ centimeters

Measurement

Standard measurements

INCHES 1 2 3 4 5 6 7

CENTIMETERS 1 2 3 4 5 6 7 8 9 10 11 12 13 14 15 16 17 18 19 20

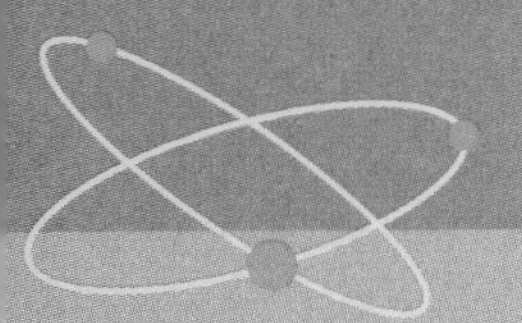

The Mad Scientists

Answer the questions. Use the measurement cards to help you with your calculations.

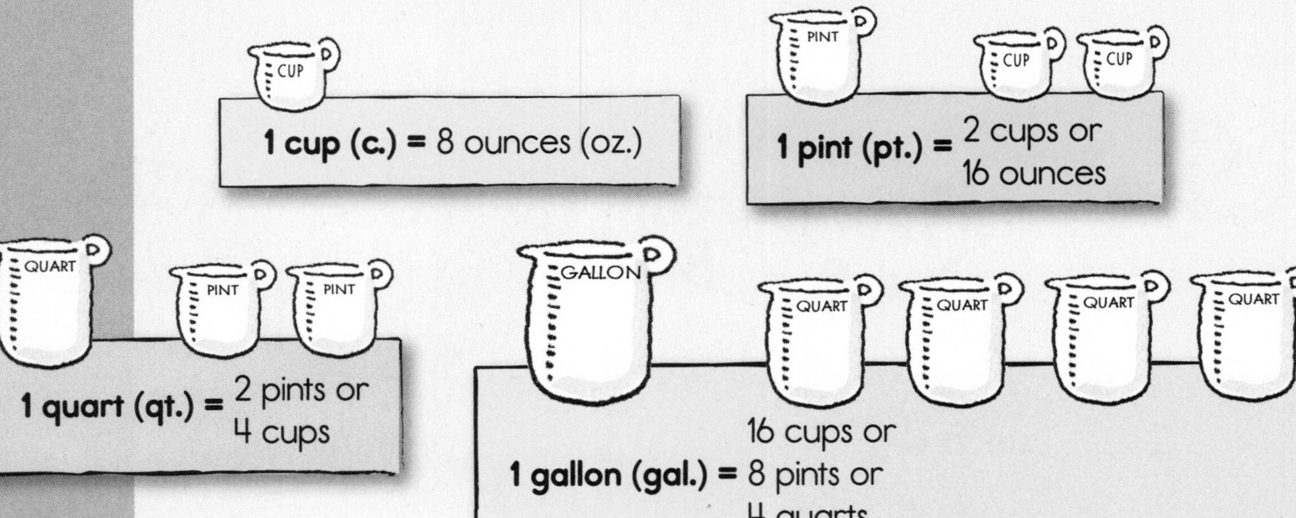

Dr. Wack, the inventor, is making a hair removal tonic.

He needs 2 pints of swamp slime.
How many cups does he need? __________

His recipe calls for 4 gallons of mud.
How many quarts does he need? __________

Dr. Frank N. Stein is developing a cure for the common cold.

His formula calls for 16 ounces of melted chicken fat.
How many cups will he need? __________

He needs 4 quarts of snail ooze.
How many pints is that? __________

Now That's Heavy!

Write **ounces, pounds,** or **tons** to tell which unit of measurement you would use to measure each thing.

16 ounces (oz.) = **1 pound (lb.)**

2,000 pounds (lbs.) = **1 ton**

a strawberry ________

a bicycle ________

a flower ________

a dog ________

a dump truck ________

a boy ________

an elephant ________

Measurement

Standard weight measurements

Brain Box

Ounces, pounds, and **tons** are the standard units of measurement for **weight** used in the United States.

Measuring Inside

Find the **area** of the figure.

How many square units are inside this rectangle?

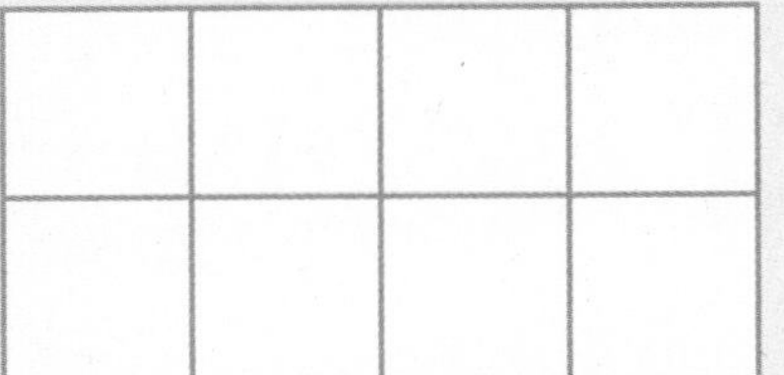

____

That means the **area** of the rectangle is ________ square units.

Write the area below each figure.

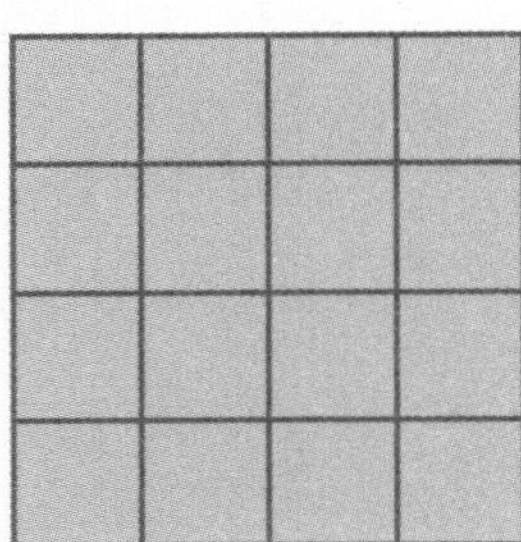

________ square units

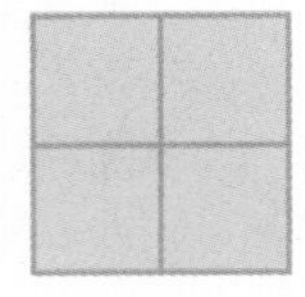

________ square units

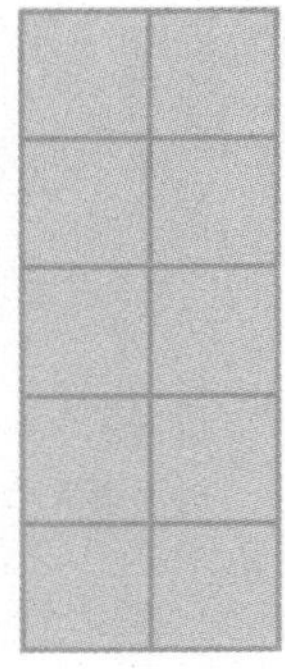

________ square units

________ square units

________ square units

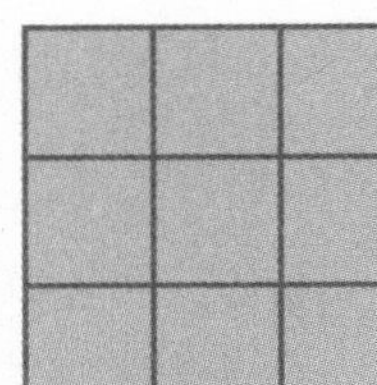

________ square units

Measurement

Area

Brain Box

The **area** of a figure is the number of **square units** inside a figure.

Answer the questions.

width

length

What is this figure's length?

_______ square units

What is this figure's width?

_______ square units

The area of this figure = _______ × _______
width length

What is the total area of this figure? _______ square units

Write the area for each figure.

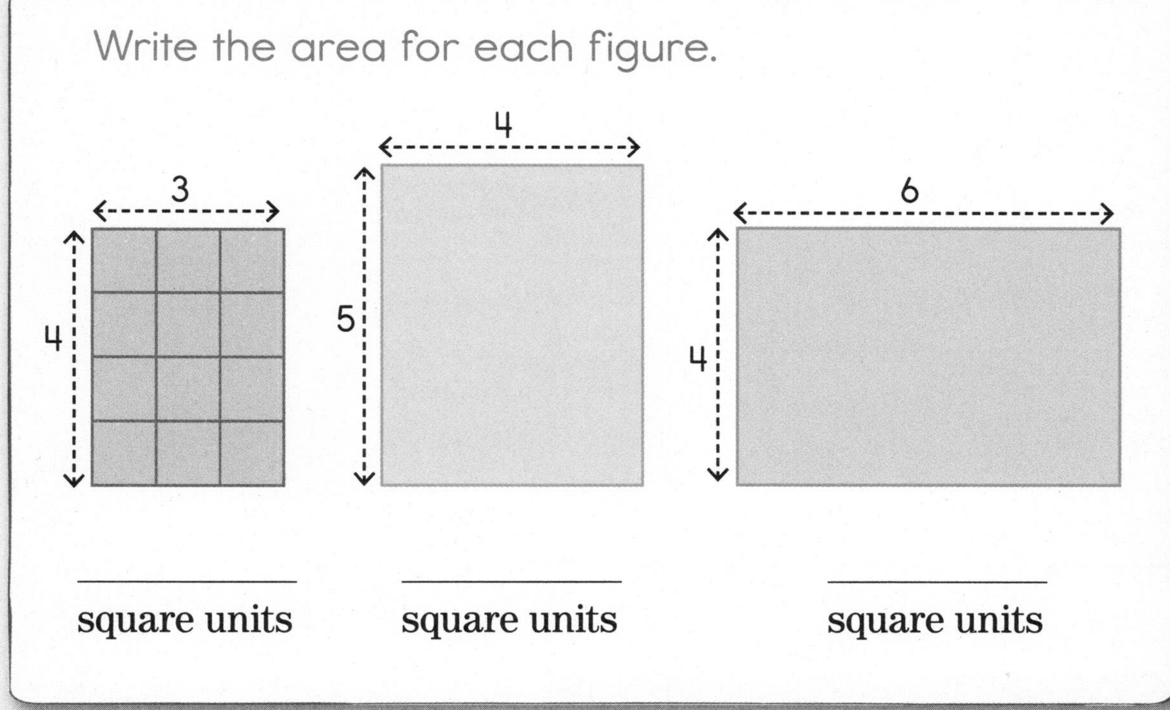

Measurement

Area

Matt has a poster of the wrestling star, the Brawler, which measures 6 feet long by 4 feet wide. What is the area of his poster? _______

Brain Box

You can find the area of a figure by multiplying its **length** by its **width.**

Let's Go Around

Write the **perimeter** below each geometric figure. Make sure to label your answer either feet (ft.) or inches (in.).

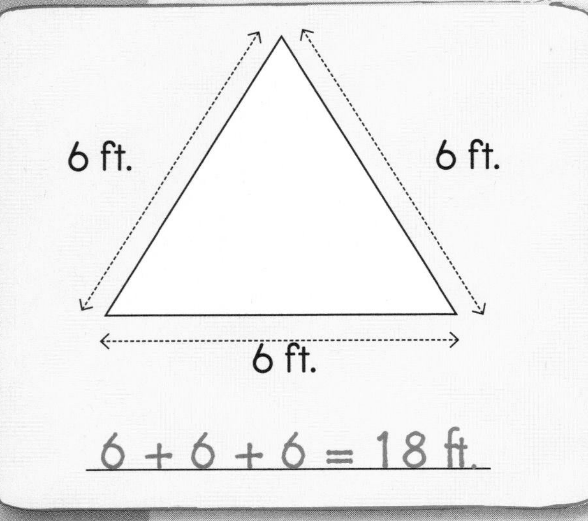

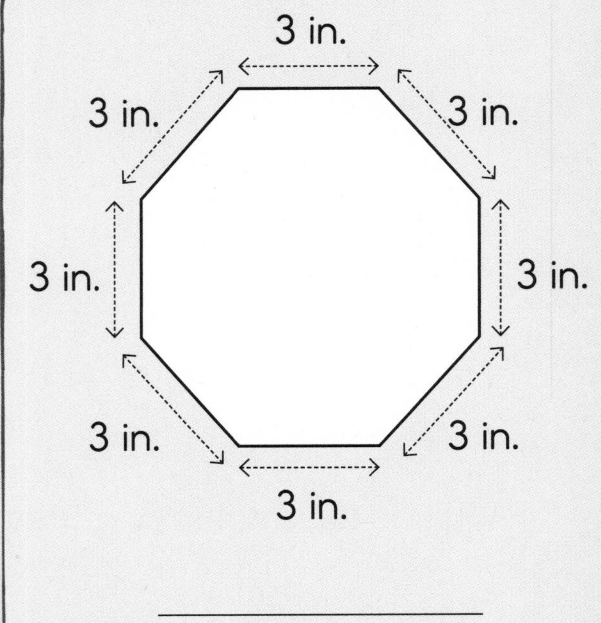

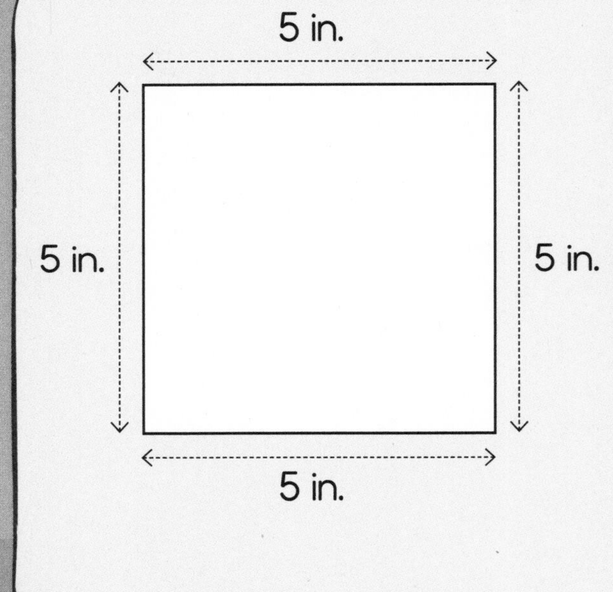

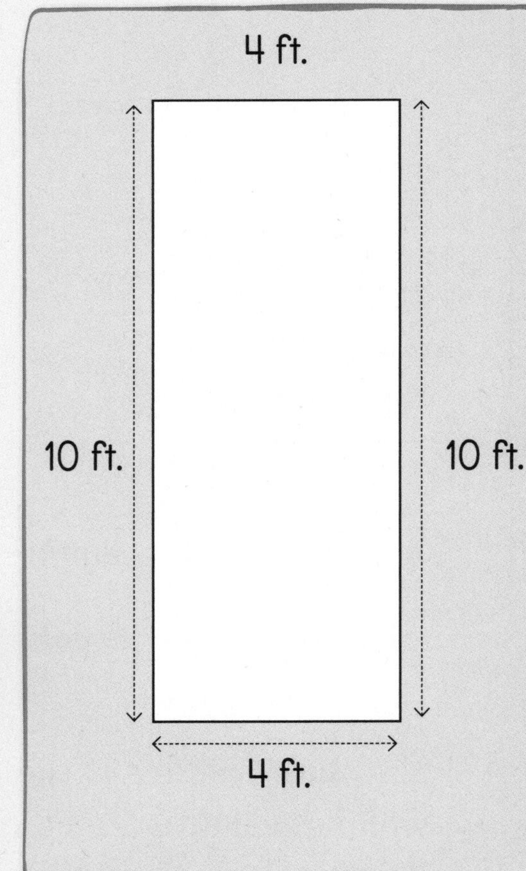

Measurement

Perimeter

Brain Box

The **perimeter** is the distance around a figure. You can find the perimeter by adding the lengths of the sides.

For example: This rug is 3 feet long and 1 foot wide. Its perimeter is 8 feet.

(3 + 3 + 1 + 1 = 8)

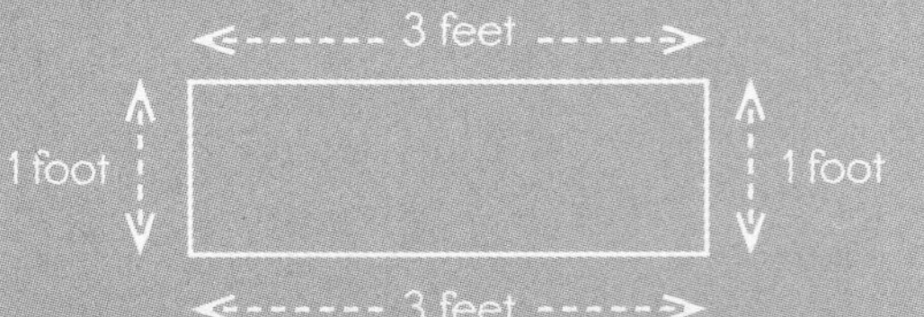

Time and Money

It's About Time

Write the **time** below each clock.

24 hours = 1 day

60 minutes = 1 hour

60 seconds = 1 minute

:

:

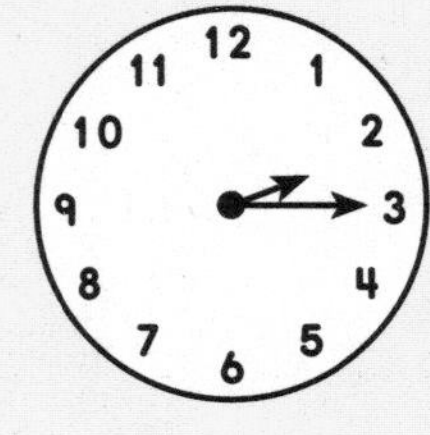

:

:

Brain Box

Seconds, minutes, and **hours** are all measurements of time.

There are several ways to read time.

For example:
This clock shows that the time is **4:50.**

You can also say or read the time as **50 minutes after four** or **10 minutes to five.**

:

:

:

:

:

:

Time and Money

Telling time

:

:

:

Answer the questions.

It's 20 minutes to 7. How does a digital clock show this time?

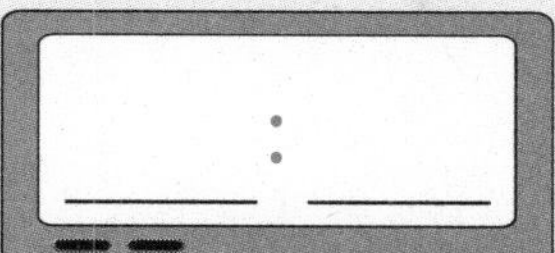

It's 7:30 a.m. How does a digital clock show this time?

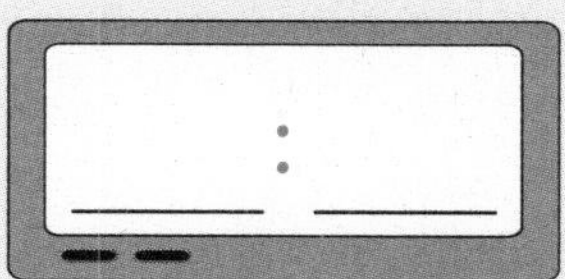

Rick's fastest time in the race was 50 seconds. Nick's fastest time was 1 minute. Who was faster?

____

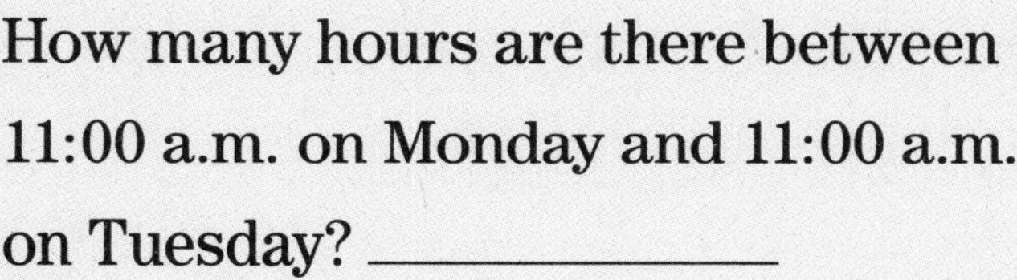

How many hours are there between 11:00 a.m. on Monday and 11:00 a.m. on Tuesday? _______________

Luke and his friends went on a $1\frac{1}{2}$ hour hike. How many minutes long was their hike?

____

Kate finished the race in $1\frac{1}{2}$ minutes. What was her time in seconds? _______________

Brain Box

- The hours between 12:00 midnight and 12:00 noon are **a.m. hours.**
- The hours between 12:00 noon and 12:00 midnight are **p.m. hours.**

Time and Money

Telling time

As Time Goes By

Answer the questions. Be sure to include **a.m.** or **p.m.** in your answer if appropriate.

Waldo the Wondrous started his magic show at 2:30 p.m. He finished his show at 4:00 p.m. How long was his show? ____________

The Dynamites started baseball practice at 3:45 p.m. If practice lasted for 1 hour and 15 minutes, what time did it end? ____________

Justin went to see a movie at Startime Cinema that was 2 hours and 5 minutes long. It started at 6:15 p.m. What time did it end? ____________

The Bohidars ate pancakes from 8:15 a.m. to 9:00 a.m. How long were they eating pancakes? ____________

Raman's bowling party lasted for $1\frac{1}{2}$ hours. If it ended at 4:00 p.m., what time did it start? ____________

Rock Daddy's radio show is on from 10:30 a.m. until 11:45 a.m. How long is his show on? ____________

Time and Money

Elapsed time

The skating party at Roxie's Rollerdome started at 6:30 p.m. and ended at 8:15 p.m. How long did the party last? ___________

Kenji went to the park at 10:00 a.m. and left at 11:55 a.m. How long was he at the park?

____

Bridget gave a 15-minute speech on her trip to Mexico. She finished her speech at 11:00 a.m. What time did she start her speech?

____

At 4:35 p.m., Bill Brawny got a flat tire. It took him 20 minutes to change the tire and get back on the road. At what time did he get back on the road? ___________

Rosa's friends came over yesterday and stayed for 2 hours. If they left at 5:15 p.m., what time did they arrive? ___________

The Money Tree

Coins are falling off the money tree! How much money did these kids find?

penny = 1¢

nickel = 5¢

dime = 10¢

quarter = 25¢

Connor found 2 nickels and 1 quarter.
How much did he find? ____________

Kareem found 2 quarters, 5 dimes, and 5 pennies.
How much did he find? ____________

Paul found 8 dimes, 4 nickels, and 1 quarter.
How much did he find? ____________

Emily found 8 nickels. Laura found 2 dimes and 1 quarter.
Who found more money? ____________

Federico found 3 nickels, 6 dimes, and 2 quarters.
How much did he find? ____________

Allison found 4 quarters and 4 dimes. Denise found 10 nickels and 5 dimes. Who found more money? ____________

Add up the coins. Write the total sum on the line.

____

____

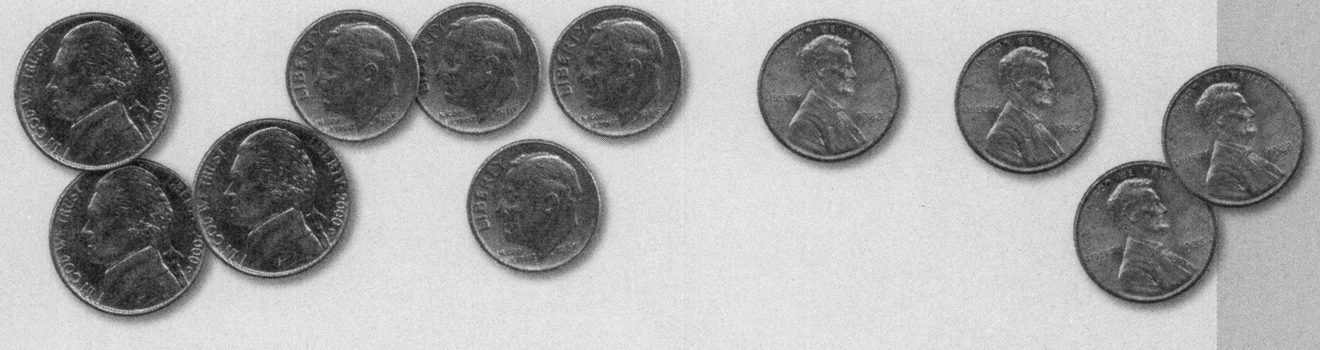

____

____

Yard Sale

Add and subtract using decimals.

\$3.57 + .12 \$3.69	\$3.00 + .42	\$2.75 – 1.15
\$3.54 – .44	\$8.99 – 7.99	\$9.99 + 2.99
\$6.28 + 5.72	\$6.50 – 1.30	\$8.70 + 1.11
\$5.24 – 3.83	\$7.07 + 2.20	\$7.31 – 6.69
\$2.52 + .35	\$4.95 – 4.93	\$10.00 – 1.33

At the Amusement Park

Add and subtract using decimals. Use the extra space on the cards as your work area.

A ticket to ride on the Thunderbolt costs $1.50. How much will it cost Daryl and his sister to ride on this ride? $3.00

$1.50
+ 1.50
$3.00

Cotton candy costs 60¢. Mrs. Gill bought one each for her son and her two daughters. She paid for them with $2.00. How much change should she get? ______

Diego bought four 80¢ tickets for rides on the Super Scorpion. How much did the tickets cost in all? ______

Melissa drove a bumper car for 75¢ and rode on the Ferris wheel for $1.25. How much did the rides cost? ______

The Whirl-a-Twirl costs $2.25. Takumi has 8 quarters and 2 dimes left. Does he have enough money for this ride?

______

Zoo Gift Shop

Ariana's third grade class bought souvenirs when they went to the zoo. Subtract using decimals to figure out how much change each student received.

Time and Money

Making change

Word Problems

All Together Now

Solve each **addition word problem.** Use the extra space on the cards as your work area. Write the answer in the white box.

There are 45 girls in the pool and 36 boys in the pool. How many children in all are in the pool?

$$\begin{array}{r} {}^{1} \\ 45 \\ +\ 36 \\ \hline 81 \end{array}$$

81

Aaron and his brother went fishing. Aaron caught 15 fish. His brother caught 9 fish. How many fish did they catch in all?

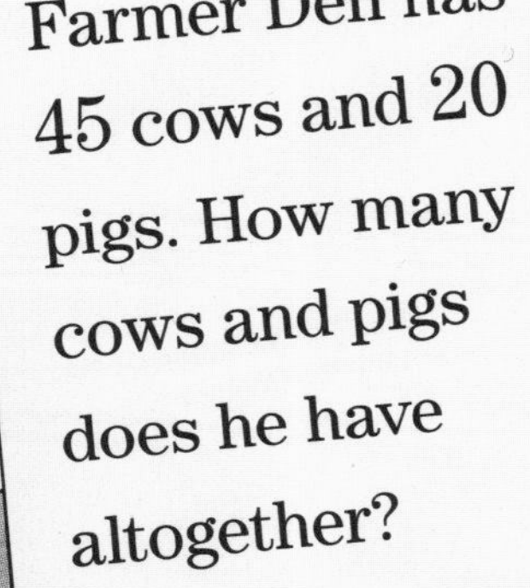

Farmer Dell has 45 cows and 20 pigs. How many cows and pigs does he have altogether?

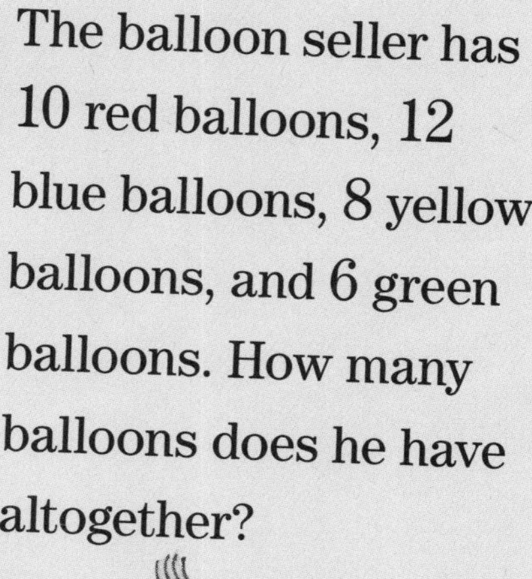

The balloon seller has 10 red balloons, 12 blue balloons, 8 yellow balloons, and 6 green balloons. How many balloons does he have altogether?

Brain Box

In **word problems** that ask about the **total** of two or more things, you need to **add.**

Word Problems

Addition

Solve the **addition word problems.**

Our school library had 55 biographies. The librarian just bought 19 more. A local bookstore donated another 31 biographies. What is the total number of biographies in the school library now?

Tamika swam 10 laps in the pool on Monday and 15 laps on Tuesday. Tony swam 18 laps on Wednesday and 20 laps on Thursday. How many laps did Tamika and Tony swim altogether by the end of the week?

Now it's time to write your own problem! Write an addition word problem and give it to a friend to solve.

Subtract It!

Solve each **subtraction word problem.** Use the extra space on the card as your work area. Write your answer in the white box.

Dulce sold 35 boxes of cookies for her Girl Scout troop. Meredith sold 47 boxes of Girl Scout cookies. How many more boxes of cookies did Meredith sell?

Rita bought a box of raisins with 88 raisins in it. She ate 26 of the raisins before passing the box to her friend Kaylee. Kaylee ate 41 raisins. How many raisins are left in the box?

Gina ran the race in 72 seconds. Kristina ran the race in 85 seconds. What was the difference between their times?

Brain Box

In **word problems** that ask about the **difference** between two numbers, you need to **subtract.**

Aunt Linda put 38 gumdrops in her candy dish. Samantha grabbed 9 when she stopped by after school. Uncle Jeff ate 10 for dessert. Aunt Linda snacked on 2 before she went to bed. How many gumdrops are left?

Word Problems

Subtraction

Solve the **subtraction word problems.**

Haji has a collection of 86 baseball cards. Ethan has 100 baseball cards in his collection. How many more baseball cards does Ethan have?

Mr. Shah is driving across the country. On Monday, he drove 320 miles. On Tuesday, he drove 375 miles. How many fewer miles did he drive on Monday?

Jake wants to earn $130 this summer. He has earned $75 so far. How many more dollars does he have to earn to meet his goal?

Write your own **subtraction word problem.** Then give it to a friend to solve!

Picture It

Solve each **multiplication word problem.** Use the extra space on the card as your work area. Write the answer in the white box.

The fourth grade at Lerner Elementary has 4 rows of desks with 6 desks in each row. How many desks are in the classroom?

Victoria has 16 pairs of socks. How many socks does she have in all?

There are 7 teams for the relay races. Each team has 4 boys on it. How many boys are participating in the relay races?

Mrs. McSugar bought 5 boxes of doughnuts. Each box has 6 doughnuts in it. How many doughnuts did she buy?

Word Problems

Multiplication

Solve the **multiplication word problems.**

Cornelius Cobb has 8 rows of corn plants with 7 plants in each row. How many corn plants does he have?

Cameron does 50 push-ups each day. How many push-ups does he do in 8 days?

Miguel has 7 pens. His sister has 3 times more pens. How many pens does Miguel's sister have?

Caroline has 9 photo albums with 30 pictures in each album. How many pictures does she have in these albums?

Write your own **multiplication word problem.** Then give it to a friend to solve!

Get a Clue

Solve each **division word problem.** Use the extra space on the card as your work area. Write the answer in the white box.

Akila divided her 55 dimes evenly into 5 piles. How many dimes did she put in each pile?

Gabby's Goofy Gifts has 81 windup mice. They are packed with 9 in each box. How many boxes of windup mice do they have?

There are 24 cookies in the cookie jar. If 8 girls share the cookies equally, how many cookies will each girl get?

Alexis has 56 pumpkin seeds. She has made 8 rows and wants to plant the same number of seeds in each row. How many pumpkin seeds should she put in each row?

Solve the **division word problems.**

There are 32 children who want to play dodge ball. Mr. Su wants to divide the children evenly into 4 teams. How many children will be on each team?

Each baseball team at the sports club has 9 players. If there are 36 players in all, how many teams are there?

Sydney is reading a biography that has 64 pages. If he reads 8 pages each day, how long will it take him to finish the book?

Hassan divided his 21 computer games evenly into 3 piles. How many games were in each pile?

Madison wants to divide her 40 balloons into 5 equal bunches. How many balloons will be in each bunch?

Piri's Pets has 16 hamsters. They keep 2 hamsters in each cage. How many hamster cages are there?

Which Operation?

Solve each **word problem** using **addition, subtraction, multiplication,** or **division.** First write which operation you are going to use in the long yellow box. Then solve the problem and write your answer in the white box.

The Snack Shack sold 87 bags of pretzels on Saturday and 65 bags of pretzels on Sunday. How many more bags of pretzels did they sell on Saturday?

87
− 65
22

subtraction | 22

There are 9 tables in Mr. Lyden's art room. If there are 5 students at each table, how many students are at the tables?

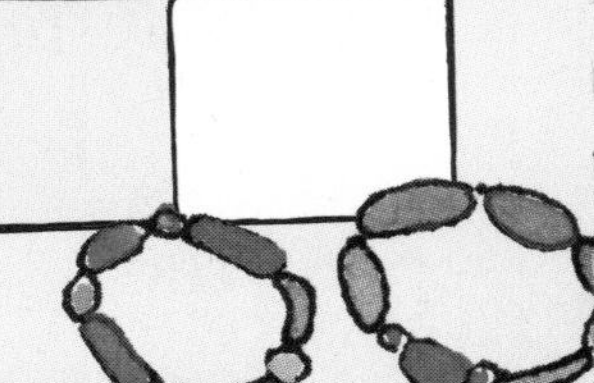

Brain Box

Word problems have clue words and phrases that tell you what operation you need to do to solve the problem.

Addition	Subtraction	Multiplication	Division
• how many • total number • in all • altogether	• how many more • how many less • how many are left • what is the difference	• how many	• each • every

Suki makes bracelets. She uses 9 beads in each bracelet she makes. How many bracelets can she make with 72 beads?

Word Problems

Mixed operation problems

At the school bake sale, Jasmine sold 26 banana muffins and 34 cranberry muffins. How many muffins in all did she sell?

Solve the **word problems.**

The camera club started with 32 members. 5 of those members dropped out. How many members are there now?

Ryan rakes leaves for $4 an hour. If he wants to make $36, how many hours will he have to work?

Jack Stalk has 8 rows of bean plants with 9 plants in each row. How many bean plants does he have?

At the school picnic there were 42 quarts of lemonade and 57 quarts of fruit punch. How many quarts of liquid are there in all?

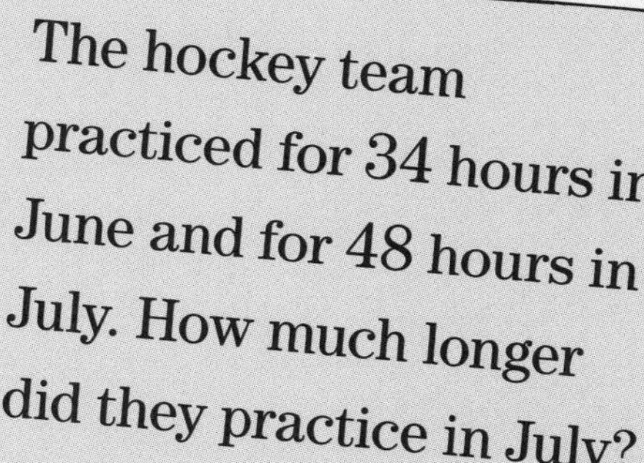

The hockey team practiced for 34 hours in June and for 48 hours in July. How much longer did they practice in July?

Noah wants to divide 48 almonds evenly into 6 little paper cups. How many almonds can he put in each cup?

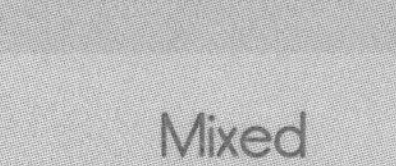

Word Problems

Mixed operation problems

Double the Fun

Solve the **word problems** below. Each problem requires that you do two math operations to find the answer.

Destiny had 31 tiny glass animals, but 5 of them broke. If her mother buys her 2 more, how many will she have then?

$$\begin{array}{r} 31 \\ -\ 5 \\ \hline 26 \end{array} \qquad \begin{array}{r} 26 \\ +\ 2 \\ \hline 28 \end{array}$$

28

Mrs. DeMauro bought 3 boxes of apricots with 6 apricots in each box. She wants to give the same number to each of 9 children. How many apricots will each child get?

Benjamin has $4 and Luis has $5. Victor has 4 times more money than the two boys together. How much money does Victor have?

Mrs. Moore divided 24 crackers evenly among 6 children. Then she gave Min 2 more. How many crackers did Min get?

Word Problems

Word problems with two operations

Solve the **word problems.**

Holly and Sabrina have made pot holders to raise money for a charity. Holly made 57 pot holders. Sabrina made 65. They've sold 93 so far. How many do they have left to sell?

Robert had his birthday party at a crowded movie theater. They needed 20 seats in all. There were 2 rows with 4 seats each and 2 rows with 5 seats each. How many more seats did they need?

Arthur's Art Shop is having a sale. Pens are \$3 each and a box of colored pencils is \$2. How much more will you pay if you buy 12 pens rather than 6 boxes of color pencils?

The Joke Shop had 59 false rubber noses in stock. On Monday they sold 4 and on Tuesday they sold 8. How many false rubber noses were left?

Special Strategies

Solve these complicated **word problems.**

Nathan has 12 video games. Martin has 4 times as many. How many video games do the two boys have in all?

Mario's class had 8 books left after their book sale. The class had sold 44 books on Monday and 32 books on Tuesday. How many books did they have at the start of the sale?

Brain Box

Some **word problems** are complicated to solve. Try these strategies to help you work through them.

- Work backward. Start with the part of the equation you know, and fill in the missing pieces.
- Make a little diagram.
- Make a chart.

Chuck now has 96 shells in his shell collection. For his birthday last week, he got 5 shells from his mother and 3 shells from his uncle. How many shells did Chuck have before his birthday?

Word Problems

Working backward and making diagrams

Social
Studies

This Land Is Your Land

Use the map of the United States to answer the questions on the next few pages.

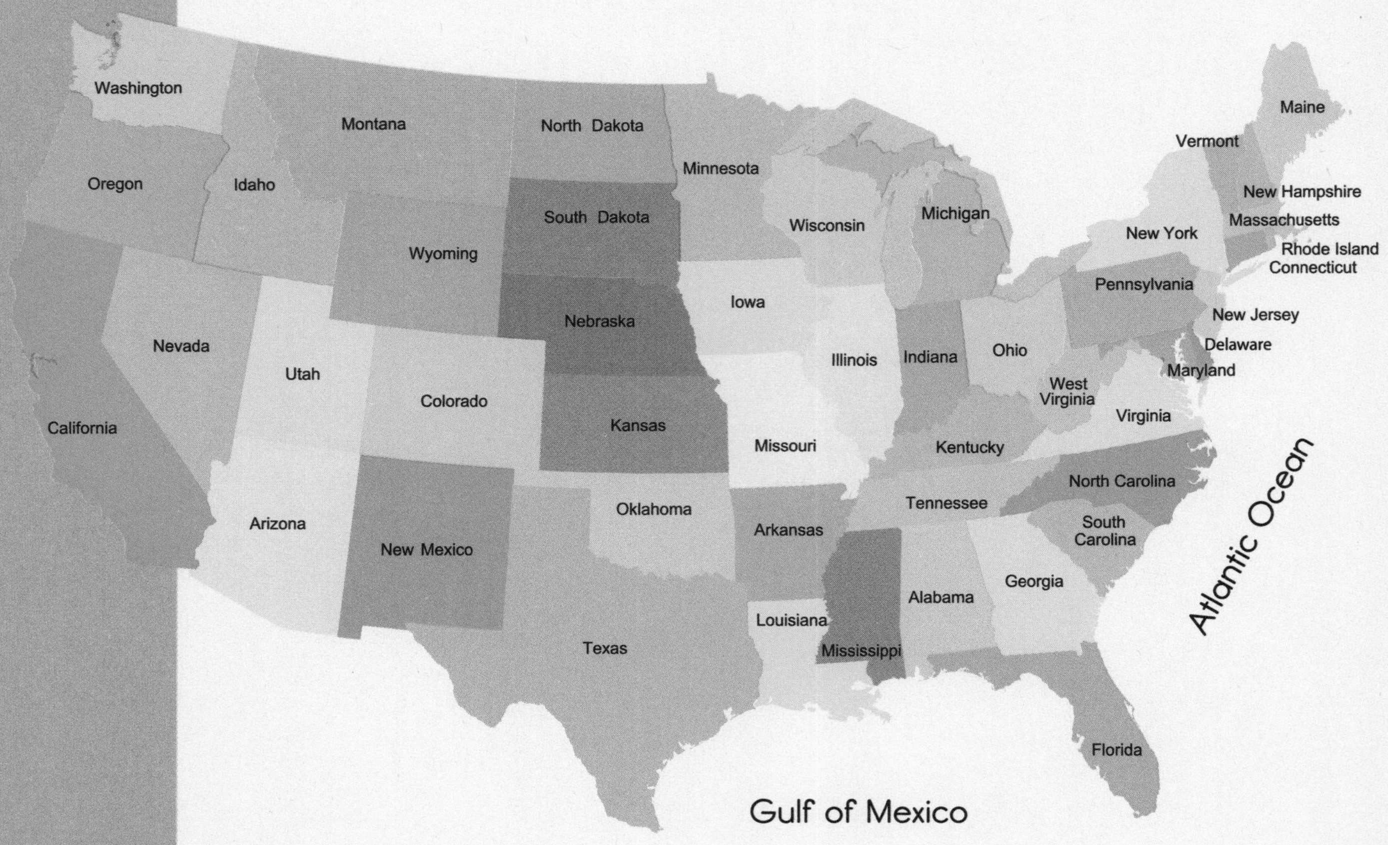

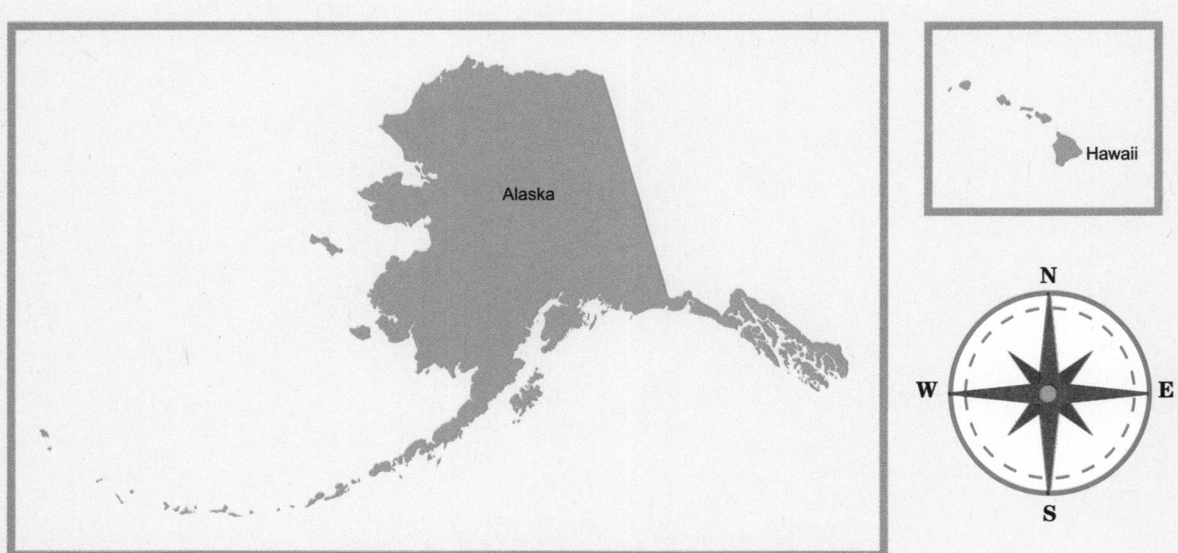

Which state is directly east of Indiana? ____________

North of Indiana? ____________

West of Indiana? ____________

South of Indiana? ____________

Which state is directly north of Arkansas?

____

Which states border Iowa?

____________ ____________ ____________

____________ ____________ ____________

Which state is bordered by only one other state? ____________

Which two states are shown separately from the other 48 states? ____________ ____________

Which state is directly west of North Dakota? ____________

What four states have corners that all touch in the same exact place? (HINT: these corners form the shape of a +.)

____________ ____________

____________ ____________

Which state is directly south of Nebraska? ____________

How many states have the word **North** in their names? ____________

Write them: ____________

How many states have the word **West** in their names? ____________

Write them: ____________

Name That State

Look at the U.S. map on page 264 to help you identify these states by their shapes. If you have trouble figuring out the state names, look up the capitals in an atlas or on the Internet.

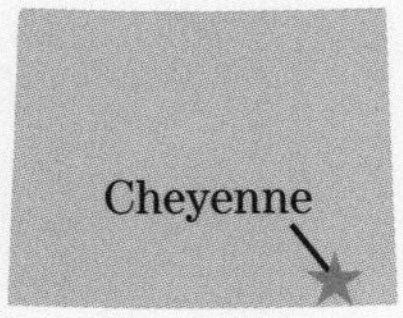

____

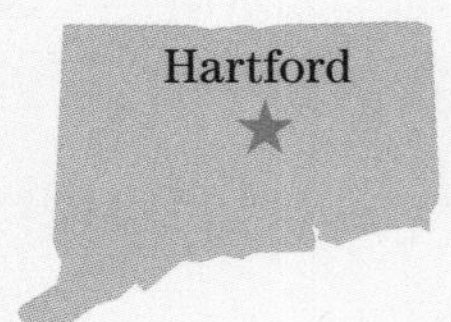

____

____

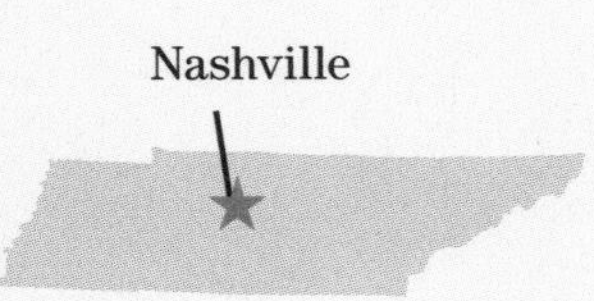

____

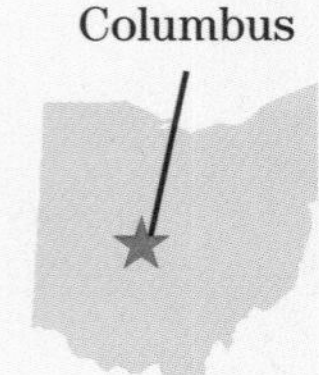

____

____

____

____

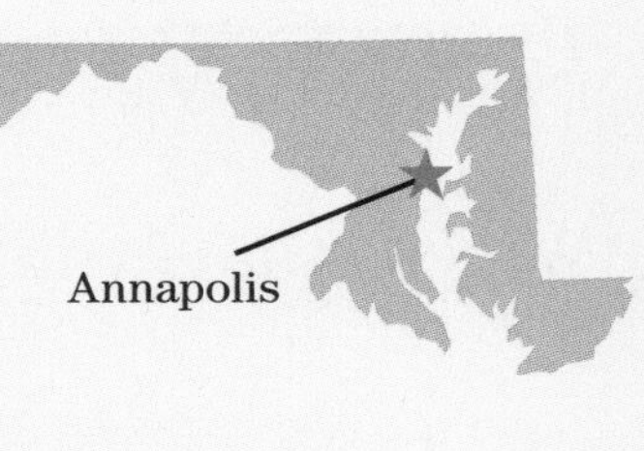

____

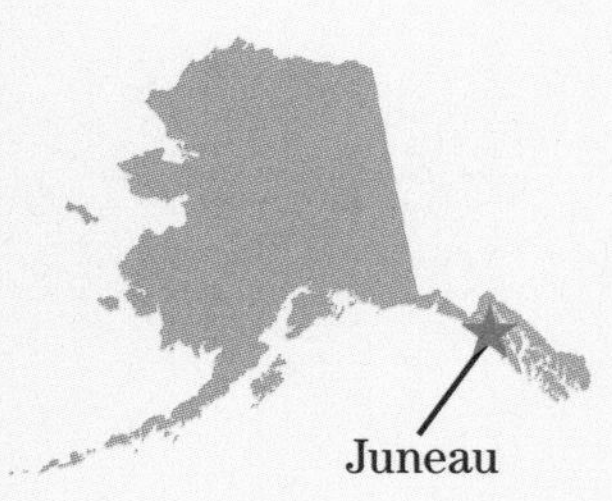

____

____

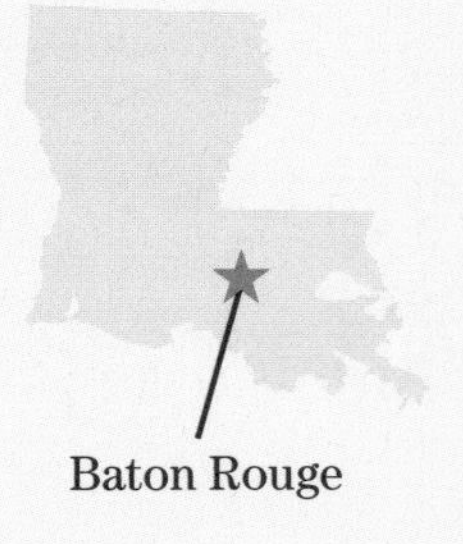

____

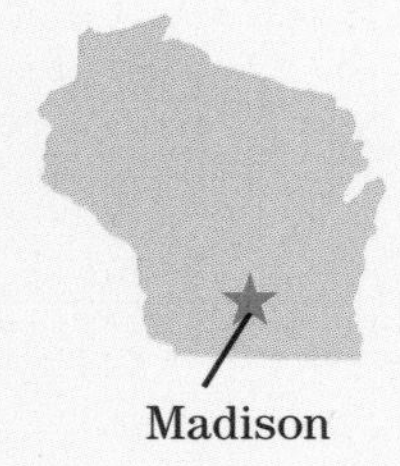

____

____

____

Play Ball

Below each baseball jersey, write the name of the state in which the team can be found.

Your State

Answer these questions about the state you live in.

You may need to do some research in an atlas, an encyclopedia, or on the Internet.

In what state do you live?

___

What is the capital of your state?

___

What is the population of your state?

___

What are three of the major industries of your state?

___

___

What states border your state?

What is your state bird?

What is your state flower?

Draw your state flag:

Shorten It Up

Each state in the United States has a two-letter postal abbreviation for its name. Use the map to write the postal abbreviation for every state.

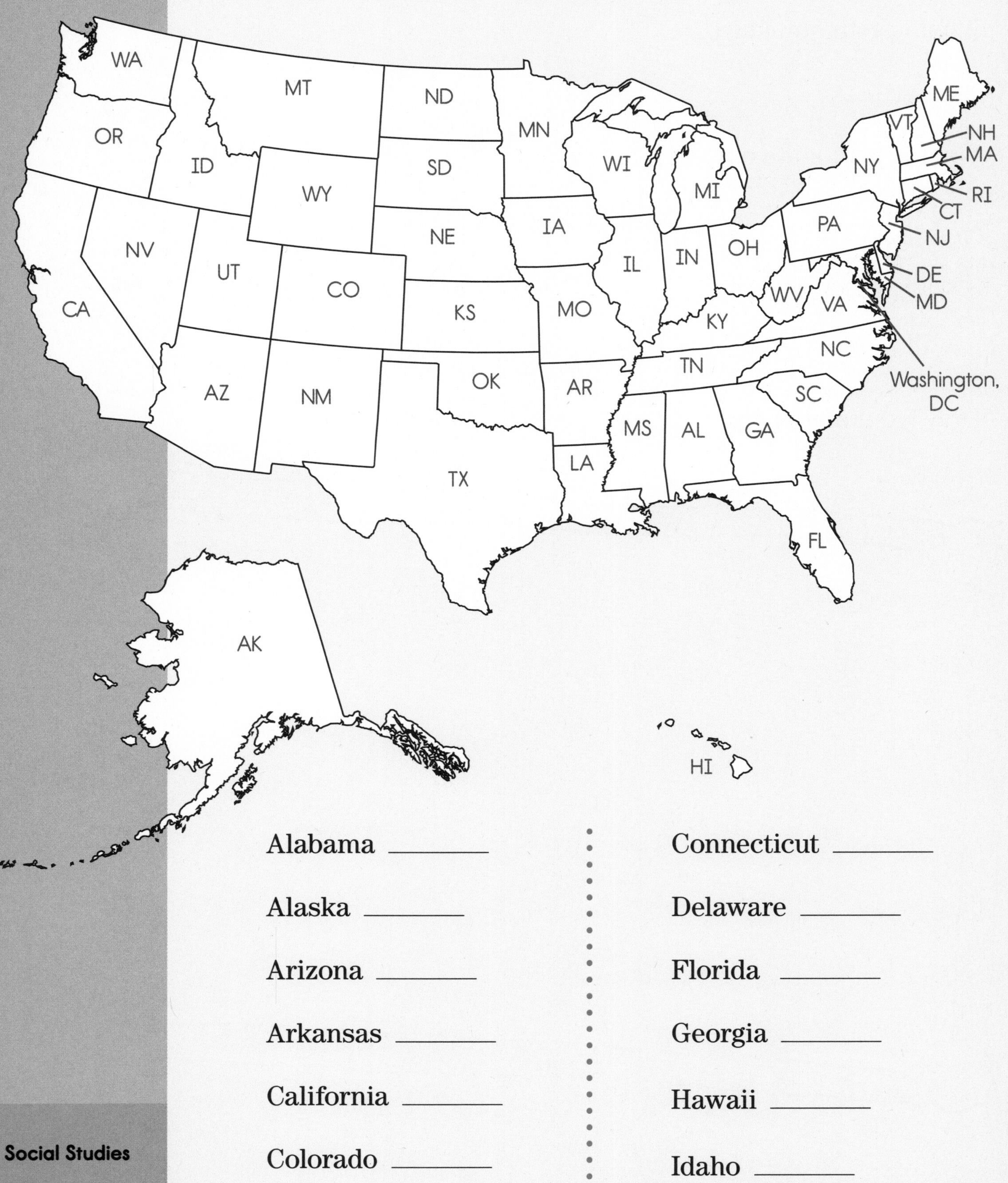

Alabama ________

Alaska ________

Arizona ________

Arkansas ________

California ________

Colorado ________

Connecticut ________

Delaware ________

Florida ________

Georgia ________

Hawaii ________

Idaho ________

Social Studies

State abbreviations

Illinois ________

Indiana ________

Iowa ________

Kansas ________

Kentucky ________

Louisiana ________

Maine ________

Maryland ________

Massachusetts ________

Michigan ________

Minnesota ________

Mississippi ________

Missouri ________

Montana ________

Nebraska ________

Nevada ________

New Hampshire ________

New Jersey ________

New Mexico ________

New York ________

North Carolina ________

North Dakota ________

Ohio ________

Oklahoma ________

Oregon ________

Pennsylvania ________

Rhode Island ________

South Carolina ________

South Dakota ________

Tennessee ________

Texas ________

Utah ________

Vermont ________

Virginia ________

Washington ________

West Virginia ________

Wisconsin ________

Wyoming ________

MAIL

The capital of the United States is ____________________________

What do the last two letters stand for? ________________________

The Constitution

The United States is a representative democracy. This means its leaders are elected by the people, and its government is meant to serve the people. Up until the creation of the United States, most countries were just the opposite: The people were meant to serve the government—usually a king who had inherited his throne, or an emperor who had seized power. But George Washington, Benjamin Franklin, and the other men who wrote the Constitution in 1787 did not want their newly independent country to be like most other governments! These men, who were called the "framers" of the Constitution, did not want a government ruled by kings or emperors. They wanted a government ruled by its people, where decisions were made by majority rule. This meant that people would vote for leaders they wanted.

The first three words of the Constitution are: "We the people…" That's because the Constitution was written to represent the voice of the people—not the president, not the politicians—but the common people of the United States.

The Constitution guarantees the citizens of the United States power to rule their own country by outlining a structure of government that protects the people's freedom. In 1791, the Bill of Rights was added to the Constitution. The Bill of Rights spells out the individual rights of American citizens: the freedom of speech, freedom of religion, freedom of the press, and the right to a fair trial.

What type of government is the United States?

Who did the framers of the Constitution want the United States to be ruled by, a king or the people? Why?

How does the Constitution protect the people's freedom?

When was the Bill of Rights added to the Constitution?

Name two freedoms that the Bill of Rights protects.

The Three Branches of Government

The U.S.A. has three branches of government: the Executive Branch, the Legislative Branch, and the Judicial Branch. Each branch holds equal but separate power so that there is a system of checks and balances.

Executive Branch

The Executive Branch is headed by the president and includes the vice-president, and the 15 presidential advisors that make up the Cabinet. The main job of the Executive Branch is to protect and serve the citizens of the United States by enforcing the laws.

Legislative Branch

The Legislative Branch is headed by Congress. Its job is to create the laws that govern the people. Congress is made up of two parts: the Senate and the House of Representatives. Both the Senate and the House are made up of leaders from every state who have been elected by the people of the states they represent. The Senate has 100 senators: two for every state—no matter how big or small the state. In the House of Representatives, the number of members per state varies according to state population. A state with a large population has more representatives than a state with a small population.

Judicial Branch

The third branch of government is the Judicial Branch. This branch is responsible for interpreting the laws of the Constitution to make sure everyone is being treated fairly. The Supreme Court of the Judicial Branch is the highest court in the U.S., and everyone—even the president!—must accept its rulings.

Name the three branches of government.

____

Why does the government have three branches of government instead of one?

____

____

Who is in charge of the Executive Branch?

____

Which two legislative groups make up Congress?

____

____

How many senators are in the Senate? How many senators does each state have?

____

Would a state with a small population have more representatives than a state with a larger population? Why?

____

____

What is the highest court in the United States?

____

Looking Back

This time line shows when our last thirteen states joined the United States (also called the Union). Use the time line to answer the questions.

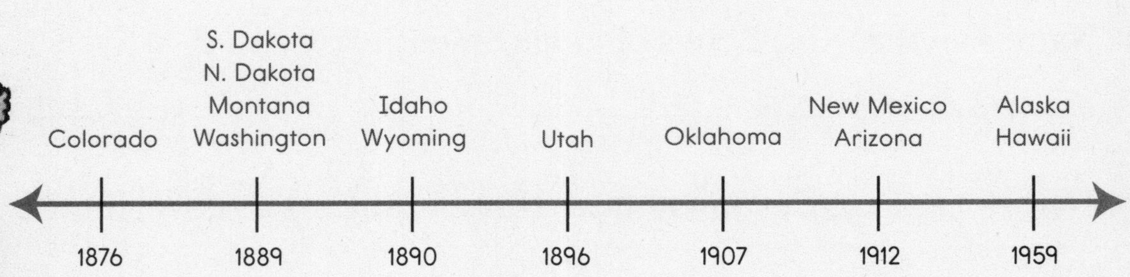

Which were the 49th and 50th states to join the Union?

____

Which state joined the Union first: Oklahoma or Montana?

____

Put these states in the order in which they joined the Union:

Utah, Colorado, Arizona, Idaho.

____

____

In what year did four states join the Union?

____

What two states joined the Union in 1890?

____

Social Studies

Understanding time lines

What Came First?

Use the time line and your knowledge of history to answer each question. Circle the correct answer.

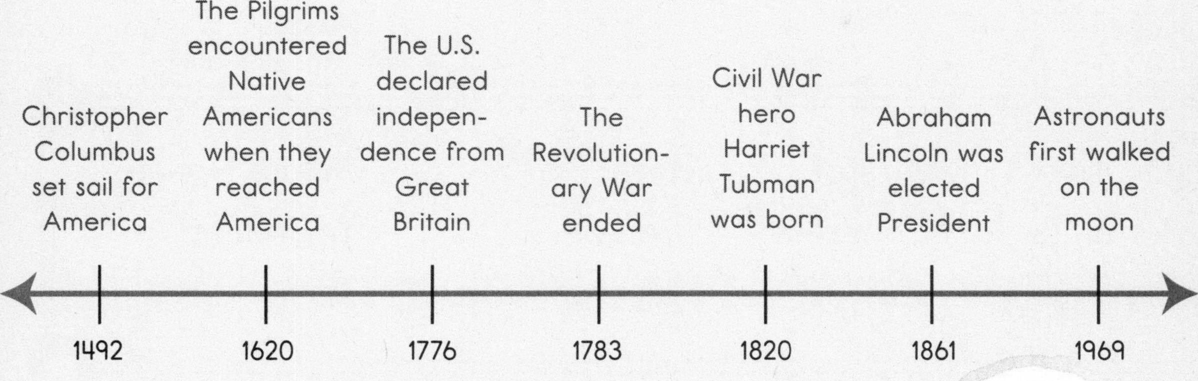

Which came first?

a. the Declaration of Independence

b. the United States Constitution

Who sailed across the Atlantic Ocean first?

a. the Pilgrims b. Christopher Columbus

Who lived in America first?

a. Native Americans b. African-Americans

Which war was first?

a. the Civil War b. the Revolutionary War

Who was born first?

a. Martin Luther King Jr. b. Harriet Tubman

Which happened first?

a. cars were being driven on the roads

b. astronauts walked on the moon

Social Studies

U.S. historical facts

Going to Washington

The Congress of the United States is the Legislative Branch of our federal government. Circle the twelve hidden words about Congress in the puzzle. The words go across and down.

legislative	capitol	term	White House
federal	Congress	Senate	president
government	state	representative	law

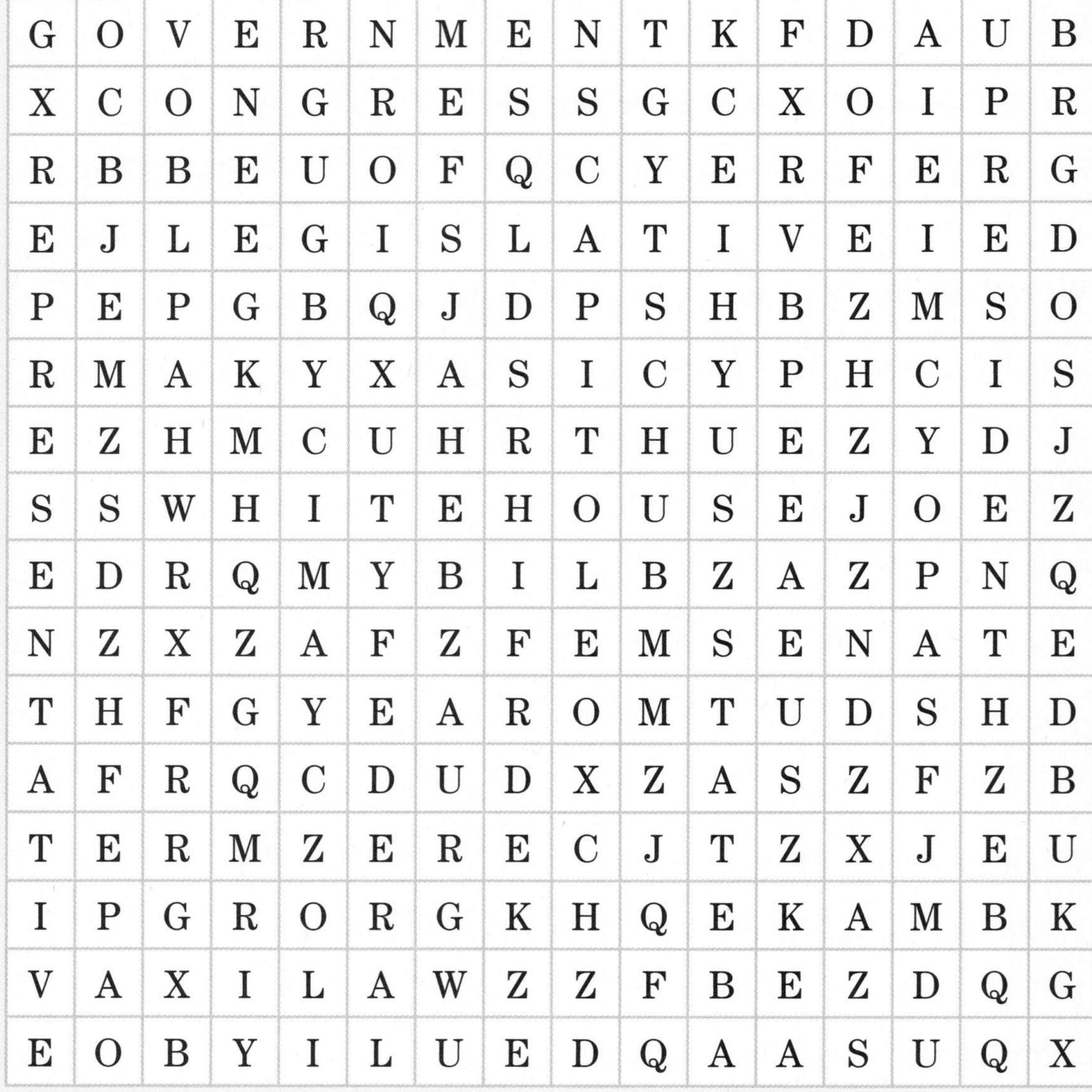

G	O	V	E	R	N	M	E	N	T	K	F	D	A	U	B
X	C	O	N	G	R	E	S	S	G	C	X	O	I	P	R
R	B	B	E	U	O	F	Q	C	Y	E	R	F	E	R	G
E	J	L	E	G	I	S	L	A	T	I	V	E	I	E	D
P	E	P	G	B	Q	J	D	P	S	H	B	Z	M	S	O
R	M	A	K	Y	X	A	S	I	C	Y	P	H	C	I	S
E	Z	H	M	C	U	H	R	T	H	U	E	Z	Y	D	J
S	S	W	H	I	T	E	H	O	U	S	E	J	O	E	Z
E	D	R	Q	M	Y	B	I	L	B	Z	A	Z	P	N	Q
N	Z	X	Z	A	F	Z	F	E	M	S	E	N	A	T	E
T	H	F	G	Y	E	A	R	O	M	T	U	D	S	H	D
A	F	R	Q	C	D	U	D	X	Z	A	S	Z	F	Z	B
T	E	R	M	Z	E	R	E	C	J	T	Z	X	J	E	U
I	P	G	R	O	R	G	K	H	Q	E	K	A	M	B	K
V	A	X	I	L	A	W	Z	Z	F	B	E	Z	D	Q	G
E	O	B	Y	I	L	U	E	D	Q	A	A	S	U	Q	X

Social Studies

Government word search

Science

Information, Please

Look at the information that is usually found in reference books. These pages are from a book about amphibians.

The **table of contents** tells you the titles of the chapters in the book and the page on which each chapter begins.

TABLE OF CONTENTS

A **glossary** is an alphabetical listing that gives the meanings of some words that are used in the book.

GLOSSARY

caecilian	a wormlike amphibian that lives underground
cold-blooded	having a body temperature that changes with that of the surrounding air or water temperature

An **index** is an alphabetical listing that tells where you can find a particular subject.

INDEX

Using references

Answer the questions.

In which chapter should you look
to find out about "colorful" amphibians? ______________

On which page does the first chapter of the book begin? ______

In which chapter would you look
to find out about how amphibians breathe? ______________

If you want to find out about tadpoles, on which page would you begin looking? ______________

Where would you look to find out what general subjects the reference book covers? ______________

Where would you look to find out on which page or pages a particular person, place, or subject is covered? ______________

Where would you look to find out the meaning of an unfamiliar word or term? ______________

Flutter in the Air

Read the passage.

Butterflies and Moths

Butterflies and moths are beautiful insects. They belong to the same group of insects, which is called *Lepidoptera*. Like all insects, butterflies and moths have six legs. But unlike other insects, they have scales that cover their wings. Both moths and butterflies have two pairs of wings. That's four wings in all.

Butterflies and moths go through four stages of development:

- **egg:** Females usually lay their eggs on a leaf or a stem.
- **caterpillar:** A caterpillar eats and eats. It sheds its skin several times as it grows.
- **pupa:** The caterpillar rests in either a chrysalis, if it's a butterfly, or a cocoon, if it's a moth. This hard shell protects it.
- **adult:** When the pupa cracks, the adult butterfly or moth emerges.

All butterflies and moths undergo this metamorphosis, or transformation, from egg to adult. Butterflies and moths also differ in several ways. Most butterflies have slender, hairless bodies. Most moths have plump, furry bodies. Many butterflies are brightly colored, while many moths have a dull color. Most butterflies fly during the day, while most moths fly at night. A butterfly's antennae are knobbed at the tips. A moth's antennae are plain or feathery at the tips. Most butterflies hold their wings upright over their backs while they are resting, but most moths rest with their wings stretched out flat.

Some species of moths and butterflies migrate. That means that they make a journey to a new place. One of the most amazing migrations is made by the monarch butterfly, which flies south to find a new home for the winter. Millions of monarchs fly thousands of miles to reach forests of fir trees in Mexico. There they rest and feed after their long journey.

Using a Venn diagram

Name the four stages of development in the life cycle of moths and butterflies.

1. ______________________ 2. ______________________

3. ______________________ 4. ______________________

Define these terms.

Lepidoptera: ______________________________________

migrate: ______________________________________

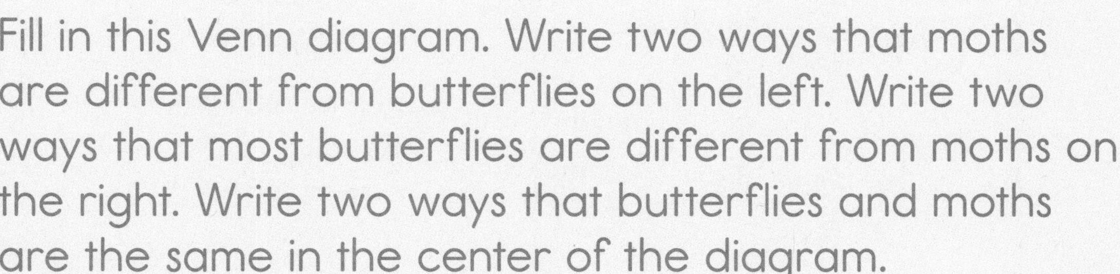

Fill in this Venn diagram. Write two ways that moths are different from butterflies on the left. Write two ways that most butterflies are different from moths on the right. Write two ways that butterflies and moths are the same in the center of the diagram.

moths

both

butterflies

Using a Venn diagram

We've Got Backbones

Read the passage.

Creature Features

Animals that have backbones are called **vertebrates.** Vertebrates include five classes of animals:

- **Mammals:** Mammals are warm-blooded animals with hair. All mammals feed their young with milk. Some examples are people, dogs, mice, dolphins, whales, horses, and chimpanzees.
- **Fish:** Fish are cold-blooded animals that live in the water. Most fish breathe with gills. Some examples are goldfish, sharks, eels, and manta rays.
- **Birds:** Birds are warm-blooded animals that have wings, feathers, and beaks. Most birds can fly. Some examples are hawks, barn owls, toucans, eagles, and swans.

- **Amphibians:** Amphibians are cold-blooded animals that live in the water and breathe with gills at the beginning of their lives. Later, they move on to land and breathe with lungs for the rest of their life. Some examples are salamanders, frogs, and toads.
- **Reptiles:** Reptiles are cold-blooded animals that have scales and lay eggs. Some examples are geckos, crocodiles, boa constrictors, snakes, chameleons, and sea turtles.

Using what you learned about vertebrates, list three examples of each class of animal.

Fill in the chart, checking off **warm-blooded** or **cold-blooded** for each class of vertebrate.

	mammals	birds	amphibians	reptiles	fish
warm-blooded					
cold-blooded					

Feathered Friends

Read about birds. Then answer the questions.

Even though they all have wings, not all birds can fly. Penguins and ostriches are among the birds that have wings but can't fly.

Whether they eat meat or plants, birds do not chew their food—that's because they have no teeth! Birds use their beak or their claws to gather food. Birds of prey, such as hawks, eagles, and owls, will spot small animals on the ground to hunt from high above in their perch. Other birds eat seeds and nectar from plants.

Many birds fly south for the winter to stay warm, and head north in the summer to stay cool. This is called migration.

Name a bird that doesn't fly.

____

Many birds fly south for the winter. What is this called?

____

Why don't birds chew their food?

____

Name three types of birds of prey.

____

Birds

Read the **essay** about owls. Then answer the questions.

Many people have never seen an owl in the wild. That's because owls are usually quiet and motionless as they roost during the day. It is at night that they become active, for this is when they hunt for their prey.

Owls are well equipped for hunting. Their huge eyes can see well in the dark, and their hearing is very sensitive. Soft-fringed feathers on their wings help them fly so quietly that most animals don't hear them coming. To catch and carry their prey, owls have needle-sharp claws called talons. Owls usually swallow their prey whole. Parts that can't be digested—hair, teeth, feathers, and bones—are spit up in pellets.

Name four things that help the owl hunt its prey.

1. ______________________________

2. ______________________________

3. ______________________________

4. ______________________________

What happens to the parts of the prey that the owl's stomach can't digest?

____

Something's Fishy

Read about fish. Then answer the questions.

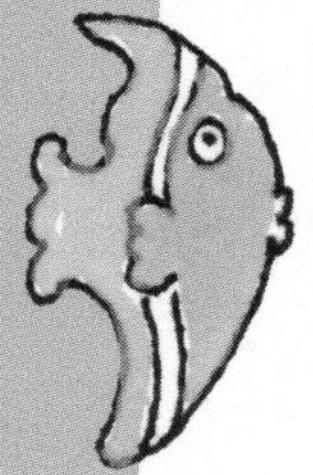

Fish do not have lungs. They take in oxygen through their gills. Unlike mammals, fish must be under water in order to breathe. Most fish are covered with scales, and they have several fins and a strong tail, which help them swim through the water.

You can find fish in just about any body of water—oceans, streams, lakes, rivers, ponds—both in salt water and freshwater. Some fish stay by themselves, but many live in a large group called a school. Many fish eat other fish or smaller sea creatures, while others survive on a diet of underwater plants called algae.

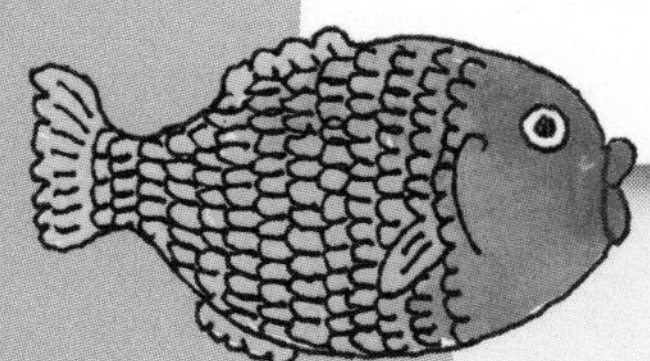

Do fish use lungs or gills to breathe? ______________________

What covers the body of most fish? ______________________

What is a large group of fish called? ______________________

What two body parts do fish use to help them move through the water? ______________________

What do some fish eat, other than underwater plants?

____

Scary or Scaly

Read about reptiles. Then answer the questions.

While not all reptiles are dangerous, some are. The boa constrictor is a long, powerful snake that wraps itself around its prey and squeezes it to death. Poisonous snakes such as rattlesnakes and cobras inject their poison into their prey through their sharp teeth or fangs.

Many people confuse two similar reptiles: alligators and crocodiles. Although they look alike, there are some differences. When a crocodile has its mouth closed, you can still see all of its teeth. When an alligator's mouth is closed, you can see only its top teeth. An alligator's snout is wider than a crocodile's. Lastly, alligators are found mostly in the southeastern United States. Crocodiles live on almost every continent.

Name two kinds of poisonous snakes.

1. ________________________________

2. ________________________________

Name three differences between alligators and crocodiles.

1. ________________________________

2. ________________________________

3. ________________________________

Facts about reptiles

Creature Crossword

Read each clue. Write the answer in the crossword puzzle on the next page.

ACROSS

1. This snake kills its prey by squeezing it.
3. Which of these animals is *not* a reptile: snapping turtle, iguana, or bullfrog?
6. Fish travel in _____.
8. This poisonous snake injects its poison into its prey through its fangs.
11. Fish breathe with _____.
12. You can tell an alligator and crocodile apart by the shape of their nose, or _____.
13. Can alligators be found in the northern part of the United States or the southern part?
15. A _____ is a bird of prey.
17. This kind of animal begins its life in the water, then lives on land.
19. Animals that have these are called vertebrates.
21. All mammals feed their young this.

DOWN

2. Reptiles are _____-blooded animals.
4. Poisonous snakes inject their venom using their _____.
5. Fish are covered with these.
7. Even with its mouth closed, you can see all of this reptile's sharp teeth.
9. This reptile sometimes hides inside its shell.
10. Baby reptiles are hatched from these.
14. Birds have no _____.
16. A _____ is a large marine mammal.
18. Both mice and men are types of_____.
20. This type of bird can't fly.

1
2
3
4
5
6
7
8
9
10
11
12
13
14
15
16
17
18
19
20
21

Take Me Home

Read about animal habitats. Then draw a line from each animal to its habitat.

An animal's habitat is the place where it naturally lives and grows. The habitat provides everything the animal needs: food, shelter, the right temperature, and protection.

giraffe

cheetah

parrot

whale

deer

shark

octopus

woodpecker

buffalo

squirrel

toucan

zebra

WOODLAND

RAIN FOREST

GRASSLAND

OCEAN

Animal habitats

Help!

Draw a line from each animal to the card that describes how it protects itself.

turtle

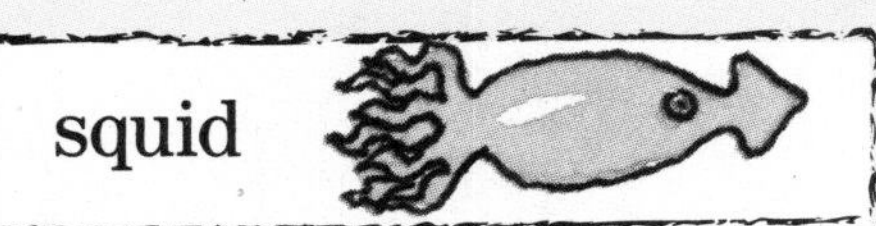
squid

chameleon

poison dart frog

skunk

moose

cheetah

puffer fish

armadillo

wasp

- runs away very fast
- is brightly colored to warn that it is poisonous
- rolls up into a ball
- shoots inky liquid to hide itself
- has a poison sting
- sprays out a smelly substance
- puffs itself up so it's too big for predators to swallow
- has large antlers as weapons
- changes colors to camouflage itself
- hides in its shell

Animal defenses

Species in Danger

Read this page about endangered species.

Save the Animals

Animals can become extinct, endangered, or threatened for several reasons, but people are the primary cause.

In many places, people are taking over the lands where animals once roamed freely. Loggers and road builders are cutting down forests. In other parts of the world, factories and businesses are polluting the air and the waters. Tankers sometimes spill oil into the oceans, killing thousands of fish and ocean birds. The destruction of their natural habitats is a big reason why animals are losing their homes, nesting and feeding grounds, and sometimes become extinct.

Another major cause of animal extinction is hunting and illegal poaching. Sadly, some people kill animals for their fur, meat, tusks, or skins, which they can sell for big profits. The majestic black rhino, for instance, is killed just for its horn, which is used to make daggers. Bengal tigers, clouded leopards, and giant pandas have been hunted to the point of extinction for their beautiful fur. Leatherhead turtles and sharks are caught to make soup! In some parts of the world, shark fin soup or turtle soup is considered a delicacy.

Some people don't understand why it would be terrible for the world if sharks became extinct, but sharks are vital to our oceans. All animals live in harmony with their environments and are part of a natural cycle that allows all creatures to flourish. Humans also need to live in harmony with their environment.

Many people and governments are taking steps to save endangered animals from extinction. One way people can help is by writing letters to the government about the issues.

Endangered animals

Choose an endangered animal from the previous page and write a draft of a letter to the President of the United States. Explain why the animal is important to you and what steps should be taken to protect it.

The White House
1600 Pennsylvania Ave.
Washington, DC 20500

Date: ____________

Dear Mr. or Madame President,

When you have finished the draft, go back and edit it. Then write it neatly—or type it—and send it to the President.

Thank You!

Plants and animals help make many useful products. Draw a line to match each product with the plant or animal that it comes from.

wood tables

rain boots

pearls

olive oil

cheese

silk scarves

olive tree

cow

silkworm

rubber tree

oysters

pine tree

Products from plants and animals

Flower Power

Read about flowers. Label the parts of the flower.

Many flowers are wonderful to smell and beautiful to look at. But flowers also have a very important job. They make the seeds that produce more flowering plants of the same type. All the parts of the flower play an important role in reproduction.

- **Stamens:** The stamens are the male part of a flower. They are tall, thin stalks with grains of pollen on their tips. Most flowers have several stamens.
- **Pistil:** The pistil is the female part of a flower. It is usually a large center stalk that is often shaped like a tall vase.
- **Ovary:** At the base of the pistil is a ball-shaped part called the ovary. This is where the plant's eggs are developed. If the eggs are fertilized by pollen, seeds will develop.
- **Petals:** Petals are usually colorful. They attract insects and birds that help spread the flower's grains of pollen to another flower of the same type so that seeds can form.

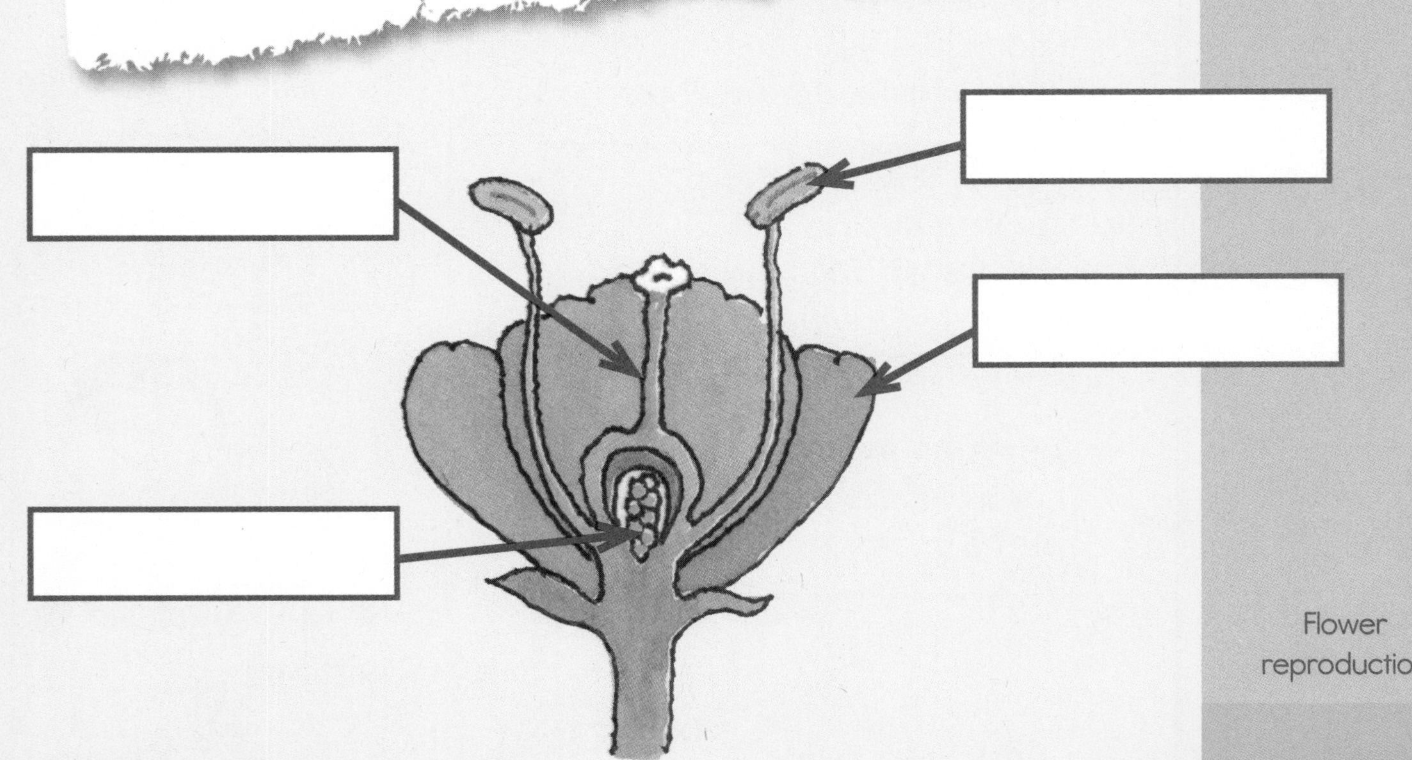

Flower reproduction

The Human Body

Draw a line from the system on the left to the part of the body that belongs to that system.

The body's organs work together in groups known as systems. Each of these systems has an important set of functions to perform.

digestive system: responsible for getting food in and out of the body.	brain
respiratory system: responsible for breathing.	ears
muscular system: responsible for movement.	blood
sensory system: responsible for seeing, hearing, tasting, touching and smelling.	lungs
skeletal system: responsible for bones and joints that support and protect the body.	stomach
circulatory system: responsible for getting blood to all the parts of the body.	biceps
nervous system: controls all the functions of the body.	spine

The Human Skeleton

Read about bones. Then answer the questions.

There are 206 bones in the human body. These bones are connected to each other at joints. The bones and joints make up the human skeleton, which is what supports and protects the human body. For instance, the skull protects the brain. The ribs protect the heart and lungs.

Half the bones in the human body are in the hands and feet. The smallest bone is in the ear. The biggest bone is in the thigh.

Bones are held together by ligaments, and they move with the help of muscles. When babies are born, their bones are still soft. This soft bone is called cartilage. As babies grow, the cartilage hardens into bone. Calcium, a mineral found in milk and eggs and broccoli, helps make bones stronger.

How many bones are there in the human body?

____

How many bones are in the hands and feet?

____

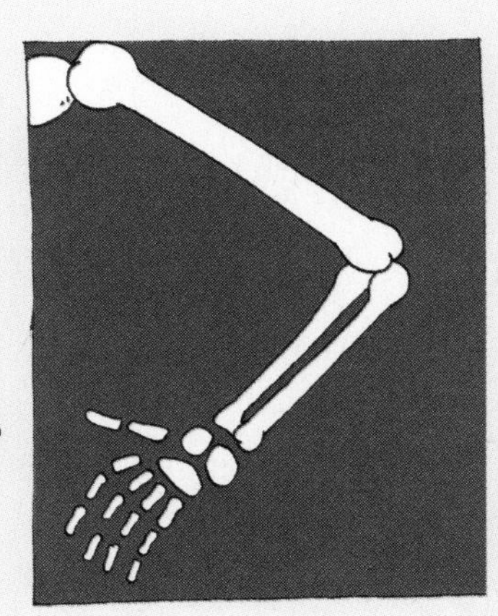

What part of the body does the skull protect?

____

What holds bones together?

____

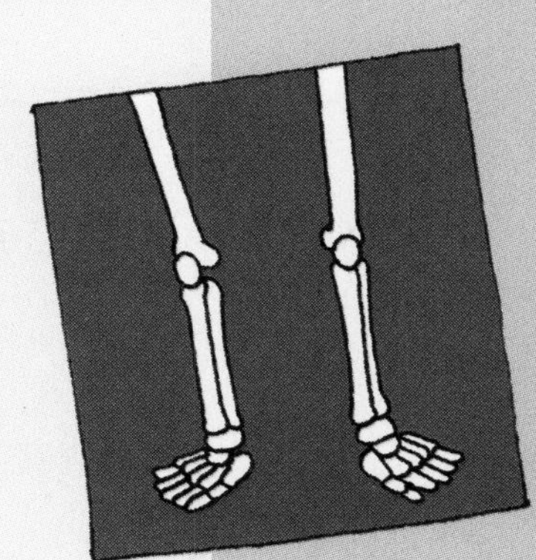

What is found in milk, eggs, and broccoli that is good for bones? _______________________

How Magnetic!

Magnets have two poles: a north pole and a south pole. When two magnets are placed near each other, their poles have a force that will either pull the two magnets together or push the two magnets apart. If the poles are the same, they will push apart (be repelled). If the poles are different, they will pull together (be attracted).

Will these two magnets pull together or push apart?

N S 

____

Will these two magnets pull together or push apart?

N S   S N

____

Magnets can attract or pick up many metal objects. Put an **M** in front of those objects that are attracted or can be picked up by a magnet.

_____ paper clip

_____ plastic fork

_____ candle

_____ bolt

_____ metal spoon

_____ safety pin

_____ rubber band

_____ nail

_____ crayon

Are all metal objects attracted by magnets? __________

Answer Key

(For pages not included in this section, answers will vary.)

Spelling and Vocabulary

pg. 6
stray
cheese
blue
tote
boat
lake
line; rhino
supply
painted; easels
key; open
huge; studio
Eight
break

long a words	long e words
stray	cheese
lake	easels
painted	key
eight	
break	

long i words	long o words
line	tote
rhino	boat
supply	open

long u words
blue
huge
studio

pg. 7
friends
ahead
umbrella
bus
bottom
red
laughed
said
grabbed
rink
pig; pink
saddle
bread
wash

short a words	short o words
laughed	bottom
saddle	wash
grabbed	

short e words	short i words
friends	rink
ahead	pig
red	pink
bread	
said	

short u words
umbrella
bus

pg. 8
school; racket; kayak
Monarch; kangaroo; chameleon
sock; castle; cake

pg. 9

night	wrong
write	gnome
autumn	climb
campaign	knowledge
comb	right
raspberry	doubt

pg. 10
swimming
dreaming

jumping	running
asking	digging
driving	changing
writing	winning

pg. 11

wished	nodded
shopped	laughed
lived	smiled
shined	scrubbed
hurried	relied

I am worried about my social studies test tomorrow.
I started sneezing when I smelled the flowers.
The father waved to his daughters as they got on the bus.
Everyone jumped when he popped the balloons.
He started slipping on the icy driveway.
The thief robbed the bank.

pg. 12
weight
receive
thief
sleigh
science
eight
piece
shriek
freight
chief

D	B	K	G	A	S	C	I	E	N	C	E	F	U
M	Y	R	U	O	Z	L	J	D	R	B	H	R	S
S	W	E	I	G	H	T	X	D	C	H	I	E	F
V	B	C	M	V	S	H	R	I	E	K	V	I	F
P	I	E	C	E	N	I	C	A	L	A	J	G	L
O	C	I	G	S	L	E	I	G	H	O	S	H	R
H	D	V	K	Q	U	F	T	B	I	X	H	T	T
X	A	E	I	G	H	T	B	O	F	B	R	C	K

p. 13

Febuary	enuf	shoping	favrit
busy	because	once	hitting
dinasor	suprise	Wensday	receive
peeple	anser	minit	docter
please	calendar	kwite	giving

February; enough; shopping; favorite; dinosaur; surprise; Wednesday; people; answer; minute; doctor; quite

pg. 14

knives	dwarves
cities	glasses
shelves	brushes
pennies	taxes
witches	candies
turkeys	rays

pg. 15
babies; houses; peaches; foxes
bunnies; boys; puppies; elves
spies
tigers

S	P	I	E	S	Y	E	Q	W	J	L	S
X	V	O	G	U	E	I	T	M	U	N	Y
P	U	B	A	B	I	E	S	H	O	Y	X
U	L	O	Q	W	K	N	E	I	B	G	S
P	J	Y	I	C	P	H	L	T	L	P	L
P	W	S	O	B	U	N	N	I	E	S	M
I	U	K	L	C	P	H	Q	G	A	D	F
E	L	V	E	S	U	Z	I	E	V	Z	F
S	D	I	Q	W	B	M	Y	R	E	R	O
M	R	H	O	U	S	E	S	S	S	B	X
C	I	K	F	M	C	K	W	V	L	I	E
B	V	Q	M	H	P	E	A	C	H	E	S

pg. 16

children	geese
mice	women
men	oxen
teeth	fish
sheep	moose

pg 17
preview
misbehaved
rebuild
substandard
misspelled
preheat
repaint

pg. 18
unhappy
unwrap
impatient
impolite
inexpensive
disagree
impossible
dislike
independent

pg. 19
powerful
thoughtful
fearless
hopeful
helpful
colorful
useless
careless

pg. 20

teacher

magician

singer

writer

artist

dancer

actor

violinist

pg. 21

rainy	forgiveness
attractive	repackage
successful	invention
transportation	childlike
reread	buyer
golden	underground
worthless	poisonous

pg. 22-23

Across	Down
sweet	small
over	low
shallow	rich
friend	soft
heavy	old
least	wild
	narrow
	asleep

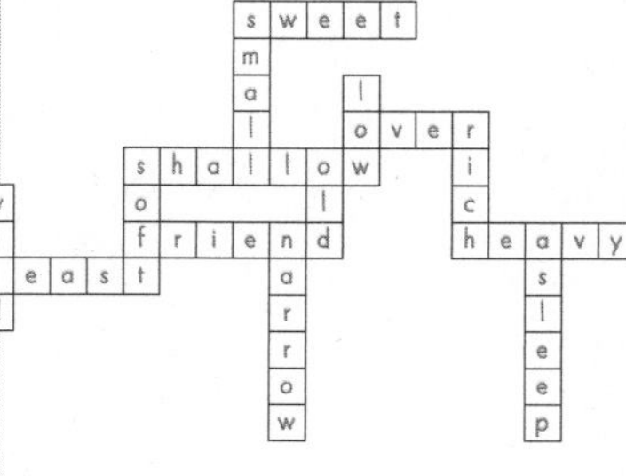

pg. 24
Good
early
nice
morning
exciting
fastest
first
happy
delicious
easy
right
won
pleased
best

pg. 25
hungry = famished
angry = mad
elevated = high
eager = excited
pal = friend
build = construct
wicked = cruel
brag = boast
wealthy = rich
damp = moist

pg. 26

cautious	reckless
sob	laugh
difficult	easy
depart	arrive
exhausted	energetic
repair	break
ill	healthy
complete	begin
alike	different
factual	false

pg. 27

threw	through
their	there
to	two
meet	meat
won	one
write	right
knight	night
fare	fair

pg. 28
creek; creak
aloud; allowed
scent; sent
toad; towed
waist; waste
principal; principle
stationery; stationary
pair; pear

pg. 29
b. very angry
c. worked hard
a. smell
a. climbed up
c. real
c. fancy
c. warned
b. busy

pg. 30
very important
dangerous
amazed
rich
lay back
calm
worn down
easily noticed

pg. 31
1 – rabbit; 2 – race; 3 – rose
1 – meat; 2 – messy; 3 – more
1 – mad; 2 – map; 3 – mouse
1 – has; 2 – hill; 3 – home
1 – read; 2 – red; 3 – ride
1 – happy; 2 – heavy; 3 – hide
1 – hall; 2 – hello; 3 – hero
1 – rest; 2 – road; 3 – rug
1 – minus; 2 – mitten; 3 – money

pg. 33
bed, behave
behave

no
noun
three

Language Arts

pg. 36
strawberry
eyebrow
wheelbarrow
sidewalk
ponytail
peppermint
butterfly
playground

H	W	K	J	W	P	O	N	Y	T	A	I	L	F	A
A	H	B	G	B	L	V	I	P	F	C	E	L	B	Q
B	E	S	T	R	A	W	B	E	R	R	Y	P	D	E
U	E	D	L	T	Y	L	M	P	J	M	E	D	I	O
T	L	F	A	H	G	E	H	P	L	C	B	E	R	A
T	B	I	B	F	R	A	C	E	B	G	R	B	G	P
E	A	N	B	U	O	D	K	R	F	E	O	N	J	V
R	R	J	P	D	U	V	J	M	P	O	W	G	U	N
F	R	G	A	K	N	K	S	I	D	E	W	A	L	K
L	O	Q	M	S	D	O	Q	N	H	S	I	V	S	R
Y	W	K	C	H	K	M	D	T	H	T	Y	B	T	F
F	A	D	L	Q	R	K	J	O	B	B	L	A	I	C

pg. 37
hallway; bedroom
necktie
everyone; basketball
jellyfish
turtleneck; wintertime
starfish
fishbowl; goldfish
snowfall; snowman
(Answers may vary)
hall + way = hallway
bed + room = bedroom
neck + tie = necktie

pg. 38
black, green, purple, yellow, orange

monkey, rhino, panda, gorilla, kangaroo

brain, lungs, heart, blood, bones

pg. 39
where
watch
shall
bead
beard
are
gone
mood

now
foot
although

pg. 40
two-syllable words:
spelling
question
ladder
birthday

three-syllable words:
dinosaur
bumblebee
accident
grandmother

four-syllable words:
operator
biography
adorable
caterpillar

pg. 41
cloak; croak; crook; brook; broom
blond; blood; flood; floor; flour

pg. 42
string
green
day
patient
girl
pounds

food
water

pg. 44
couldn't = could not
she's = she is
didn't = did not
they're = they are
what's = what is
weren't = were not
don't = do not
we'll = we will
he'd = he would / he had
it's = it is

pg. 45
I'm, I've, he's, We've, They're, weren't, couldn't, I'll, what's

pg. 46
feather
desert
ice
mouse
skyscraper
ghost
elephant

pg. 48-49
(Some answers will vary)
told all/confessed
is reading
help me
I'm listening
made me scared
easy
joking with me
two of a kind
makes me crazy

pg. 50

Madeline and her family decided to go to the shore in New Jersey. Madeline brought her best friend, Cara, along. Madeline packed extra beach towels and sunscreen. Cara packed a Frisbee and a radio.

Madeline and Cara went to the beach with Madeline's mom, dad, and sister. They also walked along the boardwalk, played games in the arcades, and went to the ice-cream parlor for dessert.

Person: Madeline, family, friend, Cara, dad, mom

Place: shore, New Jersey, beach, boardwalk, arcades, ice-cream parlor

Thing: beach towels, sunscreen, Frisbee, radio, games, dessert

pg. 51
Proper nouns: Ms. Ramos, January, Penny, Maple Street, Grand Canyon, Arizona, Dylan, Aunt Ethel, Sugar Shack, Dr. Pollock, Sunday, Labor Day
Common nouns: zoo, class, house, shoelaces, shoes, doughnuts, family, beach, pool

pg. 52
an; the; an
the; the; a
the; a; the
an; the; the

pg. 53
He
They
us
She; him
we; it
them
her

pg. 54
mine; my
his; his
ours; Our

pg. 55
your; yours
hers; her
theirs; their
its

pg. 56
My teacher's reading contest is going to start next week.
I didn't realize that was Sari's house.
Samantha's cupcakes were absolutely delicious!
My friend's Halloween party was a little spooky.
Did you know that this is Lalo's trumpet?
I promised I would clean out my dad's car.
Kody's sister won the spelling bee.

pg. 57
friends'
teacher's
tree's
Molly's
girl's
giraffes'
teachers'
bulls'
travelers'
girls'

pg. 58
three; enormous; sweet-smelling
two; delicious; meatless
five; spicy; roasted
tiny; brown; loud
large; blue
noisy; timpani
quiet; gray
Number: three, two, five
Color: brown, blue, gray
Size: enormous, tiny, large
Taste or smell: sweet-smelling, delicious, spicy
Sound: loud, noisy, quiet
Kind: meatless, roasted, timpani

pg. 60
rougher
hungriest
fastest
shorter
slowest
brightest
gooder = better
farest = farthest
badder = worse

pg. 61
bowls
figure
works
investigate
dresses
prepares
dance
read

pg. 62
go = future
eats = present
cooked = past
sings = present
hunted = past
lived = past
walks = present
will ride = future
will plant = future

pg. 64
Action verbs: play, hits, pitches, slams, walks, shouts, hurts, slides, examines, tapes, catches, win

Scramble:

slams	win
slides	pitches
walks	play
examines	catches
hits	hurts
shouts	tapes

pg. 65
were
was
are
is
have
am
would
has
could

pg. 66
is
was
am
are
feels
seems
looks
smells

pg. 67

Across	**Down**
read	drank
gave	caught
threw	wrote
rang	bought
brought	hid

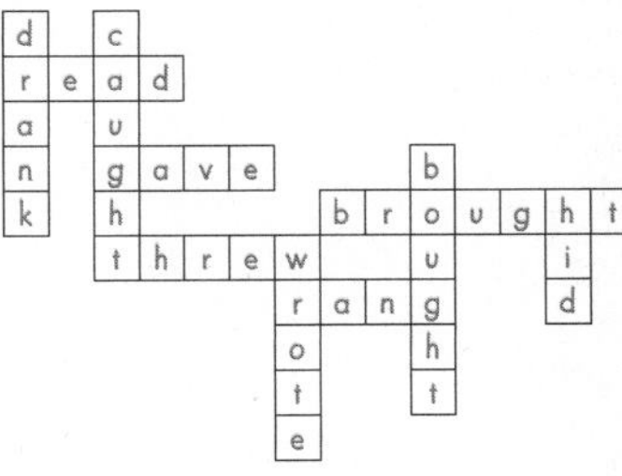

pg. 68
Present tense verbs: am, get, is, eat, spend, eat, go, choose, sing, spend, play, wear, give, promise

When I got there, I caught up with my camp friends before dinner. I ate breakfast in the mess hall and then spent the morning practicing drills.

After activities we spent more time playing soccer. On the last night of camp we all played a joke on our coaches and wore our pajamas to the game.

pg. 69
Shai plays soccer outside.
Samuel played the computer game skillfully.

Did it rain today?

There are mosquitoes everywhere.

The ballerina danced gracefully.

The boys waited patiently for their turn.

Kiko walked upstairs.

The rock star played his guitar yesterday.

Tomorrow, I will eat a burrito for lunch.

how: skillfully, gracefully, patiently
when: today, yesterday, tomorrow
where: outside, everywhere, upstairs

pg. 70
The funny clown rode on a tiny bike.

The sandy beach was very crowded.

The mothers took their children to the park.

All of the dogs began to bark.

The Peterson family is going to the mountains tomorrow.

The grumpy man yelled at the noisy boys.
Christian likes to visit his grandparents.
Dawn won a ribbon at the horse show.

pg. 73
My horse won its first race today.
I hope it's ready. I'm really hungry!
You should buy that sweater. Its color is perfect for you.
The elephant and its new baby can now be seen at the zoo.
It's time to leave for the movies.
That's a cute puppy. What is its name?
I wonder if it's hot outside today.
Hurry up! It's going to rain soon.
What a pretty bird. Its feathers are a beautiful color.
Have you seen my book? It's not in its usual place on my desk.

pg. 74
Please put the flowers there.
Have you been there before?
They're going to the zoo tomorrow.
Have you seen their new car?
I like swimming in pools when they're not too crowded.
Your pencil is over there on the desk.
Their house is right next to ours.
Will you go there with me?
On Saturday, they're having a birthday party.
I just saw their new lizard.

pg. 75
I don't know where we are going on vacation.
If we're late, he won't let us in.
What were you buying in that store?
Tomorrow, we're going to canoe on that lake.
Do you remember where Kelly said we should meet her?
We were in Florida last winter.
We're not singing in the school concert this year.
Where is your new bicycle?
Do you remember where you left your coat?
They were the winning team in the relay race.

pg. 77
Kevin said, "Let's go to the zoo tomorrow."
"Is that your new dress?" asked Chitra.
"Here we are at last!" said Ari. "I can't wait to see this movie!"
"I'm cooking spaghetti for dinner," said Rudi's father.
David asked, "Why are you laughing so hard?"
"There was one third grader," said the teacher, "who got every answer right."
"You'd better wear your coat. It's very cold today," said Philip's grandfather.
"I'm having my birthday party at the bowling alley," said Carlo.
"Are you going to play soccer this year?" asked Li.
"Watch out! There's a car coming!" yelled Alan.

pg. 78
What time is your piano lesson?
Where did you put your boots?
That is so exciting!
Julia and Jeffrey both live in North Carolina.
Hurry, the bathtub is overflowing onto the floor!
Oh no, our dinner is burning!
How long will you be gone?
That is so wonderful! OR That is so wonderful.

pg. 79
January 14, 2009
Dear Hernando,

I am so excited. We are now in our new home in Middletown, Pennsylvania. Our kitchen has a new stove, refrigerator, microwave, and sink. I have my own bedroom with a nice view.

Middletown is a lot smaller than Philadelphia, Pennsylvania, where we used to live. It is so different from living is a smaller town.

I can't wait to see you at camp this summer. We'll sail boats, go horseback riding, swim, and play tennis. I hope we'll be in the same tent like we were last year!

Your friend,
Neel

pg. 80
I watched the Red Sox play against the Yankees last night.
Sashiko lives in the United States, but she was born in Japan.
Is your Uncle Fred coming to your house for Thanksgiving?
We swam in the Pacific Ocean on our vacation last year.
I can't wait for school to start in September.
Have you read the new Harry Potter book?
Chris was born in Dallas.
We are going to Disneyland on Friday.

Person:	**Thing:**
I, Sashiko, Uncle Fred, We, Chris	Harry Potter book

Place:
United States, Japan, Pacific Ocean, Dallas, Disneyland

Reading

pg. 83
Effect:
- Coyote decided to go for a walk.
- A cloud appeared in the sky.
- It began to sprinkle.
- The creek turned into a large, swirling river.

Cause:
- Coyote wanted more rain.
- Coyote wished he could cool his feet.

pg. 85
(Some answers will vary)
- powerful; wealthy
- yes, because she becomes Queen of Egypt
- play with dolls; go to the zoo
- Tuthmosis II, her half-brother
- Neferure
- wearing a false beard and men's clothing
- directing the building of many monuments
- because the tomb that had been prepared for her was created for a queen, and Hatshepsut eventually became a pharaoh/king

pg. 87
(Some answers will vary)
- said; head
- scared, because he is afraid he will fall
- because they are so far away
- birds and clouds
- happy, because he was brave and tried to fly
- to make an effort and be brave

pg. 89
c; d; c

pg. 91
(Some answers will vary)
- to see if the heat from his body would hatch the eggs
- He sold newspapers, food, and candy
- the sole right given to an inventor to make or sell his idea
- because no one wanted it

pg. 93
- 4
- baking powder
- before
- yes, when both sides are brown
- flour, sugar, salt, baking powder
- milk, eggs, melted butter, vanilla
- one minute
- warm and with syrup

Pg 95
(Some answers will vary)
- loving, poor, kind
- a loaf of bread, a few eggs, and a cabbage
- because when they opened their cupboards they were suddenly filled with all sorts of delicious foods and fresh juices; also, their clothes turned into robes of fine linen and their hovel turned into a great palace
- because they loved each other
- to never have to live without the other
- they are different trees but grew from the same trunk

pg. 97
(Some answers will vary)
- It is difficult to please everyone.

pg. 99
(Some answers will vary)
- c
- because whoever pulls it free will become the new king of Britain
- because he is a young boy
- c
- surprised, because he did not expect to become king

pg. 101
2
6
1
4
3
5

pg. 103 (Some answers will vary)
- c
- make him a suit of the finest cloth imaginable
- because they did not want him to think that they were not smart enough to appreciate the cloth
- c
- His vanity caused him more harm than good.

pg. 105
(Some answers will vary)
Facts:
1. more than 1,000 planets the size of Earth could fit inside of Jupiter
2. Jupiter is 400 million miles from the sun
3. it has at least 64 known moons
4. Ganymede is Jupiter's largest moon
5. much of what we know about Jupiter comes from unmanned space probes

- to help them learn more about the early history of the earth
- craters
- because these names refer to the idea of exploration
- 1973

pg. 107
- survive the extreme cold of the Antarctic winter
- waddling on their feet
- one
- a fold of feathered skin that hangs down from his stomach
- 60 days
- the females return immediately and begin feeding the chicks

pg. 108
b; c; c

Writing

pg. 116
- When I go to the pool, I will swim and dive off the diving board.
- Everyone was excited and having fun.
- The boys put on their uniforms and ran out to the baseball field.
- The fans were really excited and cheered loudly for their team.

pg. 118
- Thanksgiving is my favorite holiday.

pg. 119
- Manatees have many interesting characteristics and habits.

pg. 120
Katie had a great time at tennis practice this morning. First she practiced her forehand shot with her coach. Then she worked on her backhand with the ball machine. Once she was warmed up, Katie and her coach played a few practice games, so Katie could work on her serve. Katie was exhausted when she got home, but at least she felt ready for Saturday's tournament.

pg. 121

Green card	**Yellow card**
2	4
1	2
3	3
4	1

Blue card
2
3
1
4

pg. 124
(Answers may vary)
- running is the ideal type of exercise
- opinion
- running is something almost anyone can do; running burns calories and gives your heart and legs a great workout; running is something you can do with a friend or by yourself

pg. 127
I. c. How Halloween started
II. b. Making a costume
III. b. Making a jack-o'-lantern
IV. b. Knocking on doors

pg. 133

If you travel to hawaii, don't forget to vsit the Mauna Loa Volcano. Mauna Loa is the the biggest Vol-cano on earth, and one of the most active Tourists visit from all over the World to see hot red lava flow-ing from the volcano down into the Pacific Ocean below.

Mauna Loa is located on the the island of Hawaii, and it is part of Ha-waii Volcanoes National park. The park is so big that it could take you several days just to drive arund and see all the sights. ¶Be sure to pack your raincoat and boots, because it's often cool and cloudy rainy at the top of the volcno. Of course as soon as you drive down to sea level the weather gets warmer and sun-nier that's Hawaii!

Math Skills

pg. 136
Even: 4, 2, 12, 146, 28, 70, 34, 18, 164, 500, 998, 744
Odd: 9, 17, 99, 239, 501, 23, 39, 301, 55, 87, 101, 219, 989, 3, 25
Even: 8, 10, 12, 14, 16, 18
Odd: 9, 11, 13, 15, 17
even
odd
odd

pg. 137
10 12 25
15 36 25
100 333

pg. 138
hundreds 5
thousands 2
70,208

pg. 139
Forty-eight thousand, five hundred and sixty seven
hundreds 277,539
2 75,222
thousands 4,601
3

pg. 140
2 70 8000
160 4 6
103
3 5

pg. 141
ray
line
ray
line segment

pg. 142
acute right obtuse
right obtuse
obtuse acute

pg. 143
3 8
4 right

pg. 144

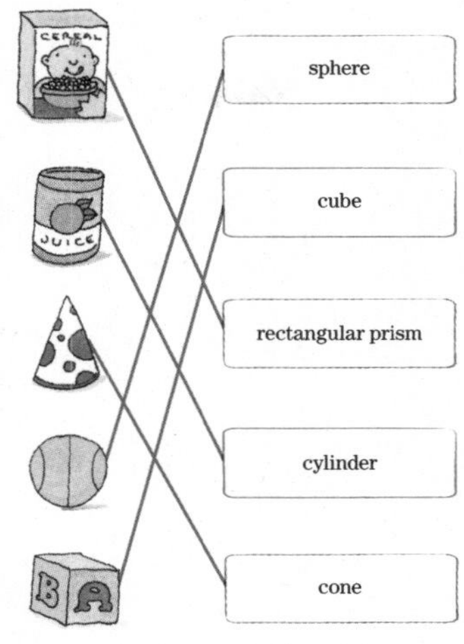

Pg. 145
square; circle; 6;
triangle, because it isn't 3-D; none
cube; 2; circle; cylinder; sphere

pg. 146
O, p
n, m
s, u
h, s

pg. 147
77; 88
44,444; 444,444
42; 49
150; 175
7; 6
23; 30
12; 16

pg. 148
60 10 30 80
60 40 40 80
20 70 20 20
500 800 700 600
900 300 700 400
300 200 100 200
400 900 900 200

pg. 149
590,000; 60,000; 3,000; 3,000,000; 8,000; 40,000; 400,000; 2,000

pg. 150
80 + 20 = 100
60 + 70 = 130
90 – 30 = 60
100 – 70 = 30
60 + 20 = 80
40 + 30 = 70
90 + 10 = 100
40 + 30 = 70
70 – 10 = 60
70 – 30 = 40
50 – 40 = 10
90 – 40 = 50

pg. 151
900 + 200 = 1100
900 + 600 = 1500
700 + 200 = 900
600 + 300 = 900
300 + 200 = 500
700 + 300 = 1000
700 + 500 = 1200
500 + 400 = 900
400 + 100 = 500
800 + 800 = 1600
900 + 600 = 1500
700 + 200 = 900

Pg. 152
May; 30; June; 5; 70

Pg. 153
8; dog;; snake; 2; hamsters; 6

pg. 154
17; 31; 15
Diving; High and low jumps;
10; Diving events

pg. 155
27 ÷ (9) = 3
(28) ÷ 4 = 7
8 + (7) = 15
4 + (56) = 60
(10) × 4 = 40
(5) × (7) = 35
(3) – 3 = 0
(6) + (3) = 9

Addition and Subtraction

pg. 158

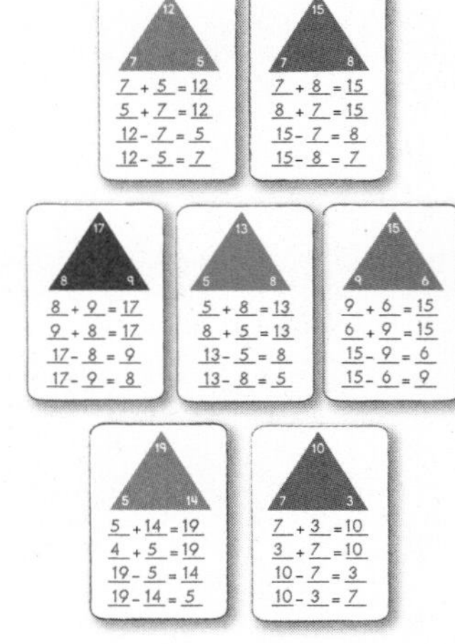

pg. 159

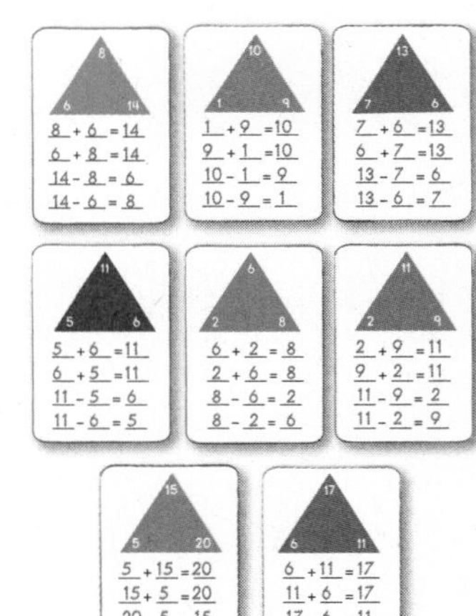

pg. 160
49 777 98 799
99 949 898 78
88 867 999 978

pg. 161
26 29 26 30
27; 26; 41; 32; 30; 35; 36

pg. 162
36 452 43 756
23 471 255 13
37 142 889 342

pg. 163
16 – 8 = 8
24 + 35 = 59
41 + 15 = 56
22 + 62 = 84
24 – 10 = 14
35 – 15 = 20
21 + 15 = 36
22 + 63 = 85

pg. 164

8	13	6
7	9	11
12	5	10

10	3	8
5	7	9
6	11	4

pg. 165

13	8	9
6	10	14
11	12	7

7	6	11
12	8	4
5	10	9

16	3	2	13
5	10	11	8
9	6	7	12
4	15	14	1

14	9	13	2
3	12	8	15
4	11	7	16
17	6	10	5

pg. 166
41 82 65
630 651 744
507 842 943

pg. 167
453 671 923
706 926 229
494 663 620
838 550 948

pg. 168
28 38 19
259 569 348
579 348 357

pg. 169
116 380 599
289 421 324
473 473 666
563 388 771

pg. 170
836 488 727
227 536 557
657 727 338

pg. 171
169 813 367
132 555 227
164 768 443

pg. 172
600 + 200 = 800
700 + 600 = 1300
800 + 100 = 900
700 + 300 = 1000
200 + 300 = 500
400 + 400 = 800
400 + 500 = 900
400 + 300 = 700
500 + 300 = 800
200 + 600 = 800
500 + 400 = 900
600 + 200 = 800

pg. 173
800 – 500 = 300
900 – 300 = 600
300 – 100 = 200
500 – 500 = 0
300 – 200 = 100
600 – 100 = 500
700 – 100 = 600
700 – 300 = 400
400 – 200 = 200
700 – 300 = 400
800 – 700 = 100
1000 – 900 = 100

pg. 174
9 + 11 = 20
11 – 5 = 6
3 + 6 = 9
125 – 75 = 50
37 – 2 = 35
68 + 12 = 80

12 + 12 – 24 = 0
150 – 100 + 14 = 64
22 – 12 + 11 = 21
21 + 33 + 3 = 57
33 + 11 – 10 = 34
47 – 15 – 3 = 29

pg. 175
388 523 977
890 378 812
545 1,079 589
825 766 896
454 524 499

pg. 176
645 211 472
443 611 782 636
324 440 642
541 701 712
685 41

Multiplication and Division

pg. 178
6 7 5 8
0 3 2 1
4 4 9 2
10 6 5 7
1 2 3 4 5 6 7 8 9 10

pg. 179
2 6 12 14
10 8 10 16
20 4 18 12
6 8 18 0
2 4 6 8 10 12 14 16 18 20

pg. 180
3 21 0 12
30 9 18 6
27 15 21 15
12 24 18 30
3 6 9 12 15 18 21 24 27 30

pg. 181
8 32 24 12
20 40
36 4
28 8 36 24
12 16 20 0
4 8 12 16 20 24 28 32 36 40

pg. 182
20 25 10 35
45 0 50 40
5 10 45 30
15 20 40 15
5 10 15 20 25 30 35 40 45 50

pg. 183
12 0 30 42
18 24 12 48
54 36 30 18
60 24 54 6
6 12 18 24 30 36 42 48 54 60

pg. 184
42 7 35 49
21 28 56 0
7 63 14 70
35 28 63 56
7 14 21 28 35 42 49 56 63 70

pg. 185
56 48 32 80
40 56 0 24
72 16 64 16
48 40 80 8

8 16 24 32 40 48 56 64 72 80

pg. 186
9 63 45 81
27 54 18 0
54 36 72 90
45 72 63 36
9 18 27 36 45 54 63 72 81 90

pg. 187
36 27
72 81
54 9
18 63
45

pg. 188
10 40 80
70 90 60
50 100 40
30 20 70
10 20 30 40 50 60 70 80 90 100

pg. 189
1 4 9 16
25 36 49 64
81 100 121 144
11 22 33 44 55 66 77 88 99 110
12 24 36 48 60 72 84 96 108 120

pg. 190
36 36 24 24
56 56 14 14
20 20 30 30
728,540

pg. 191
4 8 12 16 20 24 28 32 36 40
5 10 15 20 25 30 35 40 45 50
6 12 18 24 30 36 42 48 54 60
7 14 21 28 35 42 49 56 63 70
8 16 24 32 40 48 56 64 72 80

pg. 192
2 × 4 = 8 1 × 10 = 10
6 × 7 = 42 4 × 8 = 32
8 × 8 = 64 2× 6 = 12
5 × 7 = 35 7 × 7 = 49
4 × 9 = 36 8 × 9 = 72
6 × 8 = 48 6 × 3 = 18
3 × 7 = 21 5 × 2 = 10
9 × 0 = 0 6 × 9 = 54
4 × 7 = 28 9 × 3 = 27

pg. 193

×	0	1	2	3	4	5	6	7	8	9	10	11	12
0	0	0	0	0	0	0	0	0	0	0	0	0	0
1	0	1	2	3	4	5	6	7	8	9	10	11	12
2	0	2	4	6	8	10	12	14	16	18	20	22	24
3	0	3	6	9	12	15	18	21	24	27	30	33	36
4	0	4	8	12	16	20	24	28	32	36	40	44	48
5	0	5	10	15	20	25	30	35	40	45	50	55	60
6	0	6	12	18	24	30	36	42	48	54	60	66	72
7	0	7	14	21	28	35	42	49	56	63	70	77	84
8	0	8	16	24	32	40	48	56	64	72	80	88	96
9	0	9	18	27	36	45	54	63	72	81	90	99	108
10	0	10	20	30	40	50	60	70	80	90	100	110	120
11	0	11	22	33	44	55	66	77	88	99	110	121	132
12	0	12	24	36	48	60	72	84	96	108	120	132	144

pg. 194
28 186 155 208
84 720 488 219
98 88 156 540

pg. 195
207 288 312
225 574 78
416 594 595
564 185 384

pg. 196
20 26
0
70 36

pg. 197
36 25
200 12
48

pg. 198
8
3 3
3

pg. 199
4 2 6 5
2 10 2 11
4 3 4 6
8 7 2 9
1 9 9 10

pg. 200
100 ÷ 10 = 10 12 ÷ 6 = 2
24 ÷ 8 = 3 30 ÷ 6 = 5
10 ÷ 2 = 5 21 ÷ 3 = 7

pg. 201
40 ÷ 8 = 5
75 ÷ 5 = 15 88 ÷ 2 = 44
33 ÷ 3 = 11 35 ÷ 7 = 5

pg. 202

12 3 4: 4 × 3 = 12, 3 × 4 = 12, 12 ÷ 3 = 4, 12 ÷ 4 = 3
32 8 4: 4 × 8 = 32, 8 × 4 = 32, 32 ÷ 4 = 8, 32 ÷ 8 = 4
35 7 5: 5 × 7 = 35, 7 × 5 = 35, 35 ÷ 5 = 7, 35 ÷ 7 = 5
28 7 4: 4 × 7 = 28, 7 × 4 = 28, 28 ÷ 4 = 7, 28 ÷ 7 = 4
45 9 5: 5 × 9 = 45, 9 × 5 = 45, 45 ÷ 5 = 9, 45 ÷ 9 = 5

pg. 203

9 2 18: 9 × 2 = 18, 2 × 9 = 18, 18 ÷ 9 = 2, 18 ÷ 2 = 9
6 5 30: 6 × 5 = 30, 5 × 6 = 30, 30 ÷ 6 = 5, 30 ÷ 5 = 6
21 3 7: 7 × 3 = 21, 3 × 7 = 21, 21 ÷ 7 = 3, 21 ÷ 3 = 7
54 9 6: 6 × 9 = 54, 9 × 6 = 54, 54 ÷ 6 = 9, 54 ÷ 9 = 6
6 2 12: 6 × 2 = 12, 2 × 6 = 12, 12 ÷ 6 = 2, 12 ÷ 2 = 6
9 8 72: 9 × 8 = 72, 8 × 9 = 72, 72 ÷ 9 = 8, 72 ÷ 8 = 9
48 6 8: 8 × 6 = 48, 6 × 8 = 48, 48 ÷ 6 = 8, 48 ÷ 8 = 6
7 8 56: 7 × 8 = 56, 8 × 7 = 56, 56 ÷ 7 = 8, 56 ÷ 8 = 7
40 5 8: 8 × 5 = 40, 5 × 8 = 40, 40 ÷ 5 = 8, 40 ÷ 8 = 5
9 7 63: 9 × 7 = 63, 7 × 9 = 63, 63 ÷ 9 = 7, 63 ÷ 7 = 9

pg. 204
8 ÷ 8 = 1
6 × 5 = 30
64 ÷ 8 = 8
8 ÷ 2 = 4
8 × 8 = 64 18 ÷ 9 = 2 12 ÷ 3 = 4
7 × 9 = 63 7 × 2 = 14 3 × 7 = 21

32 ÷ 4 = 8 27 ÷ 3 = 2 49 ÷ 7 = 7
9 × 5 = 45 6 × 8 = 48 2 × 4 = 8
6 ÷ 3 = 2 9 ÷ 3 = 3 56 ÷ 7 = 8

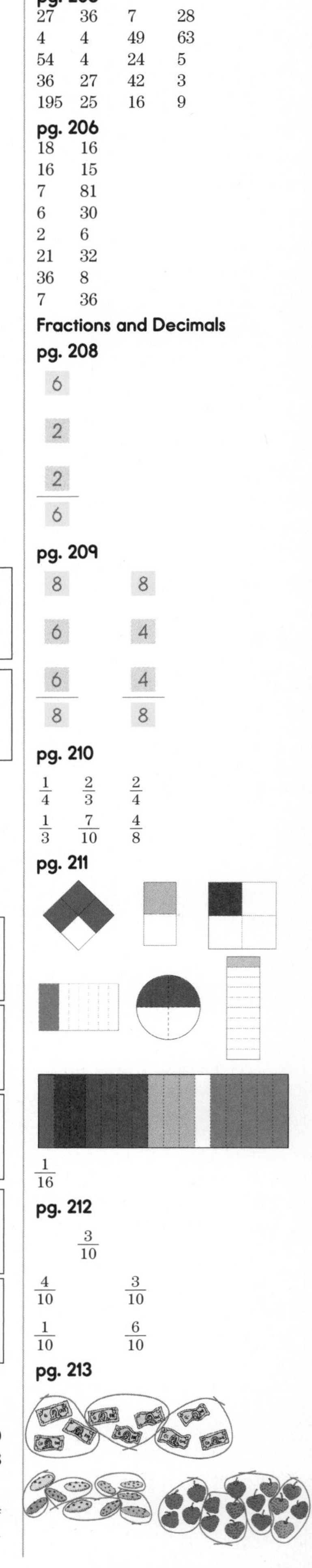

pg. 205
27 36 7 28
4 4 49 63
54 4 24 5
36 27 42 3
195 25 16 9

pg. 206
18 16
16 15
7 81
6 30
2 6
21 32
36 8
7 36

Fractions and Decimals

pg. 208
6
2
$\frac{2}{6}$

pg. 209
8 8
6 4
$\frac{6}{8}$ $\frac{4}{8}$

pg. 210
$\frac{1}{4}$ $\frac{2}{3}$ $\frac{2}{4}$
$\frac{1}{3}$ $\frac{7}{10}$ $\frac{4}{8}$

pg. 211

$\frac{1}{16}$

pg. 212
$\frac{3}{10}$
$\frac{4}{10}$ $\frac{3}{10}$
$\frac{1}{10}$ $\frac{6}{10}$

pg. 213

pg. 214

$20 \div 4 = 5$ $\frac{1}{4}$ of 20 = 5
$6 \div 2 = 3$ $\frac{1}{2}$ of 6 = 3
$10 \div 5 = 2$ $\frac{1}{5}$ of 10 = 2
$8 \div 2 = 4$ $\frac{1}{2}$ of 8 = 4

pg. 215

$4 \div 2 = 2$ $\frac{1}{2}$ of 4 = 2
$15 \div 3 = 5$ $\frac{1}{3}$ of 15 = 5
$16 \div 2 = 8$ $\frac{1}{2}$ of 16 = 8
$15 \div 5 = 3$ $\frac{1}{5}$ of 15 = 3
$12 \div 6 = 2$ $\frac{1}{6}$ of 12 = 2

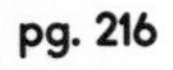

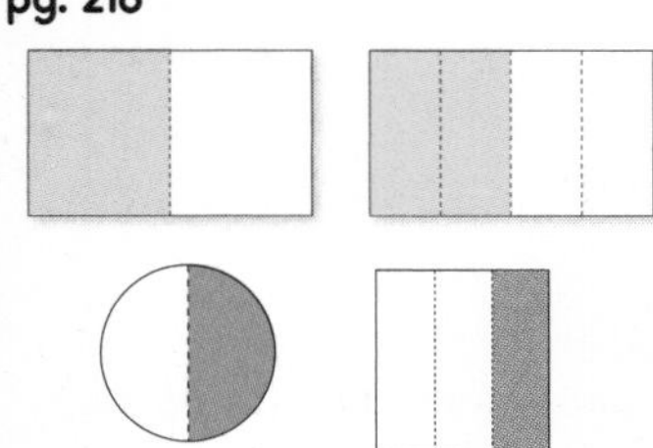

$\frac{1}{2}$ $\frac{1}{3}$

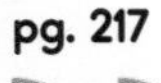

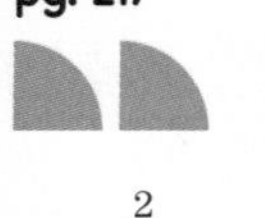

$\frac{2}{4}$ $\frac{5}{6}$

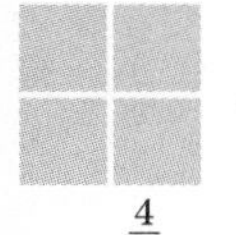

$\frac{4}{9}$ $\frac{5}{8}$

pg. 218

$\frac{2}{3}$ $\frac{4}{5}$
$\frac{4}{4}$ $\frac{3}{4}$
$\frac{9}{10}$ $\frac{4}{6}$
$\frac{9}{12}$ $\frac{7}{8}$
$\frac{2}{5}$
$\frac{2}{4}$

pg. 219

$\frac{4}{6}$ $\frac{2}{5}$
$\frac{4}{7}$ $\frac{2}{4}$
$\frac{7}{12}$ $\frac{2}{8}$
$\frac{3}{10}$ $\frac{4}{9}$
$\frac{3}{5}$
$\frac{3}{6}$

pg. 220

$\frac{2}{3}$ $\frac{8}{10}$
$\frac{1}{6}$ $\frac{5}{7}$

$21 \div 3 = 7$ 7
$16 \div 8 = 2$ 2
$18 \div 2 = 9$ 9
$20 \div 10 = 2$ 2
$24 \div 4 = 6$ 6

pg. 221

$\frac{3}{10}$ $\frac{5}{8}$

$\frac{7}{7} + \frac{7}{7} = 2$

$\frac{6}{6} = 1$

$\frac{1}{2} + \frac{1}{2} = \frac{2}{2}$

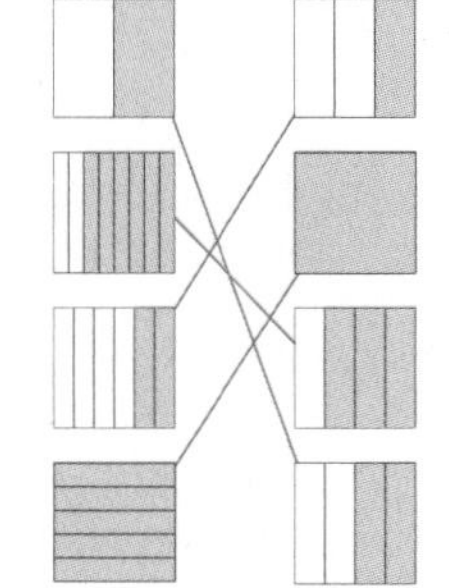

pg. 222

$\frac{4}{10} = .4$ $\frac{2}{10} = .2$ $\frac{5}{10} = .5$
$\frac{8}{10} = .8$

$\frac{9}{10} = .9$ $\frac{1}{10} = .1$ $\frac{4}{10} = .4$

$\frac{2}{10} = .2$ $\frac{5}{10} = .5$ $\frac{7}{10} = .7$

$.6 = \frac{6}{10}$ $.8 = \frac{8}{10}$ $.1 = \frac{1}{10}$

pg. 223

$\frac{8}{100} = .08$

$\frac{3}{100} = .03$ $\frac{2}{100} = .02$

$\frac{5}{100} = .05$ $\frac{9}{100} = .09$

$\frac{8}{100} = .08$ $\frac{6}{100} = .06$

$.09 = \frac{9}{100}$ $.01 = \frac{1}{100}$ $.04 = \frac{4}{100}$

pg. 224

tenths; 7; 1; Ones; $15\frac{97}{100}$

pg. 225

thousandths; 85.341; 2; 32.479;
3.01; 40.001; 5.001

pg. 226

6.8	13.9	6.5
10.47	12.87	7.96
8.07	8.55	10.94
11.60	11.57	9.49

pg. 227

3.2	2.2	.36
4.45	5.13	2.59
5.19	4.94	3.26
4.04	4.81	1.82

pg. 228

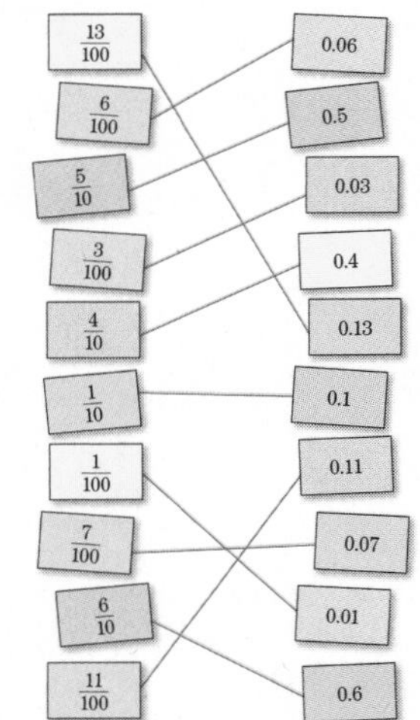

Measurement

pg. 230

inches; miles; feet
3 inches; 15 feet; 7 yards;
7 feet; 100 yards

pg. 231

20 inches < 2 feet
2 yards = 72 inches
6 feet < 3 yards
10 feet = 120 inches
1 mile > 5,000 feet
36, 30; 1; 18; 4; 10,560

pg. 232

centimeter; kilometer; meter
41 kilometers; 2 meters;
3 centimeters; 1 ½ meters

pg. 233

6 inches 15.3 centimeters
1.2 inch 3.2 centimeters
2.7 inches 7.4 centimeters

pg. 234

4 cups; 16 quarts; 2 cups; 8 pints

pg. 235

ounce; pound; ounce; pound; ton; pound; ton

pg. 236

8; 8
16; 4; 10
6; 15; 9

pg. 237

6; 4;
4 (width) × 6 (length);
24 square units
12; 20; 24
24 square feet

pg. 238

6 + 6 + 6 = 18 ft.
3+ 3+ 3+ 3+ 3+ 3+ 3+ 3 = 24 in.
5 + 5 + 5 + 5 = 20 in.
10 + 10 + 4 + 4 = 28 in.

Time & Money

pg. 240

6:00	8:35	2:15	2:45
	3:55	5:45	9:35
	10:05	5:25	12:00
	7:25	2:00	3:30

pg. 241

6:40
7:30
Rick; 24; 90; 90

pg. 242

1 ½ hours; 5:00 p.m; 8:20 p.m; 45 minutes; 2:30 p.m; 1 hour, 15 minutes

pg. 243

1 hour, 45 minutes; 1 hour, 55 minutes; 10:45 a.m; 4:55 p.m; 3:15 p.m.

pg. 244

\$.35; \$1.05; \$1.25; Laura; \$1.25; Allison

pg. 245

\$1.05; \$1.09; \$.59; \$1.23

pg. 246

\$3.69	\$3.42	\$1.60
\$3.10	\$1.00	\$12.98
\$12.00	\$5.20	\$9.81
\$1.41	\$9.27	\$.62
\$2.87	\$.02	\$8.67

pg. 248

\$3.00
\$.20
\$3.20
\$2.00
no

pg. 248

\$.05	\$.71	\$.01
\$.53	\$.75	\$3.65
\$4.03	\$1.00	\$.37

Word Problems

pg. 250

45 + 36 = 81
15 + 9 = 24
45 + 20 = 65
10 + 12 + 8 + 6 = 36

pg. 251

55 + 19 + 31 = 105
10 + 15 + 18 + 20 = 63

pg. 252

47 – 35 = 12
(88 – 26) – 41 = 21
85 – 72 = 13
38 – (9 + 10 + 2) = 17

pg. 253

100 – 86 = 14
375 – 320 = 55
\$130 – \$75 = \$55

pg. 254

4 x 6 = 24
16 x 2 = 32
7 x 4 = 28
5 x 6 = 30

pg. 255

8 x 7 = 56
50 x 8 = 400
7 x 3 = 21
9 x 30 = 270

pg. 256

55 ÷ 5 = 11
81 ÷ 9 = 9
24 ÷ 8 = 3
56 ÷ 8 = 7

pg. 257

32 ÷ 4 = 8
36 ÷ 9 = 4
64 ÷ 8 = 8
21 ÷ 3 = 7
40 ÷ 5 = 8
16 ÷ 2 = 8

pg. 258

87 – 65 = 22; subtractÚn
9 x 5 = 45; multiplicatÚn
72 ÷ 9 = 8; divisÚn
26 + 34 = 60; additÚn

pg. 259

32 – 5 = 27; subtractÚn
36 ÷ 4 = 9; divisÚn
8 x 9 = 72; multiplicatÚn
42 + 57 = 99; additÚn
48 – 34 = 14; subtractÚn
48 ÷ 6 = 8; divisÚn

pg. 260

31 – 5 = 26 26 + 2 = 28
3 x 6 = 18 18 ÷ 9 = 2
4 + 5 = 9 9 x 4 = 36
24 ÷ 6 = 4 4 + 2 = 6

pg. 261

57 + 65 = 122 122 – 93 = 29
(2 x 4) + (2 x 5) = 18 20 – 18 = 2
12 x 3 = 36 6 x 2 = 12 36 – 12 = 24
4 + 8 = 12 59 – 12 = 47

pg. 262

12 x 4 = 48 48 + 12 = 60
44 + 32 = 76 76 + 8 = 84
5 + 3 = 8 96 – 8 = 88

Social Studies

pg. 265
Ohio
Michigan
Illinois
Kentucky
Missouri
Minnesota; Wisconsin; Illinois
Missouri; Nebraska; South Dakota
Maine
Alaska; Hawaii
Montana
Utah; Colorado
Arizona; New Mexico
Kansas
Two; North Carolina, North Dakota
One; West Virginia

pg. 266

Wyoming	Connecticut	Arkansas
Tennessee	Ohio	Indiana
Florida	Arizona	Maryland
Alaska	New Mexico	Louisiana
Wisconsin	Utah	Hawaii

pg. 267

Texas	Massachusetts	Georgia
Washington	Wisconsin	Illinois
Pennsylvania	Ohio	California
Missouri	Maryland	Pennsylvania

pg. 270

AL	CT
AK	DE
AZ	FL
AR	GA
CA	HI
CO	ID

pg. 271

IL	NY
IN	NC
IA	ND
KS	OH
KY	OK
LA	OR
ME	PA
MD	RI
MA	SC
MI	SD
MN	TN
MS	TX
MO	UT
MT	VT
NE	VA
NV	WA
NH	WV
NJ	WI
NM	WY

Washington, D.C.
District of Columbia

pg. 273
- Representative democracy
- By the people, so that decisions would be made by majority rule.
- Through the Bill of Rights
- 1791
- Freedom of speech, freedom of religion, freedom of the press and/or the right to a fair trial.

pg. 275
- Executive, legislative, judicial
- So that there is a system of checks and balances
- The president
- The Senate and the House of Representatives
- 100; 2
- Yes, because the number of members per state varies according to the state population
- The Supreme Court

pg. 276
Alaska, Hawaii
Montana
Colorado, Idaho, Utah, Arizona
1889
Idaho, Wyoming

pg. 277
a
b
a
b
b
a

G	O	V	E	R	N	M	E	N	T	K	F	D	A	U	B
X	C	O	N	G	R	E	S	S	G	C	X	O	I	P	R
R	B	B	E	U	O	F	Q	C	Y	E	R	F	E	R	G
E	J	L	E	G	I	S	L	A	T	I	V	E	I	E	D
P	E	P	G	B	Q	J	D	P	S	H	B	Z	M	S	O
R	M	A	K	Y	X	A	S	I	C	Y	P	H	C	I	S
E	Z	H	M	C	U	H	R	T	H	U	E	Z	Y	D	J
S	S	W	H	I	T	E	H	O	U	S	E	J	O	E	Z
E	D	R	Q	M	Y	B	I	L	B	Z	A	Z	P	N	Q
N	Z	X	Z	A	F	Z	F	E	M	S	E	N	A	T	E
T	H	F	G	Y	E	A	R	O	M	T	U	D	S	H	D
A	F	R	Q	C	D	U	D	X	Z	A	S	Z	F	Z	B
T	E	R	M	Z	E	R	E	C	J	T	Z	X	J	E	U
I	P	G	R	O	R	G	K	H	Q	E	K	A	M	B	K
V	A	X	I	L	A	W	Z	Z	F	B	E	Z	D	Q	G
E	O	B	Y	I	L	U	E	D	Q	A	A	S	U	Q	X

pg. 278

Science

pg. 281
chapter 2
p.3
chapter 3
p.40
table of contents
index
glossary

pg. 283

1. egg	2. caterpillar
3. pupa	4. adult

Lepidoptera: a group of insects
Migrate: make a journey to a new place

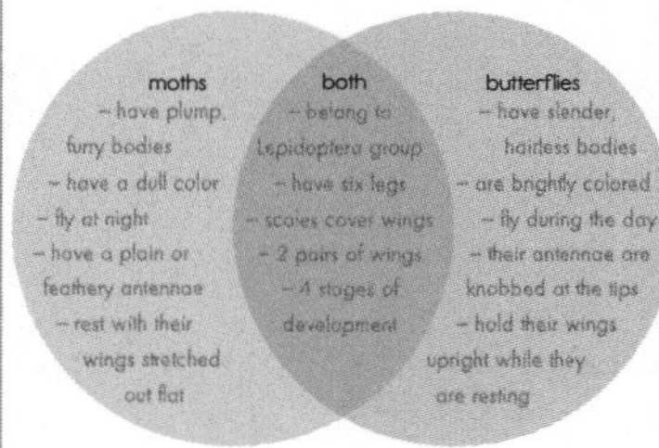

pg. 285
(sample answers)
mammals: people, dogs, mice
birds: hawks, barn owls, toucans
amphibians: salamanders, frogs, toads
reptiles: geckos, crocodiles, boa constrictors
fish: goldfish, sharks, eels

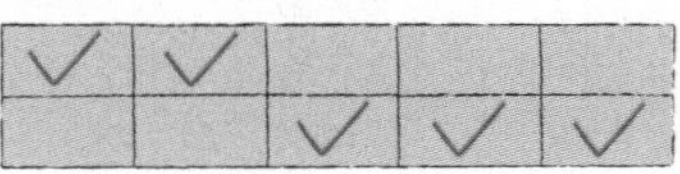

pg. 286
Penguins, ostriches
Migration
They have no teeth!
Hawks, eagles, owls

pg. 287
1. Their huge eyes can see well in the dark.
2. Their hearing is very sensitive.
3. Soft-fringed feathers on their wings help them fly quickly.
4. They have needle-sharp claws called talons.

They are spit up in pellets.

pg. 288
gills
scales
school
fins and tail
other fish or smaller sea creatures

pg. 289
1. rattlesnakes
2. cobras

1. When an alligator's mouth is closed, you can see only its top teeth. When a crocodile's mouth is closed, you can see all of its teeth.
2. A crocodile's snout is wider than an alligator's.
3. Alligators are found mostly in the southeastern United States, whereas crocodiles are found on almost every continent.

pg. 290-291

Across	**Down:**
boa constrictor	cold
bullfrog	fangs
schools	scales
rattlesnake	crocodile
gills	turtle
snout	eggs
southern	teeth
hawk	whale
amphibian	mammals
backbones	ostrich
milk	

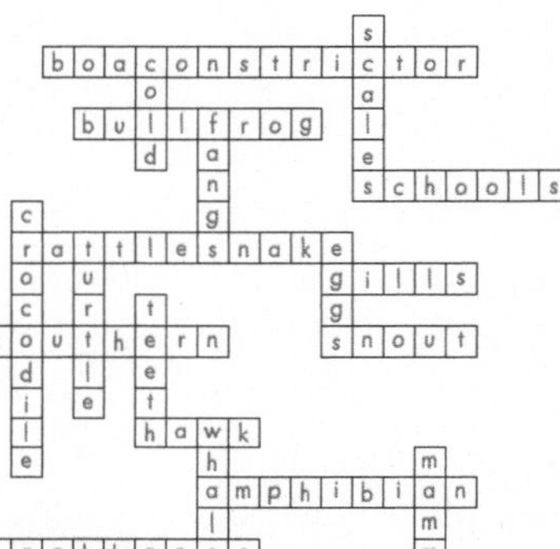

pg. 292

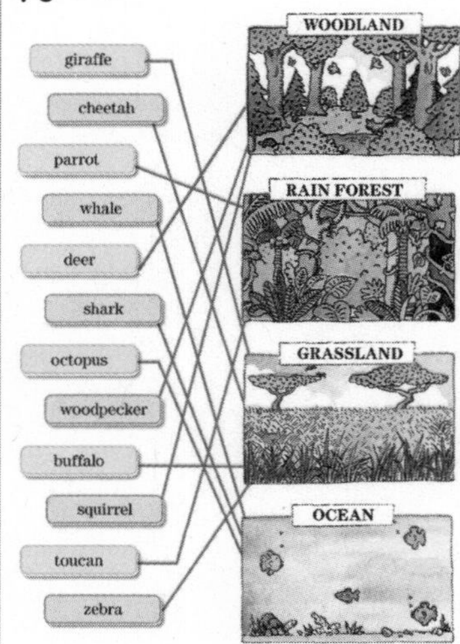

pg. 293

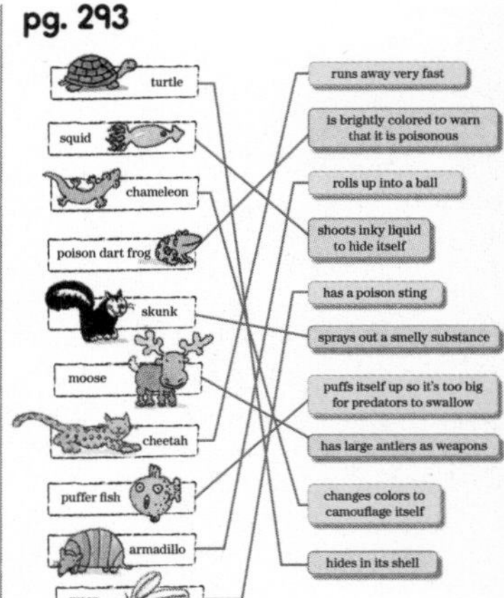

pg. 296

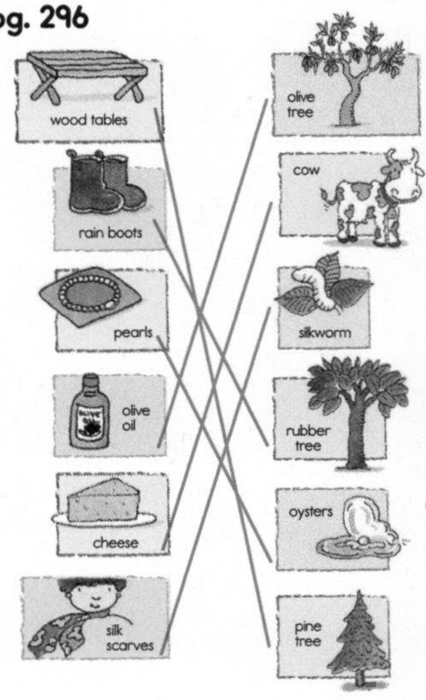

pg. 297

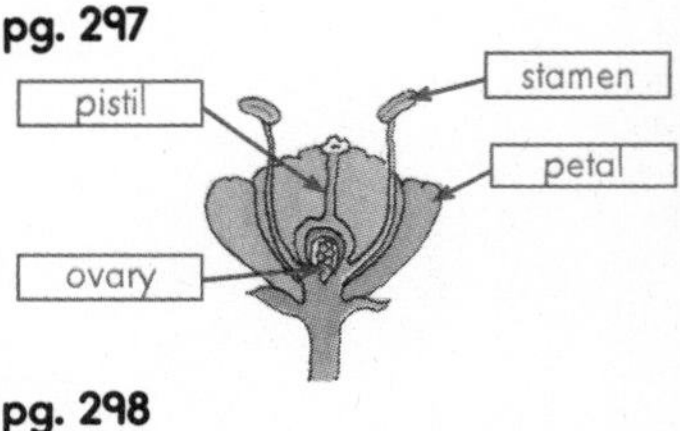

pg. 298

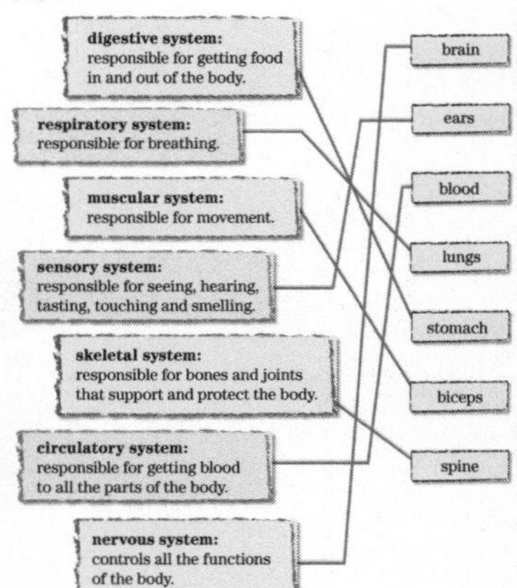

pg. 299
206
103
the brain
ligaments
calcium

pg. 300
pull together
push apart
m: paper clip
m: safety pin
m: nail
m: bolt
m: metal spoon
No

Brain Quest Extras

Congratulations!

You've finished the Brain Quest Workbook!

In this section, you'll find:

Brain Quest Mini-Deck

Cut out the cards and make your own Brain Quest deck.

Play by yourself or with a friend.

Brainiac Certificate

Put a sticker on each square for every chapter you complete. Finish the whole workbook, and you're an official Brainiac!

And don't forget to turn to the end of the workbook. You'll find stickers and a Times Tables to 12 poster!

Questions

What is the sum of 858 and 167?

Put the number words in alphabetical order: thirteen, third, three

Change this to a multiplication problem: 5 + 5 + 5 + 5 + 5 + 5 = 30

Spell the five-letter word that means the opposite of "here."

Questions

What's the sum of 224 and 551?

What do we call the person who mends clothes for a living?

Sophie has 20 buttons. Each shirt needs 6. How many shirts can she make?

Spell the name of the joint between the thigh and the calf that rhymes with "pea."

Questions

True or false: 9 + 3 = 15 – 4

Spell the plural of witch.

What is the denominator in $6\frac{4}{8}$?

Which should be written as one word: finger nail or finger puppet?

Questions

The numerator is the top number of a fraction. What is the bottom number?

Change this to a multiplication problem: 6+6+6+6=24

In the division problem 36 ÷ 4 = 9, what is the name for the number 9?

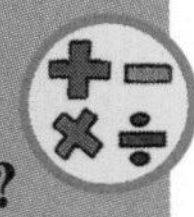

Which is a synonym of interested: uncertain, curious, talkative.

Questions

How many ounces are in a pint?

How do you spell the plural of knife?

Is home plate shaped like a hexagon or a pentagon?

Change the verb to its past form: "The dog begins to howl."

Questions

Round $762.32 to the nearest hundred dollars

"Dorothy followed the yellow brick road." What pronoun can replace the subject?

Find the difference between 127 and 98. Is it bigger or smaller than 30?

What letters do cantaloupe and celebration have in common?

Answers

False. 9 + 3 = 12 and 15 – 4 = 11

witches

8

fingernail

Answers

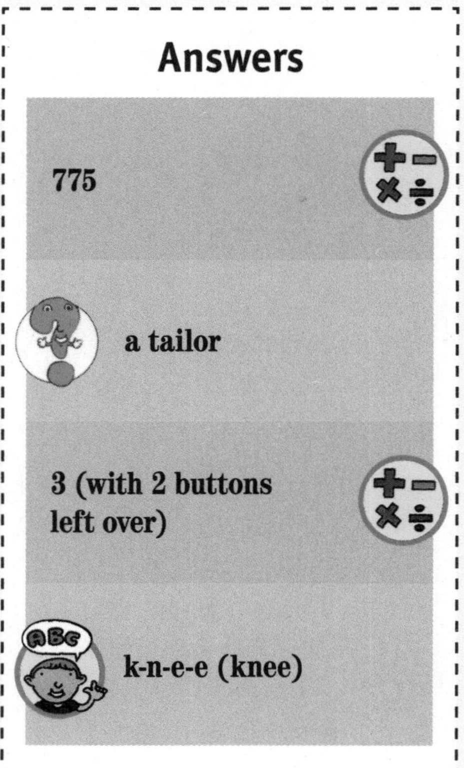

775

a tailor

3 (with 2 buttons left over)

k-n-e-e (knee)

Answers

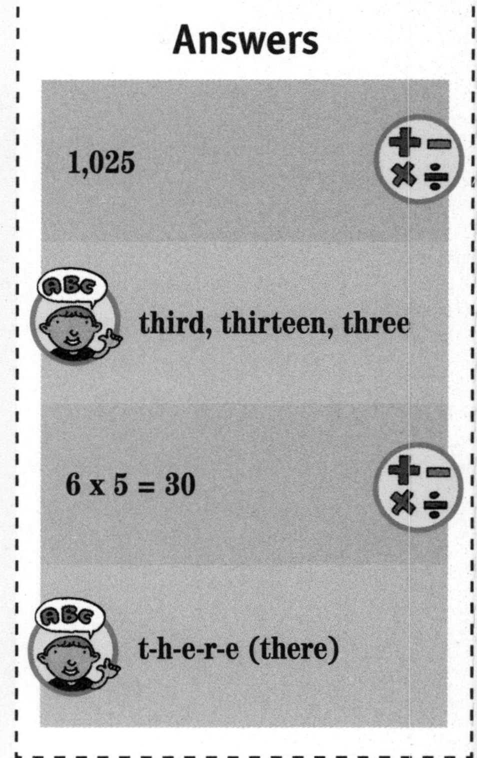

1,025

third, thirteen, three

6 x 5 = 30

t-h-e-r-e (there)

Answers

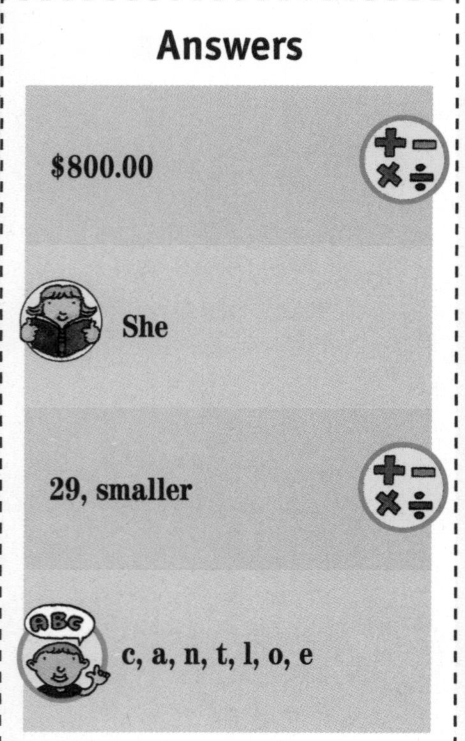

$800.00

She

29, smaller

c, a, n, t, l, o, e

Answers

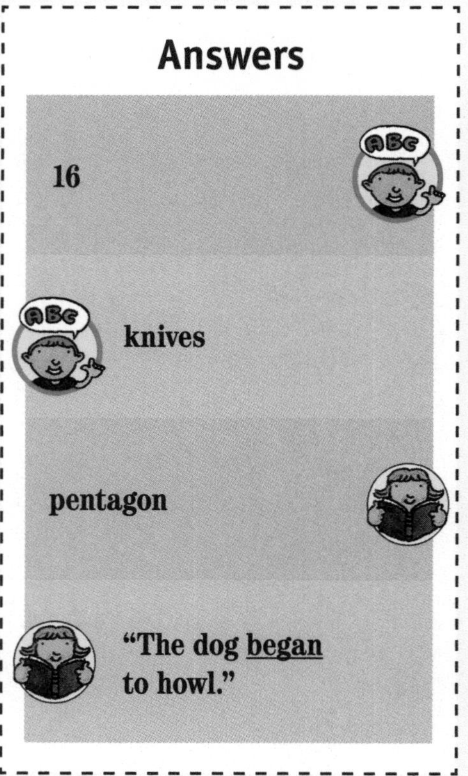

16

knives

pentagon

"The dog began to howl."

Answers

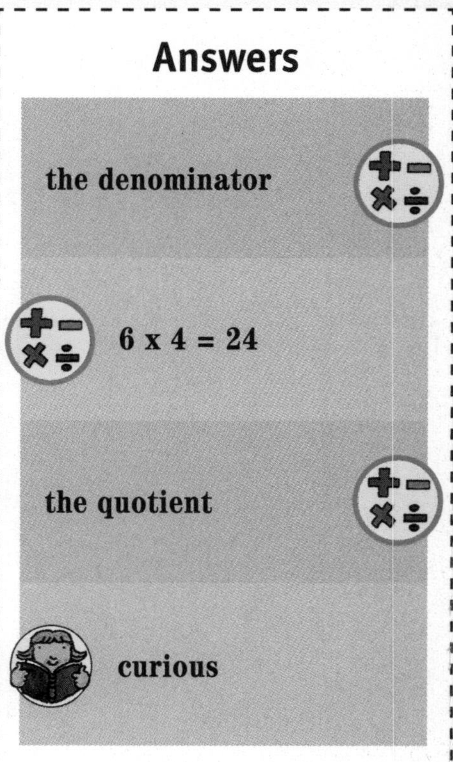

the denominator

6 x 4 = 24

the quotient

curious

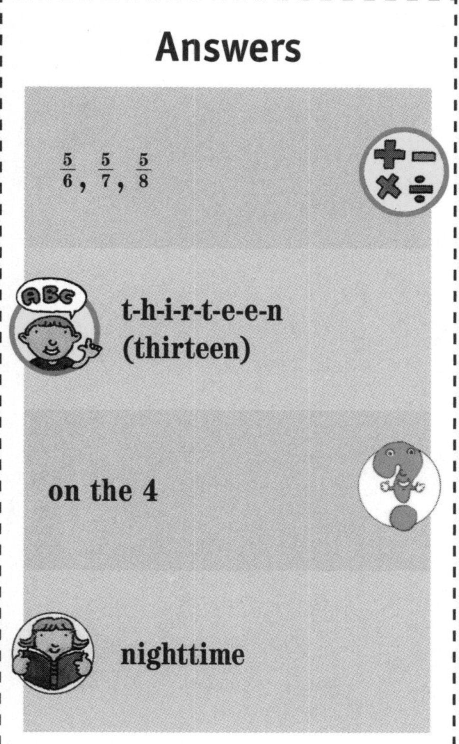

Answers

$\frac{5}{6}, \frac{5}{7}, \frac{5}{8}$

t-h-i-r-t-e-e-n (thirteen)

on the 4

nighttime

Answers

80

"Mom, Dad and I <u>saw</u> a movie last night."

10

before

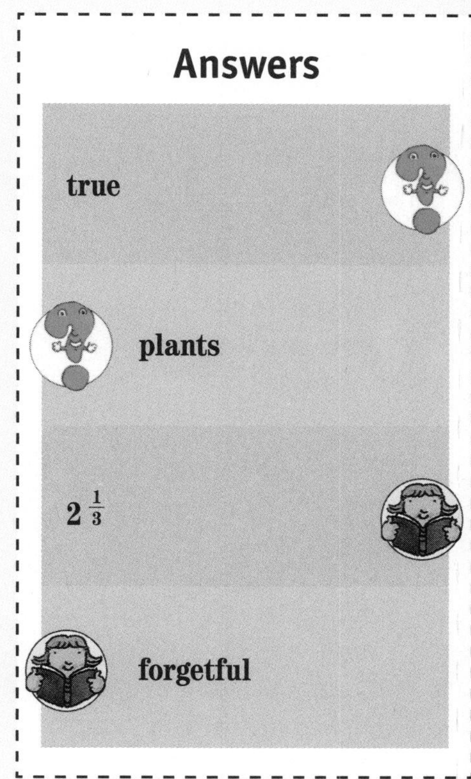

Answers

true

plants

$2\frac{1}{3}$

forgetful

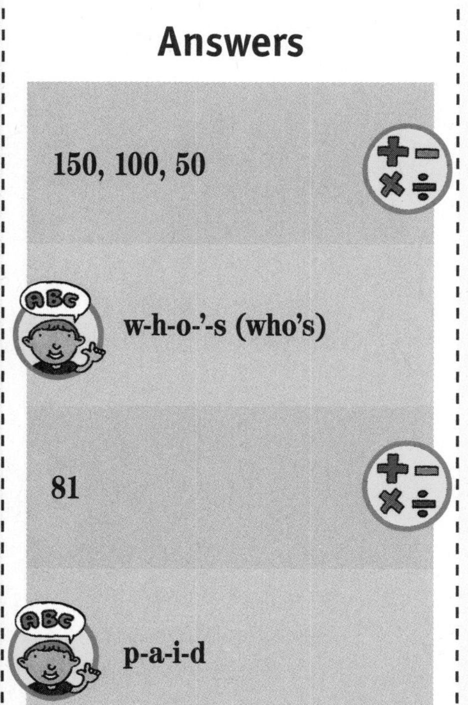

Answers

150, 100, 50

w-h-o-'-s (who's)

81

p-a-i-d

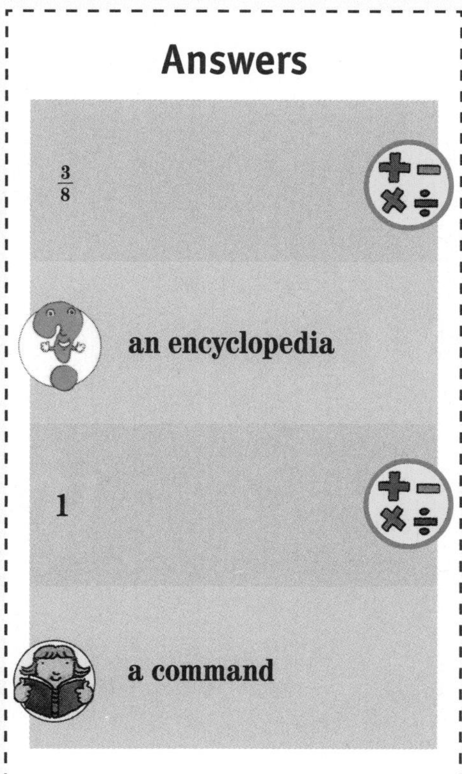

Answers

$\frac{3}{8}$

an encyclopedia

1

a command

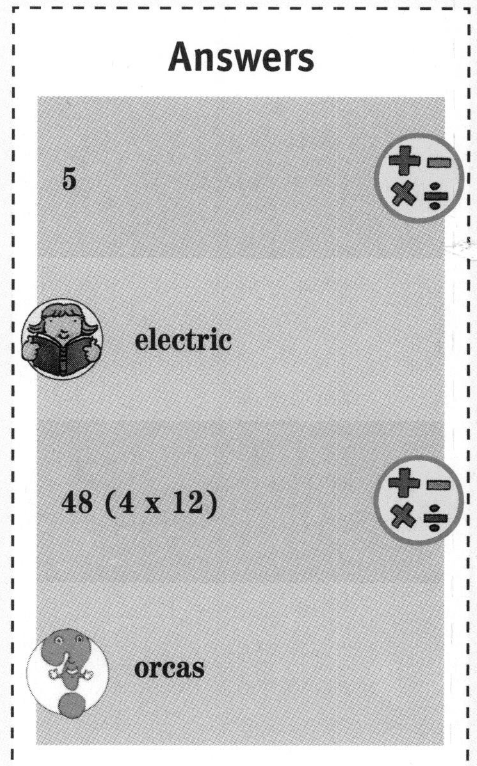

Answers

5

electric

48 (4 x 12)

orcas

Questions

The fractions $\frac{1}{6}$, $\frac{5}{30}$, and $\frac{2}{12}$ are all equal. True or false?

Is a botanist someone who studies bugs or plants?

Which of these numbers is a mixed fraction: $\frac{12}{4}$ or $2\frac{1}{3}$?

Find the adjective in this sentence: "The forgetful man left his newspaper at the diner."

Questions

Jonas has 400 pieces of paper. He uses 320 for his novel. How many are left for his short stories?

Make the verb agree with the subject: "Mom, Dad, and I seen a movie last night."

How many 100s equal 1,000?

When abbreviating the date, does the month come before or after the day?

Questions

Put the fractions in order from greatest to least: $\frac{5}{8}$, $\frac{5}{6}$, $\frac{5}{7}$

Spell the number that is one less than fourteen.

When it is 6:20, where is the minute hand on a clock?

Use two of these words to make a compound: time, arrow, night, pole

Questions

What number is 5 less than the sum of 6 and 4?

What is the root word in this word group: electricity, electrician, electrical?

How many inches are in 4 feet?

Which animal lives in the ocean: orcas, orangutans, snakes, or porcupines?

Questions

There are 5 oranges and 3 apples in a bowl. What fraction of the fruit is apples?

What kind of reference book gives information on many different topics?

We were winning 5–2. Then they scored 4 points. How many points did we need to tie the game?

"Wash your hands before dinner." Is this sentence a question or a command?

Questions

Say the next three numbers in this series: 350, 300, 250, 200.

Spell the contraction of "who is."

How much is 9 x 9?

What is the correct spelling of the past tense of pay: p-a-y-e-d or p-a-i-d?

Answers
False. 9 + 3 = 12 and 15 – 4 = 11
witches
8
fingernail

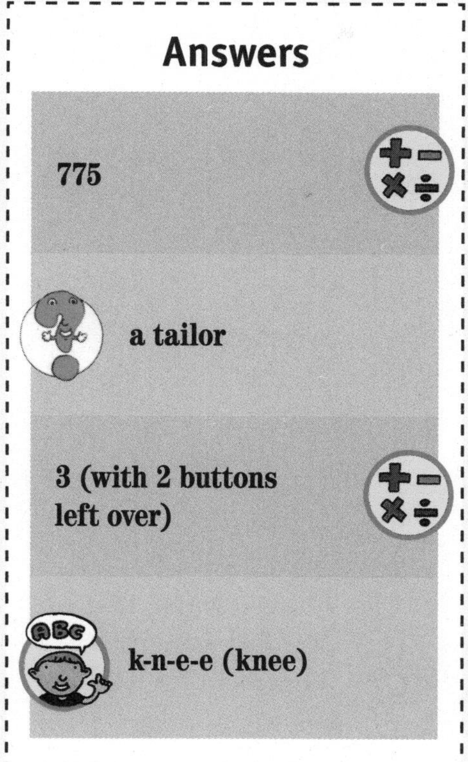

Answers
775
a tailor
3 (with 2 buttons left over)
k-n-e-e (knee)

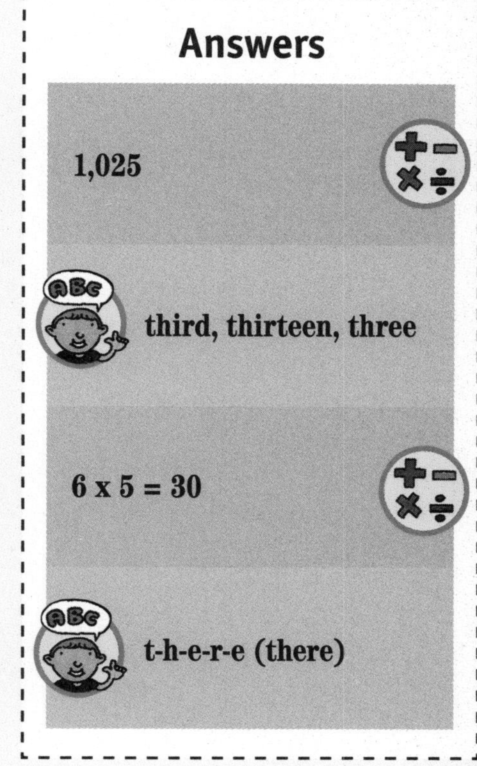

Answers
1,025
third, thirteen, three
6 x 5 = 30
t-h-e-r-e (there)

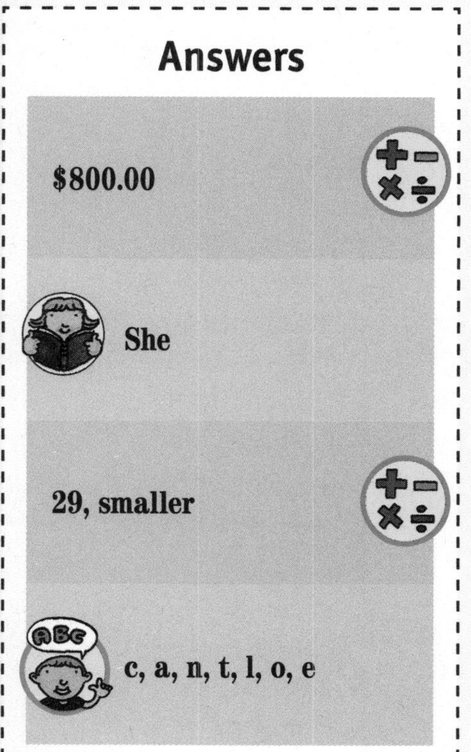

Answers
$800.00
She
29, smaller
c, a, n, t, l, o, e

Answers
16
knives
pentagon
"The dog began to howl."

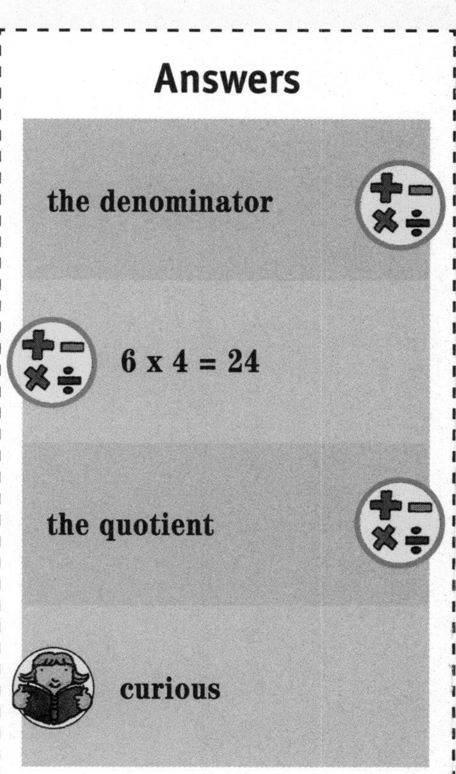

Answers
the denominator
6 x 4 = 24
the quotient
curious

Questions

What is the sum of 858 and 167?

Put the number words in alphabetical order: thirteen, third, three

Change this to a multiplication problem: 5 + 5 + 5 + 5 + 5 + 5 = 30

Spell the five-letter word that means the opposite of "here."

Questions

What's the sum of 224 and 551?

What do we call the person who mends clothes for a living?

Sophie has 20 buttons. Each shirt needs 6. How many shirts can she make?

Spell the name of the joint between the thigh and the calf that rhymes with "pea."

Questions

True or false: 9 + 3 = 15 – 4

Spell the plural of witch.

What is the denominator in $6\frac{4}{8}$?

Which should be written as one word: finger nail or finger puppet?

Questions

The numerator is the top number of a fraction. What is the bottom number?

Change this to a multiplication problem: 6+6+6+6=24

In the division problem 36 ÷ 4 = 9, what is the name for the number 9?

Which is a synonym of interested: uncertain, curious, talkative.

Questions

How many ounces are in a pint?

How do you spell the plural of knife?

Is home plate shaped like a hexagon or a pentagon?

Change the verb to its past form: "The dog begins to howl."

Questions

Round $762.32 to the nearest hundred dollars

"Dorothy followed the yellow brick road." What pronoun can replace the subject?

Find the difference between 127 and 98. Is it bigger or smaller than 30?

What letters do cantaloupe and celebration have in common?

Congratulations!

You've finished the Brain Quest Workbook!
In this section, you'll find:

Brain Quest Mini-Deck

Cut out the cards and make your own Brain Quest deck.

Play by yourself or with a friend.

Brainiac Certificate

Put a sticker on each square for every chapter you complete. Finish the whole workbook, and you're an official Brainiac!

And don't forget to turn to the end of the workbook. You'll find stickers and a Times Tables to 12 poster!

Brain Quest Extras

Questions

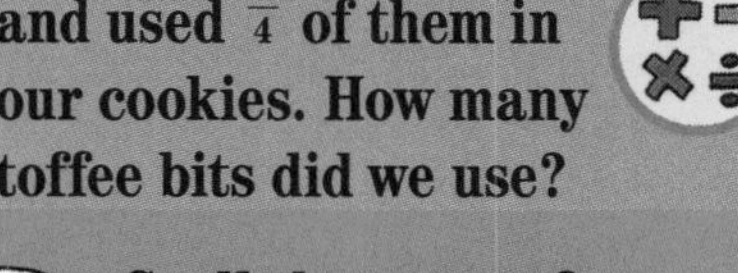

We bought 32 toffee bits and used $\frac{1}{4}$ of them in our cookies. How many toffee bits did we use?

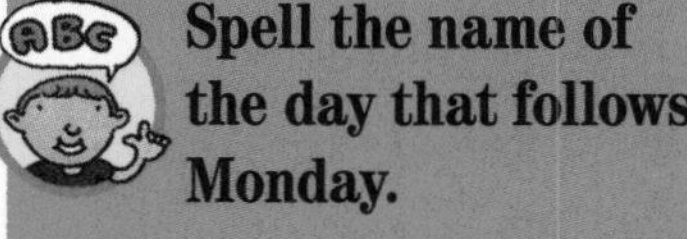

Spell the name of the day that follows Monday.

If you add two odd numbers, is the answer odd or even?

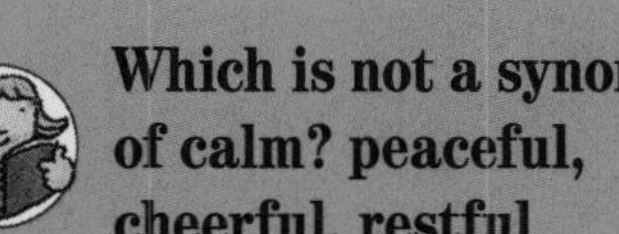

Which is not a synonym of calm? peaceful, cheerful, restful

Questions

How many corners are on a cube?

What is the name for someone who designs houses?

How many odd numbers are there between 14 and 26?

Identify the two consonants: w, u, i, y, e

Questions

How many angles are in a triangle?

What is the correct spelling: h-i-w-a-y or h-i-g-h-w-a-y?

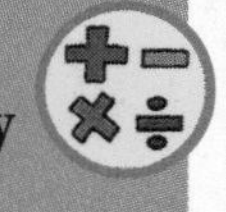

There are 50 people in line. 22 people are behind Nell. How many are in front of her?

When you don't have any responsibilities, do you feel careful or carefree?

Questions

What is the name of the period in the number 3.24?

Which words should be capitalized? "no one wants sam to move to new mexico."

Which fraction is equivalent to $\frac{1}{3}$: $\frac{3}{9}$ or $\frac{2}{12}$?

Divide the word coffee into syllables.

Questions

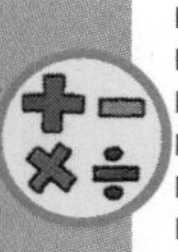

If there are 100 children and every other one is a boy, how many are girls?

Which fruit comes first in the dictionary: apple or apricot?

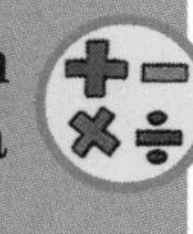

What's the best estimate for the length of a soup spoon: half a foot or 20 inches?

What punctuation usually follows the words how and what?

Questions

Is 12 A.M. at midnight or midday?

Say this sentence in the present tense: My mom weighed the grapes on the scale.

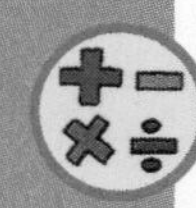

What are the next two numbers in the series 2, 4, 8, 16?

Make the nouns in this sentence singular: Put the fishes back in the tanks.

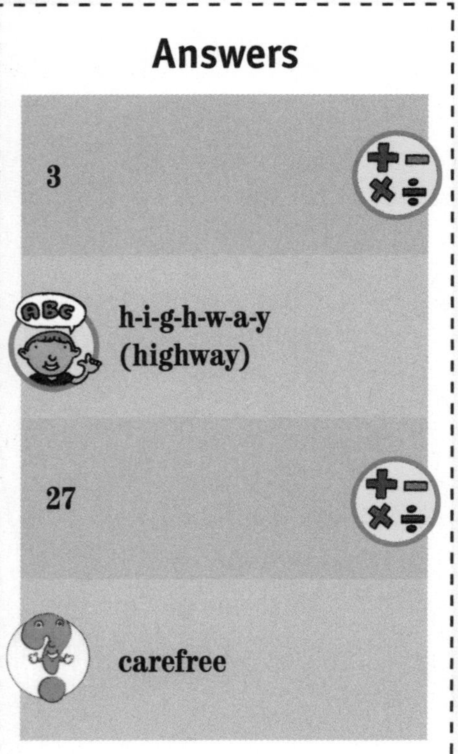
Answers
3
h-i-g-h-w-a-y
(highway)
27
carefree

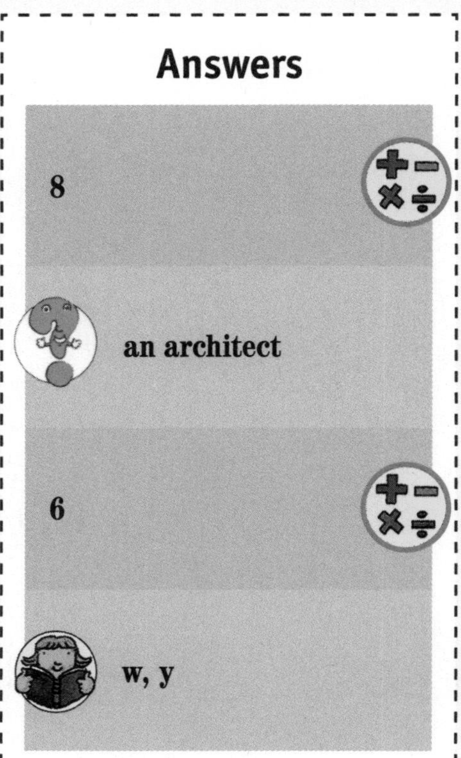
Answers
8
an architect
6
w, y

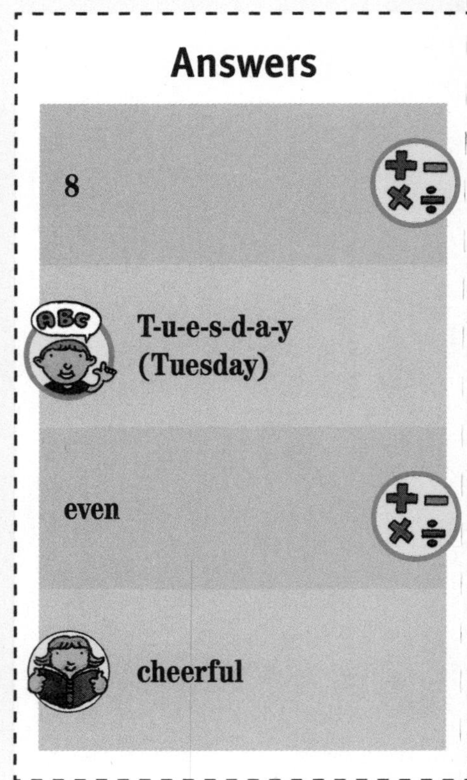
Answers
8
T-u-e-s-d-a-y
(Tuesday)
even
cheerful

Answers
midnight
My mom weighs the grapes on the scale. Or, my mom is weighing the grapes on the scale.
32, 64
Put the fish back in the tank.

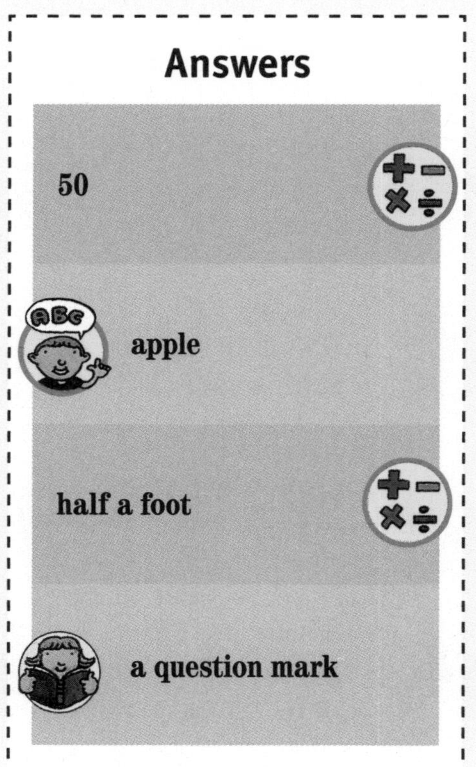
Answers
50
apple
half a foot
a question mark

Answers
a decimal point
No, Sam, New, Mexico
3/9
cof-fee

Questions

What is the product of 42 x 0?

The word ad is short for what goes on a billboard. What is the full word?

How many minutes are in a quarter of an hour?

"My mom and her partners made a business deal." What is the complete subject of this sentence?

Questions

How many quarters are in $3.00?

Is the past tense of the word "hear" spelled h-e-r-d or h-e-a-r-d?

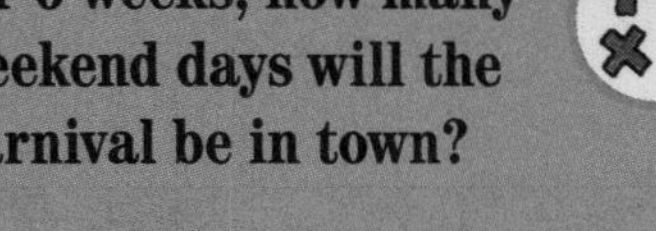

If the carnival is in town for 6 weeks, how many weekend days will the carnival be in town?

What word in a name is abbreviated D-r-period?

Questions

The Putras started driving at 11:30 A.M. and arrived at 1:15 P.M. How long was the car ride?

Which is the opposite of broader: narrower or nearer?

Change $\frac{7}{10}$ to a decimal.

Find a word that means to sketch in the word ward.

Questions

How do you write the fraction seven-eighths: 8 over 7 or 7 over 8?

Does "exaggerate" mean a) to overstate untruthfully, or b) to explode suddenly?

What is another way to write $\frac{3}{3}$?

Ship is to *sea* as *train* is to . . . what?

Questions

How much is 38 – 7 – 10 – 1?

If you step on a scale, will you learn how much you w-h-e-y or how much you w-e-i-g-h?

Which is biggest: 1 half-gallon, 1 pint, or 1 quart?

To make a word that is part of a shark, take two letters away from fiend.

Questions

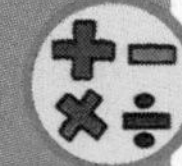

Subtract 305 from 526.

What letter is not pronounced in the word hasten?

How many seconds in $3\frac{1}{2}$ minutes?

Find the antonyms: Maisie was present, but Luke and Angga were absent.

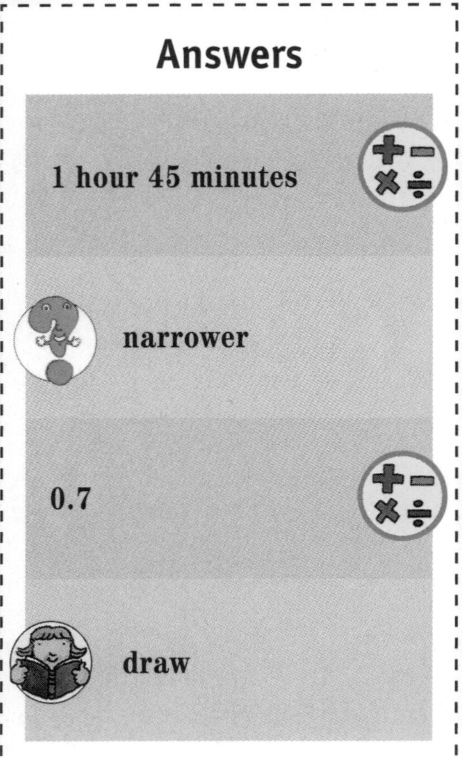
Answers
1 hour 45 minutes
narrower
0.7
draw

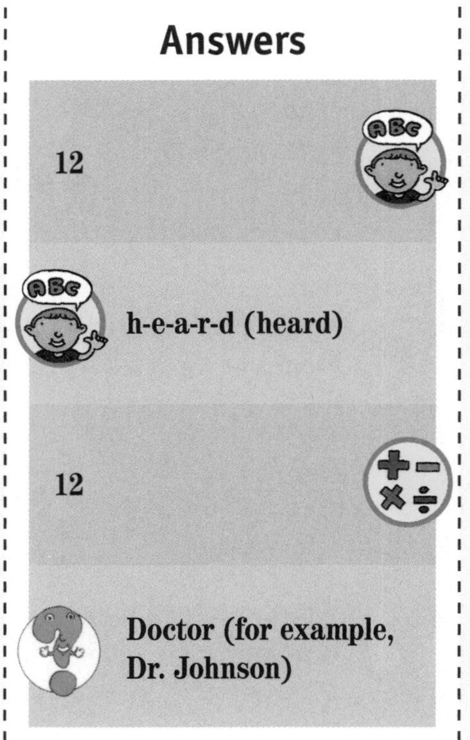
Answers
12
h-e-a-r-d (heard)
12
Doctor (for example, Dr. Johnson)

Answers
0
advertisement
15
My mom and her partners

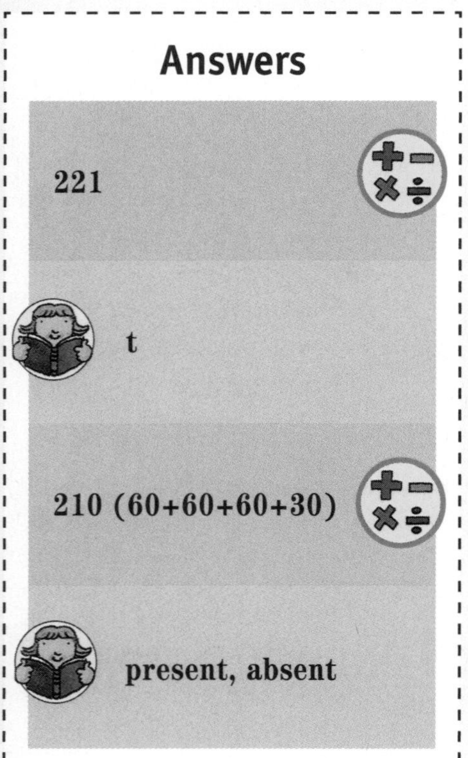
Answers
221
t
210 (60+60+60+30)
present, absent

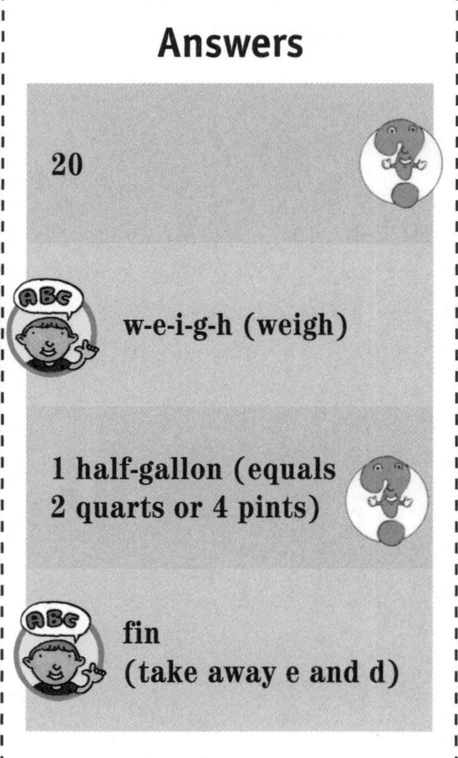
Answers
20
w-e-i-g-h (weigh)
1 half-gallon (equals 2 quarts or 4 pints)
fin
(take away e and d)

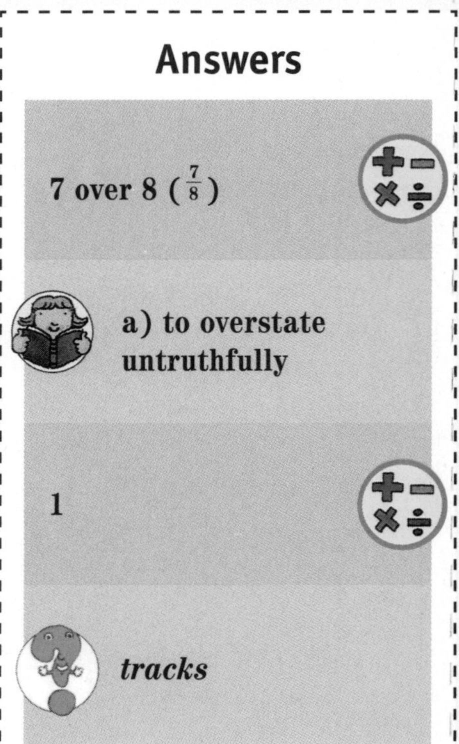
Answers
7 over 8 (7/8)
a) to overstate untruthfully
1
tracks

Brainiac Award!

Every time you finish a chapter of this workbook, choose a Brain Quest sticker and place it over the correct square on the certificate below. When all the squares have been covered by stickers, you will have completed the entire Brain Quest Workbook! Woo-hoo! Congratulations! That's quite an achievement.

Once you have a completed certificate, write your name on the line—or use the alphabet stickers—and cut out the award certificate.

Show your friends. Hang it on your wall! You're a certified Brainiac!

Great!
Hooray!
Yippee!
Cool!
Nice!
Wow!
Neat!
Yeah!
Super!
Fantastic!
Good job!
Brainiac!
Genius!
Hooray!
Yippee!
Cool!
Nice!
Wow!
Neat!
Yeah!
Arrf!
Fantastic!
Genius!
Brainiac!
Great!
Hooray!
Wow!
Yippee!
Cool!
Nice!
Wow!
Hooray!
Wonderful!
Super!
Hooray!
Good job!
Fantastic!
Grand!
Nice!
Yahoo!
Cool!
Yippee!
Great!
Excellent!
Great!
Hooray!
Yippee!
Cool!
Genius!
Wow!
Neat!
Brainiac!
Super!
Fantastic!
Good job!
Great!
Hooray!
Genius!
Cool!
Nice!
Brainiac!
Excellent!
Yeah!
Genius!
Fantastic!
Good job!
Great!
Hooray!
Yippee!
Fantastic!
Nice!
Wow!
Neat!
Excellent!
Super!
Fantastic!
Good job!
Genius!
Hooray!
Brainiac!
Fantastic!
Nice!
Genius!
Neat!
Yeah!
Genius!
Excellent!
Good job!
Great!
Hooray!
Yippee!
Cool!
Nice!
Wow!
Brainiac
Excellent!
Genius!
Fantastic!
Good job!
Great!
Brainiac!
Yippee!
Excellent!
Nice!
Excellent!
Fantastic!
Yeah!
Super!
Excellent!
Good job!
Great!
Genius!
Yippee!
Cool!
Nice!
Wow!
Neat!
Brainiac!
Super!
Fantastic!
Good job!
Great!
Hooray!
Yippee!
Arrf!
Nice!
Wow!
Neat!
Yeah!
Excellent!
Brainiac!
Good job!
Great!
Fantastic!
Yippee!
Cool!
Nice!
Wow!
Neat!
Brainiac!
Super!
Fantastic!
Good job!
Great!
Brainiac!
Yippee!
Brainiac!
Nice!
Wow!
Neat!
Yeah!
Super!
Fantastic!
Good job!